Challenging the Aid Paradigm

Rethinking International Development Series

Series Editors:

Andy Sumner, Fellow of the Vulnerability and Poverty Research Team, Institute of Development Studies, UK.

Ray Kiely, Professor of International Politics, Queen Mary University of London, UK.

Palgrave Macmillan is delighted to announce a new series dedicated to publishing cutting-edge titles that focus on the broad area of 'development'.
The core aims of the series are to present critical work that
– is cross disciplinary;
– challenges orthodoxies;
– reconciles theoretical depth with empirical research;
– explores the frontiers of development studies in terms of 'development' in both North and South and global inter-connectedness;
– reflects on claims to knowledge and intervening in other peoples lives.

Titles include

Simon Feeny and Matthew Clarke
THE MILLENNIUM DEVELOPMENT GOALS AND BEYOND
International Assistance to the Asia-Pacific

Niamh Gaynor
TRANSFORMING PARTICIPATION?
The Politics of Development in Malawi and Ireland

Eric Rugraff, Diego Sánchez-Ancochea, Andy Sumner (*editors*)
TRANSNATIONAL CORPORATIONS AND DEVELOPMENT POLICY
Critical Perspectives

Jens Stilhoff Sörensen (*editor*)
CHALLENGING THE AID PARADIGM
Western Currents and Asian Alternatives

Andy Sumner and Meera Tiwari
AFTER 2015: INTERNATIONAL DEVELOPMENT POLICY AT A CROSSROADS

Rethinking International Development Series
Series Standing Order ISBN 978–0230–53751–4 (hardback)

You can receive future titles in this series as they are published by placing a standing order. Please contact your bookseller or, in case of difficulty, write to us at the address below with your name and address, the title of the series and the ISBN quoted above.

Customer Services Department, Macmillan Distribution Ltd, Houndmills, Basingstoke, Hampshire RG21 6XS, England

Challenging the Aid Paradigm

Western Currents and Asian Alternatives

Edited By

Jens Stilhoff Sörensen
Research Fellow, Swedish Institute of International Affairs, Sweden

First published 2010 by
PALGRAVE MACMILLAN

Palgrave Macmillan in the UK is an imprint of Macmillan Publishers Limited, registered in England, company number 785998, of Houndmills, Basingstoke, Hampshire RG21 6XS.

Palgrave Macmillan in the US is a division of St Martin's Press LLC, 175 Fifth Avenue, New York, NY 10010.

Palgrave Macmillan is the global academic imprint of the above companies and has companies and representatives throughout the world.

Palgrave® and Macmillan® are registered trademarks in the United States, the United Kingdom, Europe and other countries.

ISBN: 978–0–230–57766–4 hardback

This book is printed on paper suitable for recycling and made from fully managed and sustained forest sources. Logging, pulping and manufacturing processes are expected to conform to the environmental regulations of the country of origin.

A catalogue record for this book is available from the British Library.

Library of Congress Cataloging-in-Publication Data

 Challenging the aid paradigm : Western currents and Asian alternatives / edited by Jens Stilhoff Sörensen.
  p. cm.
 Summary: "Challenging the Aid Paradigm critically examines central aspects of Western international aid policy, while at the same time exploring non-western especially Chinese aid and assesses to what extent these may be competitive or complementary" – Provided by publisher.
  ISBN 978–0–230–57766–4
  1. Economic assistance, European – Developing countries. 2. Economic assistance, Chinese – Developing countries. I. Sörensen, Jens Stilhoff.
HC60.C446 2010
338.91′401724—dc22   2010002714

10 9 8 7 6 5 4 3 2 1
19 18 17 16 15 14 13 12 11 10

Printed and bound in Great Britain by
CPI Antony Rowe, Chippenham and Eastbourne

Contents

Tables

Preface

The fall of the Soviet and socialist development model in 1989/91 meant that there was no longer any alternative to the Western neoliberal model of development. In certain regards *globalisation*, with all its meanings, can be understood as the spread of a single model of development and shaping of state and society. The end of bipolarism obviously had a profound impact on development and aid. Gradually, however, it would appear that an Asian alternative model may be emerging and especially so with China's rapidly growing and expanding economy. The emergence of an *actually existing* alternative accentuates the urgency for critical scrutiny of Western currents in development and aid, on its own terms, together with an investigation into what an *actually existing* alternative could come to constitute. Challenging the Aid Paradigm, would thereby be both to critically engage with problems in Western or mainstream aid, and to explore to which extent there is an actually existing challenging model of aid. Such a simple dichotomy should, however, not be taken too categorically: First, although it is reasonable to claim that there is a single dominant model of aid and development, which is Western as well as mainstream, there are of course variations in policy preferences and programming among various countries and donors. Second, to speak of an emerging alternative Asian model, and pose it as a challenge, is partly to presuppose an issue that is to be investigated. Is there a single Asian model or are there many; and is it a challenge or a complement, or will there be a convergence? All these layers of questions lie beneath the posed dichotomy. The selections made here explore such issues, but the reader should be made aware that the approach is not a directly comparative one; rather the contributions offer a set of critical engagements with *some* major currents and issues in Western development theory and practice, as well as with a possible Asian alternative. On the latter, there is a particular focus on China, and especially on its expanding investment and activity in Africa. One chapter offers a comparative analysis of four major Asian donors, while four chapters explore aspects of Chinese aid including its reception in Africa, one of them juxtaposing it with Western aid. Needless to say, there are other currents worthy of exploration; this volume has nothing on India, which is becoming an important actor in for example Africa. The reader will find nothing on Latin America or the Middle

East; neither on Islamic or confessional-based aid, nor on the other BRIC countries besides China (that is Brazil, Russia, India). Important as these areas are, an engagement with them would have extended the project too far.

This volume has its origins in an idea to bring together a selected group of scholars working on Western as well as Asian aid, from several disciplines, including area specialists, and to explore and engage in dialogue on above-mentioned issues and the challenges facing development and aid in the twenty-first century. A workshop, the first in a series, was organised at the Swedish Institute of International Affairs in November 2007 where initial drafts were presented. The editor wishes to thank all participants and especially the contributors to this volume for their engagement and commitment, which made for such fruitful, pleasant and stimulating discussions and collaborations across fields and disciplines. The editor also wishes to thank Riksbankens Jubileumsfond (RJ), the Special Research Programme at the Swedish Institute of International Affairs (SIIA), the School of Global Studies at Gothenburg University, and all participants in subsequent workshops at SIIA. He has gained so much from you all.

Contributors

Mark Duffield
Professor of Development Politics, University of Bristol, UK

Johan Lagerkvist
Research Fellow in Sinology, Swedish Institute of International Affairs

Henning Melber
Director, Dag Hammarsköld Foundation, Uppsala, Sweden

Yahia Mohamed Mahmoud
Research Fellow, Department of Cultural and Economic Geography, University of Lund, Sweden

Vanessa Pupavac
Lecturer in International Relations, University of Nottingham, UK

Marie Söderberg
Professor of Economics and Director of the European Institute for Japanese Studies, Stockholm School of Economics

Jens Stilhoff Sörensen
Research Fellow, Swedish Institute of International Affairs, and in Peace and Development Research, School of Global Studies, University of Gothenburg

He Wenping
Professor in the Chinese Academy of Social Sciences, and Director of the African Studies Department, Institute of West Asian and African Studies, Chinese Academy of Social Sciences, Beijing

1
Introduction: Reinventing Development for the Twenty-First Century?

Jens Stilhoff Sörensen

The challenges

The project of international development aid, which started with decolonisation after the Second World War, became from the outset deeply embedded in the logic of bipolarism and the competition between the Western and Soviet models. By the 1990s, when the Soviet Union and the socialist development model collapsed, the whole project of development had already reached a crisis. Structural adjustment, which was the latest invention of the 1980s, seemed not to be working, the development gap increased and there had been a gradual rise in civil wars since the 1960s. The so-called 'Washington consensus' around market (or 'neo') liberalism was already in question at a time when it seemed to have triumphed over a communist development alternative. Given the new opportunity offered by the fall of communism, which meant both the end of a challenging model and the opening up of a whole new space for market expansion, it was difficult to discredit the neoliberal model. Instead it was reinvented. The focus on market liberalisation remained but with an increasing attention to political liberalisation and a reshaping of the state. With the end of bipolarism, the 1990s promised a new horizon and a reinvented project for development with a growing consensus on what needed to be done; economic liberalisation and democratisation were the central themes of the 'new' paradigm, and the problem of African underdevelopment was identified as being 'poor governance', the remedy for which was of course 'good governance' or democratisation (Abrahamsen, 2000, p. 25).

The Washington consensus of economic liberalisation, privatisation and macro-economic stabilisation was equally the prescribed recipe for the transition of communist countries in Eastern Europe. But although the collapse of the Soviet, and thereby socialist, model seemed to promise a victory for market liberalism to the degree that there were fatalistic proclamations of an 'end of history' and to offer an unprecedented convergence around neoliberal solutions within international aid policy, there was, almost from its inception, a new challenge in the concern with weak or missing state institutions. In the traditional 'Third World', and especially in Africa, this was a security concern that emerged following the demise of the clientelism that had been upheld during the bipolar world order, and with the subsequent rediscovery of 'civil wars' and their connection to illiberal economies and political projects. With regard to Eastern Europe there were concerns about the catastrophic social effects of shock therapy and, especially, about the rise, expansion and consolidation of illiberal networks and crime syndicates. Where the state had previously been seen as a problem it was gradually recognised as a much-needed entity, in terms of both security and development. The emerging language of 'failed' and 'fragile' states reflected this concern. Through the 1990s the World Bank developed a new framework that designated a greater role to state institutions and the UN and Western donor governments followed suit.

In international peace-building missions and international protectorates, such as Bosnia-Herzegovina (BiH) and Kosovo, the rebuilding of institutions became the central problematic. This 'rediscovery' of state institutions reached new heights in the war on terrorism, in which failed or fragile states are considered a threat to the very stability of international order.

In all aspects, the state is now understood as a necessary security framework everywhere, and international efforts at 'state-building' have moved to the centre of the agenda in international relations and international aid and security policy.

Although such recent developments have been labelled 'post-Washington consensus' and have often been interpreted as the end or even 'death' of neoliberalism, they can be seen as the opposite. Neoliberalism is not dead, merely redressed and *secured*, through an institutional framework.[1] The state that is being fashioned and rebuilt, from the World Bank showcases in Africa to the UN and EU-led international protectorates in BiH and Kosovo, or the 'neocolonial' states in Iraq and Afghanistan, is everywhere within a neoliberal framework. A feature of this type of state is the shaping of institutions that can implement and oversee neoliberal reform, often with direct international agency intervention and supervision of the reform policies, coupled with security technologies to address the social effects on marginalised groups, or the 'risk' population. Such security technologies include poverty-reduction strategies amongst those groups that are worst off in the process. Western or mainstream international aid policy does however not allow much of a role for the state in the process of development, such as was the case in the 1950s or 1960s when modernisation and industrialisation were on the agenda. The aim of giving support to institutions, and with state-building, is rather to secure certain functions and services which in turn require a certain institutional framework and backing. Institutions are crucial to providing a legal framework, upholding law and order, securing property rights and liberal reform, providing poverty reduction and controlling borders, but they are fashioned to help shape a space for market liberalism and contain potential disturbances, thereby securing the global neoliberal project.

However, although there is, with some variation, a general Western consensus, which is also the international mainstream operating through the major institutions such as the World Bank, the IMF and the World Trade Organization, there has now for the first time since the fall of the Soviet Union emerged an *actually existing* alternative in what is sometimes called South–South cooperation. This is especially the case with Chinese aid and investment, in Asia, Africa and, to a growing extent, Latin America. Chinese aid operates differently from the international mainstream and Western aid. It offers no-strings infrastructural investment and state loans, and makes a point of not interfering with domestic political issues. It operates bilaterally, has no interest in NGOs and does not even call it aid. It shuns the idea of a single model for all countries while it appears itself to constitute perhaps the most successful example of a rapidly industrialising and modernising developing country. The strong state-led development in China is just a variation of other Asian countries with a similar reliance on the state's role in the economy; as well as the Japanese example there are South Korea and Thailand, which are themselves aid donors. To many observers the rise of Chinese involvement in Africa, the bastion of Western development aid, constitutes a threat not just in geopolitical terms but also as a non-democratic, authoritarian-capitalist and unwelcome model juxtaposed on the Western effort. For others it is a welcome exit from the unipolar, neoliberal hegemonic or imperial order, which now seems to be confronted with an alternative. While some fear geopolitical competition and challenge, others fear convergence or more of the same.

This book presents a series of critical interventions on 'Western currents' and 'Asian alternatives' in contemporary aid policy. It explores 'challenges' to the contemporary aid paradigm in a double sense: first, challenges to the international (Western) mainstream aid paradigm on its own terms, by engaging critically with theoretical and empirical problems, that is, the problems connected to the discourse and practice of the project of Western development aid, and second, in terms of examining *actually existing* challenges, in the form of an alternative 'Asian' model of aid. The various chapters address issues such as how development as a project can be understood and analysed, the relationship between development and security (hence aid and security) and the character of the present conjuncture of development-security, sustainable development philosophy and civil society within Western aid discourse and practice, whether there is an alternative Asian model of aid and what implications this has for Western aid policy and for development in Africa, the character and interests of Chinese involvement in Africa and its reception and effects there and whether there is convergence or bifurcation in international aid, that is, between Western and Asian.

The contributors represent a broad range of disciplines and fields of expertise, such as Sinology, Asian and African studies, Development and Security studies, Cultural and Economic Geography, Economics, Politics and International Relations. They do however not represent any school, nor even a necessarily shared theoretical paradigm, but are united by a shared interest and concern for the subject matter and a commitment to engaging in critical approaches within their respective fields.

The remainder of this introduction will be devoted to a short overview and interpretation of international development and aid policy since the Second World War and the relationship between state and market. This provides a historical context for development discourse and theory, and sets the scene for highlighting the contrast between Western and Asian aid that will be developed in some of the coming chapters. Finally, the last section gives a short presentation of the chapters and organisation of the book.

Development as security

International development was invented after the Second World War.[2] The usually referred starting point is Harry S. Truman's inaugural speech in 1949, when he declared the launch of a global effort to assist 'underdeveloped areas' and eradicate poverty. Here, in this 'speech act', a large part of the globe and 2 billion people on several continents became defined as 'underdeveloped' and subject to legitimised intervention by the West.[3] Now, since most of these areas were colonies or former colonies, they were of course already subject to intervention, and *international development* was in one regard a new way of relating to them. Development was not merely altruistic; the United States needed to break up the colonial system of capitalism and create a new 'fixing of space' for capitalism under US hegemony (Smith, 2003, 2005). The global political economy that had collapsed in the war was now restored with the US as the hegemonic power and with the ruined international monetary system that had been based on the gold standard now revised into a system where the US dollar, linked to a fixed price in gold, became the world's reserve currency. In order to restore the international political economy, based on this US hegemony, it was not only necessary to reconstruct Europe (aided by the Marshall Plan) and to create a new currency order and international financial institutions (the Bretton-Woods institutions), but also to reshape the global space for capitalism, 'shake loose' the colonies and re-fix the space (Smith, 2003). Thus the 'independent' nation state also became the principle for these 'emerging areas'. However, from the outset the bipolar competition and geopolitical struggle with the Soviet Union created a geopolitical security concern. Development was therefore linked to security, indeed was an instrument for security; it was a security technology designed both to prevent areas from falling into the communist camp and as a new way of managing populated territories that had earlier been under colonial administration. Development has always been connected to security in the sense of a security technology used to manage or contain the potential danger posed by the poor; this was the case with the management of marginalised urban populations in nineteenth-century Europe, and with the 'Third World' after decolonisation. However the concern has been shifting: in the 1950s development was an alternative way of dealing with areas that used to be colonies and was crucial to prevent them from falling under communism, and if the concern in the 1980s and 1990s was primarily that unstable areas risked producing refugees and developing illiberal or shadow economies, including the international drugs trade, the primary focus is now on their potentiality for harbouring and cultivating terrorism.[4] This, however, is quite general, and the *form* of managing or relating to the subject, the ideas, method and object for development (as such, a technology) have shifted.

From state to market

The struggle of the roles between the state and the market has been a defining feature of politics in the twentieth century and a central theme in the social sciences. It has in fact been so since the development of classical Political Economy. When development aid policy emerged as a state policy, and hence as a scholarly field of study, after the Second Word War, these state–market tensions inevitably became central to it. After the war the dominant economic theory and practice was Keynesianism, which allocated a central role to the state in regulation and planning. The liberalisation of international trade was gradual; regulations and fixed exchange rates shielded nation states, whereby growth was promoted with the state as a crucial agent and with social peace being ensured through a commitment to welfare programmes and full employment. Thus, state engagement, state strategies for economic development (or planning) and regulation were not just features of the communist states but also of liberal states in the West and were widely considered to be what a modern state was supposed to do. This almost universal adherence to a strong role for the state in the economy had come as a reaction to the experiences of an earlier era of laissez-faire capitalism, which had led to fateful consequences. Karl Polanyi analysed the development of the liberal welfare state, the communist state and the fascist state as variations in response to the consequences of laissez-faire capitalism and the global unleashing of market forces in the second half of the nineteenth century (Polanyi, 1944/1957). This, he argued, threatened the very fabric of society and provoked a series of counter-measures to protect societies and states. In the first instance it led to protectionism and renewed colonial expansion and competition, which eventually resulted in the breakdown of the nineteenth-century international economic system, that is a laissez-faire capitalism which was regulated through the gold standard under British hegemony and safeguarded by the balance of power system. This breakdown ultimately led to the First World War. The attempt during the inter-war years to restore the pre-war international economic order failed and the three competing projects of fascism, communism and the early signs of a liberal welfare state (including in the US with the 'New Deal') consolidated and were headed for another confrontation in the Second World War. A new organisation and framework for the international political economy came only after the Second World War.

The post-war reconstruction of the global economy, through the Bretton-Woods structure, took place within the framework of institutionally embedded 'national economies' in which the state had a central role in governing the economy and promoting welfare. This had its counterpart in the post-colonial states in the Third World where the concept of a 'developmental state' reflected the idea that the state had the leading role in promoting industrialisation and modernisation.

After the so-called 'emerging areas' – or the Third World – were invented and subjected to a project of development, there emerged a whole industry to deal with this: agencies and aid workers, academics and experts, theories and university courses. The Third World needed to change and become more like the West, that is, modern and developed, and in line with the Zeitgeist, the theoretical development of the time in the form of 'economic growth theory' and then 'modernisation theories' focused on development of national economies within nation states. The World Bank and other Western donors promoted industrialisation and the building of infrastructure, sometimes resulting in so-called 'white elephants'. Although, at a rhetorical level, there were ideas of democratisation and respect for human rights, these were not really part of the agenda. They were either premature with regard to the level of development or subordinate to geopolitical concerns; thus many states in the Third World became development dictatorships.

With such an overwhelming consensus that the state should have an active role in the economy, even be the engine for development, the debate came to crystallise around other issues. The critical perspectives of the time, with early structuralism from the 1940s and then the dependency school in the 1960s (which bifurcated into a hard version and the softer 'dependent development'), primarily targeted the fact that mainstream development theory (modernisation theories) focused on indigenous or domestic factors as the root cause of underdevelopment. Consequently these mainstream theories considered all contacts with the West, and the global economy, as primarily beneficial, whether in terms of technology transfers or in terms of trade. Conventional trade theory claimed that trade was to the benefit of all: 'specialise in what you do best and trade for the rest'. The early structuralist critique, which was first developed in Latin America, argued instead that there was a long-term decline in trade between primary goods and manufactured goods, which in turn would result in a lack of goods to finance imports and investment in technology. Therefore its proponents suggested import substitution: protectionist measures and the replacement of imports with local products. Dependency theory was even more radical in targeting capitalism, as such, and colonial exploitation as the historical problems and aimed to show how global trade was on unequal terms, thereby maintaining or extending the already established asymmetric relations. Consequently, 'delinking' with the West and trade between equal partners within the South were advocated. While such theories had a fairly large reception in the South, they remained marginalised in Western and international mainstream circles and policies, but from the 1950s until the 1970s many countries opted for import-substitution industrialisation (ISI) strategies and protectionism.

The late 1960s and early 1970s saw a new departure. Many countries had experienced problems with ISI strategies, and the emergence of the newly industrialising countries (NIC) and the new international division of labour (NIDL), in which industrial production was outsourced or involved subcontracting in Third World countries, proved that industrialisation and some development were possible. This spurred a considerable theoretical rethinking on the critical side, resulting in 'world-system analysis', but modernisation theory was also refining its positions in response to criticism. Furthermore, the 1970s saw the development of feminist critique, 'participatory development' and 'sustainable development', with various arguments against a homogeneous interpretation of underdeveloped societies, with a neglect of existing internal differences in terms of class or gender, the urban and rural; against the macro-planning of modernisation that did not involve local communities and against the whole project of industrialisation and modernisation as the ultimate and only goal. It was relatively easy though, to counter such critiques with the argument that they all had their points but could not solve the general overarching problem of lifting whole states and societies out from underdevelopment; the latter task required a macro approach of industrialisation and modernisation.[5]

The 1970s had more to offer; in the early 1970s the foundations of the international monetary system that had been laid down in Bretton Woods were destroyed when the US, in 1971, announced that it would abandon the dollar link to gold and then, in 1974, abandoned the Keynesian system within international finance, which until then had regulated the free movement around the world of private finance. The move towards a pure dollar standard and the opening up of a free capital market globally came to change the rules of the game greatly, and although there was much resentment there was little that other states could do to prevent it. In combination with the oil crises, first in 1973 and then in 1979, this laid the foundations for the debt crisis that hit much of the Third World in the 1980s, just as it paved the way for the turn to neoliberalism. The first oil crisis created the flow of petrodollars; the oil-rich states placed much of their income from oil in US banks and on the American financial market, which in turn offered loans at low interest rates. It was at the time *rational* for Third World countries to borrow money in order to finance modernisation projects, because the conditions and prospects appeared good, but following the second oil crisis (1979), when the US shifted its strategy to a restrictive monetary policy and rapidly increased interest rates, which in turn spurred a global recession, the conditions were quite different and the debt crisis was born (cf. Gilpin, 1987, p. 318).

The real challenge and definite break with the previous consensus on the role of the state came with neoliberalism. Confined to the theoretical margins and even the 'lunatic fringe' in the early 1970s, it had by the end of that decade moved centre stage. With the coming of the administrations of Reagan in the US (1981) and Thatcher in the UK (1979) neoliberalism was promoted also through the international institutions, such as the World Bank. The neoliberals wished to reduce the state to an absolute minimum and unleash the forces of the market and promote privatisation, outsourcing and deregulation. The outcome in development thinking was that the IMF and the World Bank forced 'Structural Adjustment Programs' (SAP) on the Third World. These entailed macro-economic stabilisation through fiscal and monetary restraint, devaluation and deflation, in order to suppress domestic demand and reduce imports, as short-term measures imposed by the IMF and structural adjustment measures to expand exports, as long-term measures imposed by the World Bank (see, e.g., Abrahamsen, 2000, p. 37; Hoogvelt, 1997, p. 168ff). It meant privatisation and trade liberalisation and forced many African countries to focus on primary commodity production for export, while public industries could be taken over by private foreign companies (cf. Hoogvelt, 1997, pp. 88, 138). The result of such policies in Africa was deepening poverty, widening social polarisation and increasing unemployment across the continent (Abrahamsen, 2000, p. 10; cf. Hoogvelt, 1997, pp. 170–1). In the least developed countries it seemed to result in de-industrialisation (cf. Shafaeddin, 2006). The policy has had its die-hard believers, but during the 1990s even the World Bank itself began to acknowledge some of its failures, although the blame was placed on the African governments.

By the early 1990s, when communism had collapsed in the Soviet Union and Eastern Europe, and this region itself became subjected to aid policy, similar neoliberal prescriptions were promoted there; again, the so-called *shock therapy* had disastrous social consequences (see, e.g., Amsden et al., 1998; Andor and Summers, 1998; cf. Lavigne, 1995/1999; Stiglitz, 2002).

The 1990s also meant a new possibility to promote democratisation, with the idea that democratisation and market liberalisation went together. The Bank's diagnosis for the disappointing results with Structural Adjustment in Africa was that the problem lay not with the policy but with Africa, more precisely with its states and governments. As early as 1989 it launched the idea that the solution in Africa was not just to have less government, but to have better government, or democracy (see Abrahamsen, 2000). Since then the notion *good governance* has become the catchword. In Eastern Europe the concept was *transition* (from communism). Aid agencies developed separate budgets for democracy assistance and support to civil society. Here, another feature that expanded under neoliberalism was the increasing subcontracting of NGOs as partners in aid policy and their promotion in developing countries as well as in post-communist transition countries (cf. Sörensen, 1997, 2009; the overview in Tvedt, 1998). Since the 1990s this form of assistance has been presented and construed as the promotion of civil society, which is considered an essential component of democracy. In many areas NGOs have become favoured partners, filling the space where the state in the aid-receiving society has been regarded as insufficient or undesirable as a partner.

To a great extent neoliberalism could absorb such critical discourses as 'sustainable development', 'participatory development' and feminist critiques. Sustainable development, which was largely inspired by the work of E. F. Schumacher in the 1970s, grew popular among NGOs and focused on non-material development and sustainability of local lifestyles, as opposed to industrialisation and modernisation (see Vanessa Pupavac's chapter in this volume; cf. Pupavac, 2008). Participatory development focused on local involvement, and feminists criticised the gender blindness in development and argued for the empowerment and increased participation of women. Through the stimulation of private and non-state initiatives, and through the incorporation of NGOs into the aid industry, these initially critical perspectives have all been absorbed into neoliberal aid policy. The favouring of market forces and thus reduced support to state projects and a slimming of the state has allowed more space for private initiatives. In the process the NGO sector has expanded to unprecedented levels. Various projects can be promoted by and through NGOs without affecting neoliberal policy; indeed, they merely reaffirm it. Thereby, under neoliberalism, these perspectives have themselves joined the mainstream.

However, during the 1990s the tide shifted and new policies were worked out for 'development' (in the Third World), as well as for 'transition' (to post-communism). The importance of state institutions was increasingly acknowledged. By the late 1990s the World Bank had refined its earlier focus and launched the so-called Comprehensive Development Framework (CDF), which has been presented as a more holistic approach to development that emphasises the interdependence of governance and development (e.g., World Bank, 1999/2000, 2002; Pender, 2002; Hout, 2007). Since the World Bank, according to its Articles of Agreement, is forbidden to work on political issues, this has all been cast as technical and as a strategy to promote development. Thus, the implementation of a legal framework favourable to the market is technical, not political. The good governance agenda is integral to the new approach with its focus on transparency, participation, anti-corruption, freedom of information and a well-qualified civil service. In addition the notion of country ownership has been introduced along with a number of measures to cushion social conditions for the most vulnerable parts of populations. Here, poverty reduction and poverty-reduction strategies, which are to be planned, implemented and 'owned' by the aid-receiving states, are a crucial component of the CDF. In Eastern Europe there was a similar trend moving from 'shock therapy' towards a more 'gradualist' approach to transition.

The focus on institutions has now become pre-eminent and through the 1990s there has been an increasing problematisation of what is called state fragility, and 'failed' or fragile states. This is both a security and a development concern. State institutions have been acknowledged as crucial with regard to development, and the dangers of state collapse, with its relations to war, ethnic cleansing, refugee flows, criminal economies, and even terrorism, are considered to pose a direct security challenge to the global order. There is a consensus that underdevelopment, poverty and state fragility are dangerous. With international intervention in areas like BiH, Kosovo and Afghanistan, and the US-led invasion of Iraq, the issue of *state-building* has now moved to the centre of the agenda within aid and security policy and in international relations (cf. Chandler, 2006).

Reinventing the state?

It would appear that we have moved full circle in the Polanyian perspective, where a phase of global unleashing of market forces leads to disastrous social consequences that in turn give rise to counter-movements and have to be met by a new phase of institutional *embedding* of the market. For Polanyi the earlier attempt with globalisation in the late nineteenth century had such consequences. Today we could see a parallel in recent (neoliberal) globalisation, which has challenged formal economies, disrupted and destroyed social safety networks for millions of people in the South and thereby helped to stimulate alternative forms of protection including non-liberal forms of political economy and social protection. To some extent ethno-nationalist projects as well as Islamic fundamentalism can be seen in this context (cf. Duffield, 2001; Gray, 2003/2007; Hoogvelt, 1997; Sörensen, 2009). So too can the recent re-emergence of state institutions and the project of state-building within Western and mainstream international development and security thinking and practice. The Polanyian counter-movements that developed to protect society were state based (the liberal welfare state, fascism/Nazism, communism). Similarly, the focus on institutions and state-building in contemporary development aid policy can be seen as a counter-measure, but today the scale is different. Today, capitalism can no longer be locked into a stable path of growth at the scale of the nation state. Neoliberal globalisation is promoted, but in order to secure the project, neoliberal aid policy and development aim to manage the effects and consequences on populations that are marginalised, and thus vulnerable and potentially dangerous.

Here we can introduce a biopolitical reading of development; biopolitics is concerned with populations and with humans as *species life*, rather than with territory, borders and states.[6] It aims to promote certain forms of life, administer life processes, develop knowledge about life – statistics, techniques of surveillance – and manage risk, not on the level of the individual but on the level of population. Biopolitics is integral to liberalism. If liberalism is understood as a technology of government and an ethos of government, which aims to promote life though freedom, then biopolitics is a necessary condition of liberalism and concerns the administration of life processes at the aggregate level of population (cf. Dean, 1999, p. 113; Duffield, 2007, ch. 1). It is very much about security and aims to control *circulation* and the effects of circulation, to promote good circulation and prevent bad. Neoliberal globalisation promotes certain forms of global circulation (free circulation of capital, trade, etc.), but with it comes the risk inherent with 'bad circulation' (uncontrolled migration and refugee flows, movement of terrorists and their financial networks, the drugs trade, etc.), which has to be managed while the former is promoted (cf. Dillon, 2006; Dillon and Lobo-Guerrero, 2008).

Contemporary development aid policy has moved from its previous focus on building nation states and promoting industrialisation and modernisation within states, to operate directly on populations; this is reflected in radical interventions in the South and in the promotion of NGOs that can operate in societies directly rather than through states. Rather than being concerned with the development of states, and with inequality within the international system, development has come to focus on various forms of self-sustainability; while market liberalism is promoted, development concerns *surplus life* or such life as has become superfluous to liberal development, and either secures its survival or alternatively disallows such life not deemed worthy in a liberal world, while at the same time securing the liberal project from interference (cf. Cowen and Shenton, 1996, ch. 4; Duffield, 2007).[7] Mark Duffield has put it in clear and simple terms: 'development is a technology of security that is central to liberal forms of power and government', it expresses a 'will to manage and contain disorder rather than resolve it' and 'it provides a liberal alternative to extermination or eugenics: modernity's other solution to the problem of surplus population' (Duffield, 2007, p. viii). However, rather than being a universalising biopolitics, scaled up from the level of the state to that of the globe, development is the opposite and operates on biopolitically separated surplus life (ibid., p. ix). Sustainable development, for example, promotes non-material development as an alternative to modernisation (cf. Pupavac, 2008). The recent reorientation towards institutions and state-building is not a departure from this trend, but a strategy to re-territorialise populations and create an institutional framework that can help to promote this policy and form of governance, as well as to control circulation.

Contemporary state-building is neoliberal state-building. It is not a return to the developmental state of the 1960s or early 1970s, as in the conceptual world of Keynesianism or Third Worldism, where the state was regarded a crucial and leading agent in development and towards modernisation. The neoliberal framework within which the newly discovered focus on state institutions is taking place can be read from the *character* of the state being rebuilt, the approach to institutions and the reforms imposed in order to adapt to markets. This type of state is what Graham Harrison has labelled a 'governance state' (Harrison, 2004). His work on the World Bank's new policy towards selected African showcases, such as Uganda, Mozambique and Tanzania, demonstrated that the bank's policy was stimulated by the failure of the implementation of SAPs in the 1980s and that the new emphasis on institutions was a remedy to enable, implement and 'lock in' neoliberal reforms. The failure of SAP and so-called 'first generation reforms', with their focus on rolling back the state, gave way to 'second generation reforms' focusing on the state's capacity to receive and implement aid programmes, civil service reform, introduction of new information technology, technical assistance, management and the facilitation of public participation in policy monitoring, evaluation and development. A central feature of the 'governance state' is the involvement of international agencies in shaping the policy reforms. In this context Harrison also urged us to reconsider the fixed distinction between national and international and instead suggested the concept of a 'sovereign frontier' for exploring how various political agents, local and external, engage in alliances and struggles to capture the sovereign frontier and shape policy outcomes (ibid.).

The World Bank's continuous commitment to neoliberalism has further been discussed by Gordon Crawford who has analysed the conception of 'good governance' and the shift in terminology from 'minimal state' to 'effective state' through a review of the World Bank's key texts on the state, and compared its assumptions and premises with those of classical political liberalism, especially as revived by Friedrich Hayek (Crawford, 2006). He concludes that the merit of a free-market economy, inclusive of private property and property rights, remains a fundamental assumption, that ongoing economic liberalisation continues to be emphasised, including the introduction of market-like relations into public institutions and that there is particular hostility to state interference in the economy. Further, there is an ambivalence to democracy in the sense that it is the liberal component of liberal democracy that is emphasised, while the scope of democratic decision-making is circumscribed to exclude the sphere of economic policy (ibid., p. 136).

For the Bank 'good governance' equals neoliberal governance and 'effective state' means effective for business, notably for international companies (ibid., p. 136). Thus, rather than constituting a break with neoliberalism, or a 'bringing the state back in', the policy aims to ensure that government remains limited and the scope of state power restricted, or in other words, to consolidate neoliberalism.

This is also the pattern if we look at international protectorates and contemporary international state-building projects, such as BiH, Kosovo or Iraq. Here, when post-conflict reconstruction and 'state-building' is the concern, we should perhaps expect more focus on the state than elsewhere, with an investment in unifying institutions that could be utilised in post-war economic recovery and thereby attract some popular cross-ethnic legitimacy. Nevertheless, there is an undaunted reliance on private enterprise and market forces as the engine for economic recovery, even where the formal economy has been laid in ruins. Not only is 'market economy' written into the constitutions, through the detailed guidance of the international community, as in the Dayton Peace Agreement that regulates BiH and the UN recommendation on Kosovo and subsequent constitution, but international aid and reconstruction programmes have emphasised and executed rapid privatisation in all cases.[8] Regardless of whether the lead has been taken by the IMF and World Bank, the EU or the US, reconstruction programmes have had the same emphasis on rapid and wide-ranging privatisation and liberalisation, often seeking foreign investment and takeovers if possible (for BiH see Donais, 2005; for Kosovo see Sörensen, 2009; for Iraq see Allawi, 2007; Ricks, 2006).

The general neoliberal framework of contemporary aid policy can also be seen in the accompanying focus on civil society. There is a strong Anglo-Saxon and neoliberal bias in how the World Bank and bilateral Western donor agencies conceptualise civil society (cf. Sörensen, 2006). The conception of state and civil society builds on the notion of the economic sphere as being ungovernable. It is not just that government planning and control of the economy is wrong, but that it is against the 'laws' of the market, indeed against nature itself; this understanding is of course essential in biopolitics as a technology of government (Foucault, 2008, ch. 12 and *passim*).

Contemporary international development aid policy is thereby firmly embedded in neoliberalism, as are state-building projects. Here, the recent focus on institutions represents an effort to secure, 'fix' and shape the space for neoliberal globalisation, by providing the institutional framework for both ensuring that the market can operate and managing such life as has become superfluous; such management, *development*, requires institutions that can oversee and help to implement, for example, poverty-reduction programmes and non-material 'sustainable development'.

Structure and content

While the 1990s and the end of bipolarism brought an unprecedented opportunity to depart from geopolitical concerns and extend neoliberal globalisation to the full planetary scale, it would appear that there now is emerging an actually existing alternative to neoliberal development and aid policy. Several of the coming chapters will explore to what extent there is such an alternative, what it means in terms of opportunities and challenges, in general to the West, but in particular with regard to Africa. The book is divided into two parts and ten chapters, including this introduction. Part 1 (Chapters 2–4) analyses 'Western currents' in development primarily at a theoretical and conceptual level. Then, Chapter 5 opens Part 2 by reviewing Asian models of aid. This is followed by three chapters (6–8) devoted to Chinese aid and investment in Africa, one focusing on China, one examining Chinese and African perceptions and perspectives and one looking at the effects and perceptions in Africa. Chapter 9 analyses both Western and Chinese aid from the perspective of its consequences in Africa, and Chapter 10 provides a short conclusion.

In Chapter 2, Mark Duffield explores the connection between development and security from an historical perspective and analyses development as a liberal relation of governance. He uncovers the relationship between development, liberal imperialism and racism and then considers decolonisation in relation to the emergence of a global biopolitical divide between 'developed' and 'underdeveloped' populations. This is in practical terms life supported by social insurance as opposed to life expected to be self-reliant. Development, he argues, is a security technology that polices this divide. He further argues that a post-Cold War re-expansion of the West's external sovereign frontier has been possible through the ability to declare a humanitarian emergency in 'ineffective states'. This frontier is consolidated through 'development' and although judicial territorial sovereignty remains, sovereignty over life within 'ineffective states' is internationalised, negotiable and contingent.

In Chapter 3, Vanessa Pupavac examines the shift from material to non-material development. Taking the Truman's inaugural speech as her departing point, she analyses the subsequent elaborations of economic growth and modernisation theories and the shift to sustainable development theories. She traces the emergence of sustainable development, critically scrutinises its spreading advocacy among NGOs and discloses its heritage, connections and continuities with European Romanticism; after having provided a critical investigation of this major current in contemporary Western development theory and practice, she concludes with a contrast to Chinese (material) aid policy, thereby leading the way for several of the coming chapters.

The critique of aid policy in relation to NGOs is further pursued in Chapter 4, where I analyse how 'civil society' is conceptualised by aid agencies and within the aid industry, especially in relation to ethnicity and post-conflict reconstruction. I engage with the concept 'civil society', by situating it historically, in a social-political as well as an intellectual historical context, and then scrutinising it in relation to aid policy.

Then, drawing on the example of international support to 'civil society' in Kosovo, I suggest that civil society is communitarian and polarised, and that the current Western paradigm of supporting NGOs, as civil society, within ethno-plural post-conflict settings may contribute to ongoing polarisation and fragmentation rather than promote reconciliation or democratisation.

In Chapter 5, Marie Söderberg poses the question of whether there is an 'Asian model' of aid. She provides a comparative overview of Asian perspectives of development aid and shows how both China and 'new' donors, such as South Korea and Thailand, have been influenced by the Japanese model but that there also are important variations, not least with regard to Japan's particular position as a member of the OECD's Development Assistance Committee. Nevertheless, there are crucial common features shared by these states, such as a continuous commitment to the role of the state in the process of development, which should be understood, not least, in relation to their own historical experience with development.

In Chapter 6, He Wenping outlines the evolution and characteristics of Chinese aid to Africa and provides a periodisation based on, primarily, changes within China, where, crucially, she identifies a break between a more ideologically driven orientation and a more pragmatic and economically motivated one following China's economic reforms in the late 1970s.

She looks at the recent expansion of China's role and proceeds to discuss challenges and potential problems facing Chinese aid and foreign relations, with regard to Africa as well as to Western donors. The concluding section highlights key structural problems with and within Chinese aid institutions.

The question of a potential Chinese challenge to Western and international mainstream development is taken a step further in Chapter 7, where Johan Lagerkvist poses it directly and proceeds to investigate how Sino-African relations, economic development and assistance, as well as democratisation processes, are perceived among elite segments within China and two selected African states: Zambia and Tanzania. While he agrees that Chinese aid and investment in Africa is driven by economic concerns, he is critical of the simplistic perspective represented in Western research based on secondary sources, as well as in the media, and points out that in order to really find out what is going on we need to listen to African and Chinese voices and writings. He concludes that there is a challenge, but one that is not necessarily bad, and one in which China itself is open to learning; crucially, although there are strictures, there may be a moment for Africa in which it is increasingly in the spotlight and with the potential to manoeuvre between alternatives.

A similar approach and concern about the tendency towards simplistic presentations within the West are shared by Yahia Mohamed Mahmoud, who in Chapter 8 studies the effect of Chinese aid in Africa. Apart from considering Chinese interests and impacts on African development, he looks at the perceptions in Africa and notes some variations between different groups. He presents a brief case study on Mali and Mauritania and finally considers some of the consequences of Chinese aid, in relation to Africa as well as to Western countries.

In Chapter 9, Henning Melber studies the effects of both Western and Chinese aid on African development, assesses local and regional dynamics and, while opposing a simple dialectical presentation of an emerging anti-thesis, questions both the very question of an alternative and the possibility of a convergence leading to more of the same. While he would perhaps object to the suggestion that he is attempting a synthesis, this is in fact as good a synthesis as we may hope for at this stage and his analysis could be taken as an invitation to revisit the 're-challenge' of the sovereign frontier in Africa.

Chapter 10 offers a short concluding commentary.

These contributions constitute a set of inroads or critical stances towards contemporary mainstream aid policy and a shared curiosity about what an *actually existing* alternative could come to constitute and mean; if there is an Asian alternative or even just a Chinese one, does it then constitute a challenge or an opportunity? An obvious answer would of course be that it is both and we have a task at hand in studying the various effects in its unfolding. If the experience with bipolarism was hardly glorious, with its geostrategic manoeuvring, occasional violent confrontations, clientelism, authoritarianism and repression, then its replacement is not much of an improvement and recent encounters with unipolarism have offered little cause for rejoice or optimism. A new emerging strategic framework, as is crystallising in Africa and gradually becoming apparent elsewhere, may therefore not be unwelcome although the various contributions here reveal that once again we must refrain from uncritical enthusiasm; we need to scrutinise both the Western mainstream and Asian alternatives continuously, as they are – of course – moving targets. The contributions in this volume provide a state of the art of, and critical insights into, major currents in contemporary development and aid thinking and practice. Furthermore, the volume hopes to offer help in identifying, refining and posing open questions, to assist in furthering and opening a scholarly – as well as public – debate and to provide an invitation for further critical investigation into the issues at hand.

Notes

1. Writing in the midst of a global financial crisis, it is now possible to see tendencies from the perspective of a break from the most fundamentalist aspects of neoliberalism. The crisis of 2008 emerged as a crisis of the financial sector. This sector has generated a series of crises since its deregulation in the 1970s (most recently the Asian crisis in 1997), but the current one is the most devastating and threatens the core states and the whole capitalist economy itself. Therefore, even the US and the UK have moved towards rapid programmes of nationalising banks or providing considerable state investment in order to save capitalism from itself. Neoliberalism is now coming under increasing pressure and disrepute even among neoliberal advocates themselves. Certainly, the financial disaster of 2008 will bring a rethinking, and global capitalism will not be the same after the crisis (cf. the excellent collection of articles in Brand and Sekler, 2009, especially Alvater 2009) However, within development and aid policy there are as of yet no such breaks in trends to be recorded.
2. That is with an emphasis on *international*, and on development as a relationship between states in the international system. Development, as an idea and project, is, however, centuries older (see Cowen and Shenton, 1995, 1996; cf. Abrahamsen, 2000; Escobar, 1995; Esteva, 1992; Sachs, 1999). The section is indebted to these sources and with the general perspective influenced by the work of Michel Foucault and (later) Edward Said.
3. The concept of a 'speech act' draws on speech act theory as developed by Austin (1962) and Searle (1969), and which has been applied by the Copenhagen school in studies on *security*, that is, Waever (1989, 1995).
4. The intimate relationship between development and security is now widely assumed by politicians and increasingly studied in academia. During the Cold War there was a bifurcation with separate discourses and problematisations of development and security, which since have become (re)merged into a development-security problematic. On development as a security technology in nineteenth-century Europe see Abrahamsen (2000, ch. 1); Cowen and Shenton (1996, ch. 4) and extensive analysis by Duffield (2001, 2007).
5. It is possible to write 'a brief history of development' in more than one way; good overviews can be found in, for example Hoogvelt (1997); Leys (1996); Martinussen (1997); So (1990).
6. It is thereby different from geopolitics. The concept was developed by Michel Foucault and has been further elaborated within Development and Security studies; my interpretation is indebted to and draws on Dillon (2006); Dillon and Lobo-Guerrero (2008); Dillon and Reid (2009); Duffield (2007); Esposito (2008); Foucault (1976/1978, 2004, 2007, 2008); Gregory (2008); Reid (2007).
7. While promoting life, liberalism has – of course – a tremendous capacity to disallow life as well as to exterminate such life it renders unworthy of living (cf., Dillon and Reid 2009; Duffield, 2007). The term 'surplus population' is

from Karl Marx, and was a category created in the process of capitalist disruption of landed labour and is then continuously recreated; it constituted an essential reserve army for capital. Such a reserve army ensured that labour wages were kept low. Cowen and Shenton (1996) have elaborated on 'development' as a technology to manage surplus *population*. Through a Foucauldian biopolitical reading, Mark Duffield (2007) has extended the analysis of 'development' as a technology to address surplus *life*.

8. Unlike the Kosovo and BiH Constitutions, the Iraqi Constitution does not use the specific wording 'market economy', but such terms as 'modern economic principles' and 'develop the private sector'.

References

Abrahamsen, Rita (2000). *Disciplining Democracy*. Zed Books.

Allawi, Ayad (2007). *The Occupation of Iraq*. Yale University Press.

Alvater, E. (2009). Postneoliberalism or Postcapitalism? The Failure of Neoliberalism in the Financial Market Crisis. *Development Dialogue* no. 51, January 2009, The Dag Hammarskjöld Foundation.

Amsden, A. et al. (1994). *The Market Meets its Match*. Harvard University Press.

Andor, L. and M. Summers (1998). *Market Failure*. Pluto Press.

Austin, J. L. (1962) *How to do Things with Words*. Oxford University Press.

Brand, U. and N. Sekler (2009) (eds). Postneoliberalism – A beginning debate. *Development Dialogue* no. 51, January 2009, The Dag Hammarskjöld Foundation.

Chandler, David (2006). Introduction, in *State-Building* (ed.) D. Chandler, Routledge.

Cowen, M. and R. Shenton (1995). The Invention of Development, in *Power of Development* (ed.) J. Crush, Routledge.

Cowen, M. and R. Shenton (1996). *Doctrines of Development*. Routledge.

Crawford, Gordon (2006). The World Bank and Good Governance, in *The IMF, World Bank and Policy Reform* (eds) A. Paloni and M. Zanardi, pp. 115–42. Routledge.

Dean, Mitchell (1999). *Governmentality: Power and Rule in Modern Society*. SAGE Publications.

Dillon, Michael (2006). Governing through Contingency: The Securing of Biopolitical Governance. *Political Geography* 26, no. 1, pp. 41–7.

Dillon, M. and L. Lobo-Guerrero (2008). Biopolitics of Security in the 21st Century: An Introduction. *Review of International Studies*, 34, no. 2, pp. 265–92.

Dillon, M. and J. Reid (2009). *The Liberal Way of War*. Routledge.

Donais, T. (2005). *The Political Economy of Peace-building in Post-Dayton Bosnia* Routledge.

Duffield, Mark (2001). *Global Governance and the New Wars*, Zed Books.

Duffield, Mark (2007). *Development, Security and Unending War*. Polity Press.

Escobar, Arturo (1995). *Encountering Development*. Princeton University Press.

Esposito, Roberto (2008). *Bios: Biopolitics and Philosophy*. University of Minnesota Press.

Esteva, G. (1992). Development, in *The Development Dictionary: A Guide to Knowledge as Power* (ed.) W. Sachs, Zed Books.

Foucault, Michel (1976/78). *The History of Sexuality Vol. 1.* Penguin.
Foucault, Michel (2004). *Society Must Be Defended.* Palgrave Macmillan.
Foucault, Michel (2007). *Security, Territory and Population.* Palgrave Macmillan.
Foucault, Michel (2008). *The Birth of Biopolitics.* Palgrave Macmillan.
Gilpin, Robert (1987). *The Political Economy of International Relations.* Princeton University Press.
Gray, John (2003/2007). *Al-Qaeda and What It means to be Modern.* Faber & Faber.
Gregory, Derek (2008). The Biopolitics of Baghdad. *Human Geography,* vol. 1, issue 1, Bolton, MA: Institute for Human Geography.
Harrison, Graham (2004). *The World Bank and Africa.* Routledge.
Hoogvelt, Ankie (1997). *Globalization and the Post-Colonial World.* Macmillan.
Hout, W. (2007). *The Politics of Aid Selectivity: Good Governance Criteria in World Bank, US and Dutch development assistance,* Routledge Studies in Development Economics. Routledge.
Lavigne, M. (1995/99). *The Economics of Transition.* Palgrave Macmillan.
Leys, Colin (1996). *The Rise and Fall of Development Theory.* Indiana University Press.
Martinussen, John (1997). *Society, State & Market.* Zed Books.
Pender, John (2002). Empowering the Poorest? The World Bank and the Voices of the Poor, in *Rethinking Human Rights: Critical Approaches to International Politics* (ed.) D. Chandler, pp. 97–114. Palgrave Macmillan.
Polanyi, Karl (1944/1957). *The Great Transformation.* Beacon Press.
Pupavac, Vanessa (2008). A Critical Review of NGO Sustainable Development Philosophy in *China's Opening Society: Non-State Sector and Governance* (eds) J. Fewsmith and Y. Zheng. Routledge.
Reid, Julian (2007). *The Biopolitics of the War on Terror.* Manchester University Press.
Ricks, T. (2006). *Fiasco: The American Military Adventure in Iraq.* Penguin.
Sachs, W. (1992) (ed.). *The Development Dictionary: A Guide to Knowledge and Power.* Zed Books.
Sachs, W. (1992). One world, in *The Development Dictionary* (ed.) W.Sachs, Zed Books.
Searle, J. (1969). *Speech Acts.* Cambridge University Press.
Shafaeddin, M. (2006). Trade Liberalization and Economic Reform in Developing Countries: Structural Change or De-industrialization? in *The IMF, World Bank and Policy Reform* (eds) A. Paloni and M. Zanardi, pp. 162–90. Routledge.
Smith, Neil (2003). *American Empire: Roosevelt's Geographer and the Prelude to Globalization.* University of California Press.
Smith, Neil (2005). *The Endgame of Globalizaton.* Routledge.
So, Alvin (1990). *Social Change and Development.* Sage Publications.
Stiglitz, Joseph (2002). *Globalization and its Discontents.* W. W. Norton.
Sörensen, J. S. (1997). Pluralism or Fragmentation. *War Report, May 1997.* IWPR.
Sörensen, J. S. (2006). Biståndets Biopolitik: Civilsamhälle, enskilda organisationer och styrning på distans, in *Det Civila Samhället som forskningsfält* (eds) L. Svedberg and L. Trägårdh, Gidlunds.
Sörensen, J. S. (2009). *State Collapse and Reconstruction in the Periphery.* Berghahn Books.
Tvedt, Terje (1998). *Angels of Mercy or Development Diplomats.* Africa World Press.

Waever, Ole (1989). *Security the Speech Act: Analysing the Politics of a Word,* COPRI Working Paper no. 1989/19.

Waever, Ole (1995). Securitization and Desecuritization, in *On Security* (ed.) R. Lipschutz, pp. 46–86. Columbia University Press.

World Bank (1999). *Entering the 21st century: World Development Report 1999/2000.* New York: Oxford University press.

World Bank (2002). *Attacking Poverty: World Development Report 2000/2001.* New York: Oxford University Press.

Part I
Western Currents

2
The Development-Security Nexus in Historical Perspective: Governing the World of Peoples[1]

Mark Duffield

It is now commonplace for policy-makers to assert that 'if we help people who are less fortunate than ourselves, not only is it good for them, it is also good for us' (see Blair, 2001). This enlightened self-interest summarises how the current relationship between development and security is understood. That is, in fostering 'their' development, we simultaneously improve 'our' security. While often presented today as a new policy departure (DAC, 2003), the development-security nexus has a much longer genealogy. As part of his inaugural address in January 1949, for example, President Truman is credited with making one of the first calls for an inter-state development regime tailored to the new post-war world. Besides drawing attention to a situation in which 'half the people of the world are living in conditions approaching misery', he pointed out that their poverty 'is a handicap and a threat to both them and to more prosperous areas' (Escobar, 1995, p. 3).

Since this enunciation of the development-security nexus, however, the regularly promised annulment of global poverty has proven elusive. More familiar has been a recurrent and indignant rediscovery not only of this poverty's persistence but of the growing wealth gap between the developed and underdeveloped worlds (Brett, 1985; Myrdal, 1957; OECD, 1972; UNDP, 1996). After more than fifty years of strenuous development efforts, it is estimated that up to a third of humanity still lives in 'chronic poverty' (CPRC, 2005). Rather than simply focus on the reasons why poverty persists, it is important to examine the political function that its constant rediscovery serves, in particular, how it validates liberal order. While poverty did not directly cause, for example, the Third World's attraction to communism during the 1950s, the refugee crisis of the 1970s or the new wars of the 1990s – or even today's threat of international terrorism – in each case it has been discovered to lie at the root of the problem (DAC, 2003; Morawetz, 1977; Wilson, 1953). From communism to terrorism, through its marginalising effects and its ability to foster resentment and alienation amongst ordinary people, poverty has monotonously been rediscovered as a recruiting ground for the moving feast of strategic threats by which liberal order is constantly menaced.

At the same time, as William Easterly has argued, since Truman's 1949 address, apart from the development-security nexus, one can detect a number of recurrent practical measures that have shaped development policy. This includes a regular 'call for a new program, the rationale in terms of poverty, the optimism that foreign aid programs can make a difference' (Easterly, 2002, p. 227). Since the 1950s, aid organisations have exhibited an enduring tendency to define outputs in terms of money disbursed rather than services delivered; to produce low-return but observable outcomes such as framework reports, attractive brochures and high-level meetings rather than less observable but more important independent, ex-post programme evaluations; a tendency towards institutional amnesia and, not least, a willingness to engage in obfuscation and spin control 'like always describing aid efforts as "new and improved"(ibid., p. 288).

To substantiate his argument, Easterly uses a table containing three columns headed 'Stone Age' (roughly 1950s to 1970s), 'Iron Age' (1980s to 1990s) and 'Silicon Age' (the 00s) (ibid., p. 237). The rows are represented by different aid declarations such as the need to *improve donor coordination*, the need to *increase aid volumes*, that *aid works in good local policy environments*, the need to *increase emphasis on poverty*, the importance of *debt relief*, that *Africa desperately needs reform* and that *Africa is already reforming*. The resulting boxes are filled with appropriate Stone, Iron and Silicon Age quotes from UN reports, US presidential statements, World Bank documents and G7 briefs. The table reveals that what we take as today's informed policy position (aptly summarised by the above row descriptors) was also cutting-edge thinking during the 'Stone Age' of the international aid system. Rather than a steady, experience-based refining and progression of policy, the table suggests an institutional 'Groundhog Day' where every decade or two similar pronouncements are repackaged by a new generation of policy-makers and presented afresh as the way forward. When, since the eighteenth century, for example, has international development not been linked with economic growth and how its benefits can be made to work for the poor? With a few basic tools and a problem it has yet to solve, what is singular about development is its institutional ability both to survive and prosper. Despite periodic crises of confidence, it unfailingly reinvents itself as 'new and improved'. Development is able to insist on being judged by a yet distant future, rather than a past that has been lived and experienced.

While Easterly attempts to explain this recurrence institutionally, that is, as deriving from shared organisational interests, the practical Groundhog Day that development policy is trapped within is connected with its intrinsic association with security. It is with regard to the constant threats from non-Western peoples – from the zones of savagery and barbarism – that development as security is continually reinventing itself as a new and improved solution to the problems that liberalism unfailingly discovers beyond its borders. Consequently, it is possible to trace the genealogy of the development-security nexus much further than the birth of the post-Second World War inter-state development regime.

Liberalism and Empire

Despite continuing to shape our present predicament, the formative connection between nineteenth-century liberalism on the one hand, and imperialism on the other, has been neglected in mainstream International Relations and Development studies (Biccum, 2005; Cooke, 2003; Jahn, 2005; Mehta, 1999). This disregard has helped conceal and hence sustain liberalism's enduring paradox: the ability to support liberty, equality and democracy as the necessary benchmarks of civilised society while, at the same time, accepting illiberal forms of rule as necessary or sufficient for a barbarian, backward or underdeveloped one. Robert Cooper puts a contemporary gloss on this long-standing paradox when he claims that among European states, 'we keep the law but when operating in the jungle, we need to also use the laws of the jungle' (Cooper, 2002 p. 15). Liberalism's early architects, for example, James and John Stuart Mill, Lord Macaulay and Sir Henry Main, as well as many practitioners of Empire, were not only aware of the liberal paradox, but consciously sort to normalise it and interpret the emergence of representative government in Europe as proof of the unlikelihood of its occurrence elsewhere and, consequently, as justifying varying degrees of despotic, paternalistic or ameliorative rule abroad (Jahn, 2005; Mehta, 1999; Pitts, 2003). This *liberal imperialism* also informed the emerging social democratic movement. Conscious of the European need for tropical raw materials, the ' "Fabian" imperialists', for example, argued that such economic dependence carried a justifiable concern that resources were properly managed and developed, ideally using appropriate industrial technologies and educational measures that stimulated a desire for social progress within the backward country. Given this need to promote rational development, 'there can be no inherent natural right in a people to refuse that measure of compulsory education that shall raise it from childhood to manhood in the order of nationalities' (Hobson, 1938, p. 229).

While the terms used to code the civilised/barbarian dichotomy have changed over time, moving from its nineteenth-century variants, through the twentieth century's concern with development/underdevelopment, to today's effective/ineffective state anxieties, this underlying paradox has been reproduced continually. It interconnects, for example, with the widespread left-liberal support for the upsurge of Western humanitarian interventionism following the end of the Cold War (Douzinas, 2003). At the same time, in a threatening world, the idea of an imperial order, tempered with calls for voluntarism and partnership, has been rehabilitated under the rubric of *liberal interventionism* (Coker, 2003; Cooper, 2002; Ferguson, 2003). As a supporter of such order, Michael Ingnatieff argues that such an urge is not 'discreditable in itself, provided the empire does more than reproduce itself, provided that it does eventuate in self-rule for nations and peoples' (Ignatieff, 2003, p. 22).

Reflecting its Enlightenment heritage, liberalism equates culture and government. For J. S. Mill, the cultural level and moral outlook of a people – its social character – set the limits and possibilities of its governance. From this culture-government perspective, there is a necessary and intrinsic relationship between civilisation and representative government. At the same time, the political expression of barbarism is despotism. Because the social character of a people limits the possibilities for its governance, it follows that the same model of government and its associated legal codes and moral expectations cannot be applied unilaterally across what is, in practice, a human species internally divided according to its potential for political existence. For Mill, articulating the necessary politico-cultural discontinuities between nations and peoples represented a major advance over the ideas of many Enlightenment theorists, especially those believing in the universality of European laws and institutions.[2] This 'advance' not only makes a connection between development and security – as a means of managing an orderly transition between discrete politico-cultural stages – it also connects development with scientific or state racism.

Racism and development

Racism underpins liberalism's acceptance of a global dispensation that assigns freedom and representation to 'us' while declaring illiberal government as a characteristic of 'their' existence. There is a both chronological and ontological connection between the civilisational division of humankind into politico-cultural stages and, alternatively, its hierarchical ordering into biologically determined races. Following the abolition of slavery, which created the possibility of a universal humanity, both cultural and biological schemata emerged during the first half of the nineteenth century as ways of re-dividing humankind, thus nullifying this possibility (Hall, 2002). While the turn towards an outwardly biological or so-called scientific racism has attracted wide attention (Arendt, 1994; Foucault, 2003), any attempt to divide the human species according to different modalities and potentialities for existence, including political existence, is ultimately biological in essence. Although cultural and biological approaches to the ordering of humankind are outwardly different they share the same biopolitical foundation and together constitute an interconnected racist dynamic (Duffield, 2006). While forming separate and often opposed conclusions, both approaches agree that nations and peoples are inherently different, either culturally or biologically. Where a cultural coding informs a liberal developmental logic, a biological one is linked to an exterminatory impulse. Sharing the same foundation, moreover, they interconnect and move in and out of each other. Although Mill, for example, held that the politico-cultural differences between peoples and nations were mutable and thus open to change through developmental means, that is, through education and guidance (and in so doing he opposed an outwardly biological determinism), he still found it necessary to describe these differences through such dichotomies as civilised/barbarian, advanced/backward, active/passive, industrious/sensuous and so on, while assigning the former terms to 'all the English and Germans and the latter terms to the Irish, French, Southern Europeans, and the "Orientals" (more and more so as one moved south and east)' (Pitts, 2003, p. 222).

A culturally coded racism supports the liberal will to govern, ameliorate or otherwise compensate for the limitations of an inferior politico-cultural existence. Development – its practical expression – constitutes a liberal alternative to extermination, claiming a greater utility and efficiency over violence as a means of governing subject races.[3] While not the same as development, cultural racism informs it. The dichotomies that liberalism establishes between the civilised/barbarian, developed/ underdeveloped and effective/ineffective, for example, have been experienced as *developmental* challenges since the dawn of modernity (Cowen and Shenton, 1996). Development is intrinsic to *liberal imperialism* and its subjectification in politico-cultural racism. In this respect, rather than extermination, through protection and education, liberalism seeks to compensate and ameliorate the differences and vulnerabilities within the human species that it ceaselessly problematises. Liberalism's will to govern is framed through its claim to speak on behalf of people, their rights, freedoms and well-being (Mehta, 1999, p. 198). In championing equality and democracy, liberalism not only justifies the Western genius, it also defines the West's own moral self-identity and its place in the world (Biccum, 2005). Rather than reducing the social and political distance between developed and underdeveloped species-life, development constantly reproduces it.

Compared to Easterly's (2002) institutionally determined analysis of development's recurrent post-Second World War features, Uday Singh Mehta (1999) teases out development as a design of power by addressing three interconnected questions to nineteenth-century liberalism. First, *how does a liberal understand life that is unfamiliar by virtue of it existing in a different realm of custom and experience?* Understanding the unfamiliar is 'to see those experiences, those life-forms, as provisional' (ibid., p. 191). The task then is to connect that provisional, incomplete or even repugnant species-life to a more accurate science, a more consistent morality, a more just politics or a higher social teleology. To judge unfamiliar life as incomplete (and the interventions that this judgement allows) 'is the conceptual and normative core of the liberal justification of the empire' (ibid.). Second, *from what perspective is this provisional life judged to be incomplete?* It is a perspective from which experience 'is always viewed and assessed from a future point' (ibid., p. 192). Because of this forward vantage position, it is possible to claim to know the future history of an incomplete life form and how it will gestate into a better or more complete existence. Because of this longitudinal perspective, development is given to gradualism, paternalism and education in order to achieve the required gestation. Finally, *how is such knowledge of the future possible?* It is possible to know an *a priori* future when 'the soothsayer himself causes and contrives the events he proclaims in advance' (ibid., p. 210). As a strategisation of power, development is an interventionary technology of protection and betterment that, over time, seeks to fashion a more complete and meaningful future for an unfamiliar life form experienced as provisional or incomplete.

For Mehta, it is the developmental response to unfamiliar life, rather than liberalism's endorsement of empire as such, that lies at the heart of the liberal paradox (ibid., pp. 200–201). This is an important observation since it frees our understanding of development from otherwise being permanently attached to its contingent institutional anchor points, for example, nineteenth-century imperialism or the post-Second World War aid regime. Development is a liberal strategisation of power and tutelage that has a viral ability to reinvent itself, allowing it to leap institutions and act across generations. It was at work, for example, in the colonial practice of indirect rule or Native Administration (Cooke, 2003; Duffield, 2005). During the process of decolonisation, an adaptive development took on its modern institutional form as an inter-state relationship of 'development'. In the will to make unfamiliar and hence provisional life more complete, development reappeared as a way of mediating the biopolitical dichotomy at the heart of an emerging world of independent territorial nation states, that is, the politico-cultural distinction between developed and undeveloped worlds.

Decolonisation and containment

While the design of development can be recognised in both the colonial and post-colonial periods, the nineteenth century and today are very different. In addressing this problem of change within continuity, the idea of a negotiated 'sovereign frontier' is useful (Harrison, 2004). Frontiers present themselves in many different forms. For example, there are the fixed and mutually recognised borders of countries; at the same time, frontiers can be fluid or spatial, as with a shifting line of conquest and exchange, capable of advancing and retreating in time as a moving politico-cultural 'sphere of influence'. Samuel Huntington describes such a frontier in the fourteen-hundredyear history of the constant ebbing and flowing over the countries, regions and peoples of Europe, North Africa and the Middle East of the politico-cultural border between Christianity and Islam (Huntington, 1993, 7). From this perspective, the nineteenth-century European distinction between civilisation/barbarity also represents a moving politico-cultural frontier, this time on a planetary scale. Colonisation, decolonisation and today's liberal interventionism can be interpreted as the expansion, contraction and re-expansion of the West's external sovereign frontier. In relation to this fluid, contested and negotiated line of demarcation, development functions as a security mechanism that acts on populations or life itself. As a liberal design of power, development functions in order to protect and better life. It acts as a technology of security, consolidating the West's sovereign frontier by supporting and including that life which is deemed useful and capable of self-organisation while excluding the useless and destabilising (Duffield, 2005).

The so-called New Imperialism of the late nineteenth century, typically associated with the Scramble for Africa, completed the closure of the 'global commons'. Speaking in the interests of humanity, its authors swallowed whole those largely tropical and subtropical regions of the planet still unclaimed by an external power. Since this act of seizure, all geographies have become relative (Smith, 2003). Late colonialism embodied a genocidal expansion of the West's external sovereign frontier (Hochschild, 2002). The liberal will to govern was rejuvenated in the disgust and horror of this 'insane imperialism' (Hobson, 1938, p. 246; also Morel, 1920). At issue however, was not conquest and acquisition as such, *it was the manner in which the new territories and peoples acquired were to be properly and effectively governed.* In dividing and apportioning the world, late colonialism was a necessary precursor of the territorial nation state that became the desired global political architecture following decolonisation. While attempting to consolidate the sovereign frontier through the decentralised technologies of indirect rule or Native Administration (Lugard, 1965), an essentially hegemonic and gradualist developmentalism could, however, never complete the nation-state project. This task fell to an insurgent nationalism.

While the UN had precedents in the League of Nations, its formation in 1945 heralded a world of independent territorial nation states that, for the fist time, enjoyed formal or *de jure* equality within international law. Driven by nationalism, independence represented a 'pushing back' of the West's external sovereign frontier. Hitherto limited to civilised peoples, Mill's advice that equality and non-intervention should guide relations between nations in theory became applicable to humankind as a whole. However, the immediate re-division of the world into developed and underdeveloped states worked against this possibility from the beginning. The political architecture of the world of states, reinforced by the Cold War, was based upon the principle of territorial integrity and respect for domestic sovereign competence (Elden, 2005). Between the 1950s and 1970s, through state-led industrialisation, centralised health and education initiatives and rearmament programmes, nationalist elites pursed counter-hegemonic modernisation strategies. Unlike development, modernisation aimed at narrowing the differences between the developed and underdeveloped worlds rather than reproducing them. In this respect, while modernising states were still evolving in Asia, even in Africa, up to the 1970s, they were not without some success in the field of public welfare (Bloom and Standing, 2001). Regarding the negotiated sovereign frontier, this period was synonymous with nationalist elites being able to frame the terms of their engagement with the outside world (Harrison, 2004).

Despite wide support from progressive and social democratic forces, from the moment of decolonisation, state-led modernisation and its associated militarisation were subject to a liberal critique by international actors speaking on behalf of the peoples and communities in the territories concerned (Pupavac, 2005). Modernisation's wasteful, urban-biased, 'top-down' policies, for example, were unfavourably contrasted with the benefits of people-centred 'bottom-up', community-based sustainable development (Schumacher, 1974). As heirs of the liberal tradition, international NGOs played an important role in contesting state-led modernisation and shaping the biopolitical technologies to re-expand the external sovereign frontier. Reflecting colonial concerns over social breakdown, a major issue was that modernisation, by encouraging urbanisation, would undermine community and family bonds. By the end of the 1970s, contrary to Third World ideas of convergence, as a means of strengthening local self-reliance and thereby containing the effects of poverty, NGO-pioneered 'sustainable development' had begun to shape Western policy discourse (Duffield, 2005). Development's unease with independent modernisation was also reinforced by another concern.

During the nineteenth century, the liberal experience of unfamiliar life as provisional was sufficient to justify intervention and Empire. Arguments among British liberals based upon right to conquest or immanent external threats 'are almost entirely absent or, when invoked, are of a secondary status' (Metha, 1999, p. 191). This stands in marked contrast to the situation today, where fears are constantly aroused concerning the vulnerability of mass consumer society to disorder beyond its porous borders. One explanation for this difference concerns the world-historic change in the Western perception of human circulation. In general terms, as part of the expansion of European empires and spheres of influence, for several centuries the broad movement had been North to South, that is, outwards to the non-European world (Held *et al.* Decolonisation, however, altered this dynamic. The emergence of a world of independent states called forth millions of new citizens living for the first time within their own national borders. However, each new state with its fresh batch of citizens necessarily increases the number of potential non-citizens, stateless persons and refugees (Arendt, 1994, pp. 230–1). Besides a world of states, decolonisation also gave rise to a vibrant but threatening 'world of peoples'. This new world, moreover, in terms of human circulation triggered 'the reversal of population movements between old colonies and the old metropolises' (Balibar, 1991, p. 21). Acting as a planetary biopolitical hinge, decolonisation swung the direction of migration from South to North, that is, inwards towards the metropole. For the first time, growing numbers of non-Europeans, either looking for a better life or fleeing trouble, were able to move legally or illegally across international borders and head towards the West's emerging mass consumer societies. Consequently, human circulation is no longer associated with opportunity. On the contrary, since the 1960s, unchecked migration has been regarded as a threat to the Western way of life. Decolonisation announced a long-term crisis of population containment of planetary proportions. The nineteenth-century liberal urge to protect and better has been supplemented by a contemporary developmental need to secure unfamiliar and incomplete life.

The politico-cultural categories of liberalism provide a means of striating, classifying and managing the circulatory world of peoples. The reversal of international flows marks a shift in racial discourse from a colonial preoccupation with 'biological-types in location' to the contemporary concern with 'cultural-types in circulation'. The immigrant – the embodiment of cultural difference in motion – became the new racism's first iconic figure. An initial response to decolonisation and the pushing back of the external sovereign frontier was the creation of an 'internal frontier' associated with the increasingly urgent need to control immigration into Europe's emerging mass consumer societies. In it's 1964 manifesto, for example, the Labour Party promised to further restrict immigration from Britain's former colonies. To offset this restriction, a raft of legislation, special measures and training schemes followed that created an internal development regime aimed at redressing imbalances, compensating for disadvantage and promoting tolerance through ameliorating the effects of cultural difference within the home population (Duffield, 1984). Regarding the external development frontier, the manifesto also set out proposals to establish a new Ministry of Overseas Development to tackle world poverty and the 'growing danger that the increasing tensions caused over gross inequalities of circumstances between rich and poor nations will be sharply accentuated by differences of race and colour' (Labour Party, 1964). This Ministry centralised previous ad hoc and mainly colonial institutional initiatives in this field. The manifesto argued that the new Ministry would work for the expansion of international trade, increase government aid spending, support the UN and encourage the work of NGOs. The latter's proven enterprise, it was suggested, must be matched 'with Government action to give new hope in the current United Nations Development Decade' (ibid.).

Sovereignty and humanitarian emergency

With hindsight, the world of independent states seems more a temporary aberration rather than the culmination of a world-historic trend (Derlugian, 1996). By the 1980s, as if confirming liberal scepticism over Third World modernisation (Pupavac, 2005), the era of 'state failure' had begun and with it a huge compensatory expansion of the international NGO movement. Encouraged by increasing apprehension over the violent and regressive character of the 'new wars' appearing within ineffective states (Kaldor, 1999), the liberal divide between civilised and barbarous peoples has once again been re-invigorated. Since the end of the Cold War, barbarity in the shape of warlords, militia leaders, criminalised elites, age-old animosities, non-integrating regions, tribal hatreds – the reassertion of the pre-modern more generally – has been noted, analysed and re-analysed (Fukuyama, 2002; Huntington, 1993; Kaplan, 1994).

Within policy discourse, sustainable development and internal war both take a self-reliant species life as their reference point. In this respect, however, they are opposites; whereas sustainable development seeks to strengthen self-reliance, internal war is depicted as undermining and eroding it, indeed, 'it is development in reverse' (Collier et al., 2003, p. ix). The destruction of development and erosion of self-reliance fuels destabilising forms of global circulation and adds to the crisis of containment. From a Schmittian perspective, sovereignty can be understood as that power able to declare a state of emergency and, in so doing, act without the restraint of law (see also Agamben, 1998). The ability to declare a humanitarian emergency also has sovereign implications. Rather than an emergency of the state, however, with its corresponding programme of bans, exclusions and extra-legal detention centres, this is an emergency at the level of people and population. In this case, ruling beyond the law means governing beyond international law, especially the post-Second World War settlement that supported non-intervention and *de jure* sovereign equality (Douzinas, 2003). Within post-Cold War development discourse, the civilised/barbarous dichotomy has been realised in terms of the humanitarian differences between *effective* and *ineffective* states. This humanitarian division throws into relief the different and opposing capacities of states to protect and better the lives and livelihoods of people. Prompted by the threat of bad international circulation, that is, the human and criminal by-products of the new wars, the ability of effective states to declare a humanitarian emergency within ineffective ones has been instrumental in the re-expansion of the West's external sovereign frontier.

The seventeenth-century solidarist position has once again moved into the foreground of international relations (Wheeler, 2000). Since the end of the Cold War, in the shape of the 'responsibility to protect' (ICISS, 2001), solidarism has increasingly informed the emerging custom and practice of international intervention and the direction of UN reform (Weiss, 2004). The responsibility to protect holds that if an ineffective state is unable or unwilling to protect the human security of its citizens, following a supreme humanitarian emergency, as a last resort, this responsibility passes to the international community of effective states. For solidarism, moral and ethical considerations trump the restrictions of international law, which 'can be overridden in cases of supreme humanitarian emergency' (Wheeler, 2000, p. 61). The ending of the Cold War eroded political support among effective states for the principles of non-intervention and international legal restraint. The 1990s saw a major upsurge in the number of large-scale humanitarian, peace-enforcement and peace-keeping operations, many of them combined in different ways (Macrae, 2002). As a measure of its success, this interventionism has helped to reduce markedly the number of civil wars in the world. Having climbed steadily since the 1950s to peak at more than fifty in the mid-1990s, their number has declined significantly to fewer than thirty today (HSC, 2005, p. 23). However, as Kosovo, Afghanistan and Iraq suggest, ending 'wars' within ineffective states is relatively easy, far more difficult is securing the 'peace' among the people living within them. Whereas Third World states enjoyed a formal *de jure* equality with those of the First and Second Worlds during the Cold War, since the end of the 1980s effective states have increasingly assumed the moral authority to intervene within what are now judged to be ineffective ones. An informal or *de facto* condition of state inequality now shapes the international arena (Pupavac, 2001). Humanitarian intervention, with its concern for protecting life, was the blunt instrument used to demolish the *de jure* sovereign equality of the world of states. The ineffective state and how it can be reshaped in order to discharge its international duties better, especially supporting the human security of its citizens, is now the central focus of international security and development policy.

There is 'a secret solidarity' between humanitarianism and sovereign power (Agamben, 1998). While asserting a radical right of intervention in civil war, in the interests of maintaining political neutrality, humanitarian actors focus on tending the victims of sovereign power while leaving that power unchecked. In practical terms, humanitarian intervention aims to 'have as limited an effect on the authority structure of the concerned state as possible' (Riseman and McDougal, 1969, quoted in Wheeler, 2000: pp. 42–3). Exposing the divide between effective and ineffective states, humanitarian intervention avoids directly addressing the deficiencies of the latter; for the development critics of humanitarianism, it 'resists engagement with the state and capacity-building on the grounds that it breaches humanitarian independence and neutrality' (Leader and Colenso, 2005, p. 40). As a consequence, humanitarian action on its own has been found lacking in terms of addressing the crisis of containment; although it can save lives, humanitarian intervention cannot reconstruct states or govern populations. In other words, the shortcomings of humanitarianism create a developmental space. This apparent developmental critique, however, is less a critique and more a mutual dependency that rests on the sovereign nature of development itself. Humanitarianism and development are two sides of the liberal urge to protect and better life that otherwise lacks the perquisites of a proper or complete existence. Between humanitarian protection and developmental betterment, there is a mutual conditioning, each depending upon the other. This formative relationship rests upon the moral ability to override existing sovereignties while, at the same time, being able to assert a liberal will to govern the newly exposed life. It is typically presented as a moral dilemma attaching to the iconic figure of the hungry child (Campbell, Clark and Manzo, 2005). The onlooker is faced with choosing between feeding the starving child who will die tomorrow, or helping the many more destitute children whose entire lives will be blighted by chronic poverty unless their 'conditions are bettered: this is the most painful of tasks' (Jones, 1965, pp. 43–4). This recurrent moral dilemma, arising from a condition of permanent emergency, is continually resolved in favour of the greater efficiency of development. However, in an uncertain world, one thing is certain; tomorrow there will be more starving children on our TV screens.

This dilemma conceals a biopolitical choice between 'the right to make live and let die' (Foucault, 2003, p. 241). To decide the point of exception – the child who can be allowed to die so that others may live – is not only a tough moral choice, it is a sovereign act that unites the humanitarian urge to protect with the developmental will to better.

In deciding the exception, aid agencies and NGOs become non-state or petty sovereign powers able, through routine administrative choices, to decide between supporting life or allowing death (see Butler, 2004, p. 56). During the 1990s, funded and orchestrated by Western states, the administrative sovereign power of aid agencies and NGOs among the world of peoples has increased. It has fallen to development to consolidate the external frontier and, in a fresh round of 'new and improved' programming, to govern it more effectively. This process of consolidation is examined in relation to the idea of human security.

Human security, non-insured life and ineffective states

Given the centrality of the responsibility to protect for Western interventionism, we can ask the question – protect what exactly? In providing an answer, the concept of 'human security' needs to be considered. It is now accepted by policy-makers that international security needs to be understood more widely than the traditional geopolitical register linking state, territory, defence and alliance. Territories also come with populations, and modern effective states take care to ensure optimal levels of social fitness and resilience. Human security highlights a range of biopolitical variables associated with underdevelopment that threaten the equilibrium of population – chronic poverty, environmental breakdown, economic marginalisation, forced migration, bad government, health pandemics, social exclusion, and so on. Such factors are not only serious in themselves; in an interdependent world they are capable of threatening international stability.

In biopolitical terms, the developed/underdeveloped dichotomy can be seen as signalling a metaphorical distinction between 'insured' and 'non-insured' life (Duffield, 2007). Citizens within mass consumer societies are supported by centralised welfare technologies associated with social insurance that translate into universal health, education, employment and pension provision. While the quality and quantity of such welfare support is subject to constant debate, in contrast, the subjects of underdevelopment are non-insured. To put this another way, under the rubric of sustainable development those populations existing beyond the borders of mass consumer society are expected to be self-reliant in terms of their basic economic, social and welfare needs. However, in a globalised world, self-reliance is in a state of permanent emergency. This suggests that a biopolitics of underdevelopment is a combination of self-reliance plus international humanitarian assistance. From this perspective, humanitarian assistance functions as a form of non-contractual, international insurance of last resort. Faced with the generic dichotomy between insured and non-insured species life, human security embraces the hope that sustainable development will secure the latter while, at the same time, drawing attention to those factors that threaten its containment and hence menace global society. Not least is the prospect of non-insured migrants making asymmetric demands on mass society's welfare systems. While optimistic for the future, human security cautions the West that underdevelopment is dangerous.

Concern over human security emerged following the end of the Cold War and, by the close of the 1990s, had produced a growing number of dedicated networks, research programmes and international commissions (Duffield and Waddell, 2006). One only has to scratch the surface of the extensive literature on human security, however, to realise that it encapsulates, indeed, is built upon, the humanitarian distinction between effective and ineffective states; some states are better than others at supporting the human security of their citizens. While the word *human* in human security might imply a universal or cosmopolitan ethic, policy discourse is unequivocal; the territorial nation state is, and will remain, the single most important institution for guaranteeing human security (Boutros-Ghali, 1995, p. 44; UN, 2004, p. 11). The idea of human security is embodied within the responsibility to protect. Indeed, protecting human security has become 'one of the fundamental objectives of modern international institutions' (ICISS, 2001, p. 6). However, while speaking on behalf of the security of humans, interventions under this dictum are not really interventions at all, merely a time-limited international substitution for the original state. In other words, the international community is only responsible 'until it can find a responsible agent to replace the failed state itself' (Warner, 2003, p. 114). With the collapse of the small-state Washington Consensus and scepticism over the transforming ability of humanitarian assistance, concern over human security signals that the ineffective state, and its circulatory consequences, has moved centre stage in international security.

In a radically interconnected world, ineffective states, with their limited ability to police borders and support populations, pose a threat that is no longer captured within a traditional geopolitical register. Indeed, geopolitics is being reframed in biopolitical terms (Strategy Unit, 2005). Magnified by weak and ineffective government, threats to the national interest of effective states now primarily arise from the circulatory political, economic and security effects of continuing underdevelopment. Such disturbances do not threaten the survival of Western states directly; they menace the fragile livelihood systems, public infrastructures and centralised food, energy and transport networks of mass consumer society – massified and interconnected systems that support the Western way of life. Even in the course of its normal working, however, mass society is prone to recurrent breakdown and chronic system failure impacting on millions of people. In relation to this intrinsic vulnerability, the circulatory effect of underdeveloped, that is, non-insured, life is a further identifiable threat. Within the territories covered by ineffective states, the world's chronically poor, and with them the ills of underdevelopment, are concentrated (Leader and Colenso, 2005, p. 9). Exacerbated by the neglect and wilful acts of bad government, this stubborn concentration is itself questioning whether the UN Millennium Development Goals of halving world poverty by 2015 can be met (Benn, 2004). Although chronic poverty does not cause conflict, for policy-makers it increases the risk of human rights abuse and instability (Collier et al., 2003). Indeed, as policy-makers are now arguing (Strategy Unit, 2005, pp. 4–9), while the overall numbers of internal wars and battle deaths have declined since the early 1990s, if human security together with non-battle deaths due to poverty, health crises, displacement, economic collapse, and so on, are factored into the equation, human *in*security is argued to be a growing factor that will continue to exacerbate the problem of winning the peace.

Apart from making the achievement of foreign policy objectives more difficult, this instability at the level of population affects Britain's way of life in a number of ways. For example, political tensions can 'trigger large unmanaged flows of refugees and asylum seekers. In already disadvantaged communities in the UK large inflows of transient populations can be damaging to social cohesion' (ibid., p. 11). Although migrants from ineffective states represented only 20 per cent of total immigration in 2003, 'those states yielded 65% of asylum seekers, and 90% of those granted asylum or leave to stay in the UK' (ibid.). In terms of energy security, the Strategy Unit points out that those countries regarded as unstable held 60 per cent of the world's oil reserves in 2003, a proportion projected to rise over the following decade. The UK's vulnerability to price shocks is expected to increase; it became a net importer of natural gas in 2006 and is projected to do so for oil in 2010. As can be seen from the experience of Afghanistan, ungoverned territories can also provide base areas where international terrorist organisations can train recruits and launch attacks. In such areas, lack of public oversight makes the extra-legal movement of money and commodities easier, while poverty, inequality and alienation make a good recruiting ground for terrorist organisations. At the same time, there is a danger that 'national terrorist and insurgent groups, radicalised by military intervention, may become aligned with international terror groups' (ibid., p. 12).

The liberal culture–government connection is again being restated. Rather than a relationship between barbarism and despotism, it is between a culture of human *in*-security and its corresponding *ineffective* government that policy discourse now conjures up through terms like failed or fragile states, difficult partnerships, low-income countries under stress (LICUS), and so on (see Torres and Anderson, 2004). Non-insured life is incomplete because it has yet to master its own self-reliance. Since decolonisation and the emergence of the world of states, however, liberal tutelage can no longer take the form of direct territorial acquisition. Although international respect for territorial integrity remains strong, instead of non-interference, the *de facto* inequality of states means that in practice sovereignty over the lives of people living within ineffective states has become internationalised, negotiable and contingent (Douzinas, 2003; Elden, 2005). Interventions in Kosovo, Sierra Leone, East Timor, Afghanistan, and so on, did not challenge the principle of territorial integrity, indeed, they upheld it. Speaking in the name of people, freedom and rights, what is more important is how life is supported and maintained, and brought to a more complete and secure existence. In addressing the limitations of humanitarianism, this contingent sovereignty is being enacted through state reconstruction that has spawned a new institutional *Empire Lite* that, depending on location, variously links donor governments, militaries, UN agencies, NGOs and private companies (Ignatieff, 2003). In this respect, the disastrous neocon intervention in Iraq is the exception that proves the rule. Liberal governance works through the control of core economic and welfare functions. Market access, meeting basic welfare needs and supporting self-reliance, promises to contain the circulatory effects of a poor and non-insured existence.

Since the state that is being reconstructed is not the independent, modernising 'top-down' state that development denounced during the Cold War, this begs the question – in furthering human security, what sort of state is being called forth? Taking a lead from the donor-declared success stories of Africa, the process now underway is that of attempting to transform failed or fragile states into what have been called 'governance states' (Harrison, 2004). Uganda, Mozambique, Ghana, Tanzania, and so on, are now regarded as 'functioning' underdeveloped states. They are synonymous with 'an internationally managed and regulated society' in which core budgetary and human security functions, through such tools as World Bank-led but jointly agreed Poverty Reduction Strategy Papers (PRSPs), are subject to a high degree of international oversight and control (Pender, 2005, p. 15). Effectively blurring the national/international dichotomy, donor governments, international financial institutions and NGOs are so closely involved in the work of key ministries that rather than being external actors 'it would be more useful to conceive of donors as *part of the state itself*' (Harrison, 2001, p. 669, emphasis in original). Essential to this process of internalisation has been the socialisation of a neoliberal technocratic elite into the role of official interlocutor. Rather than a marked improvement in life-chances, 'success' in such countries appears more associated with the degree to which core biopolitical functions are controlled by the international community, in other words, the degree to which the West's external sovereign frontier has been consolidated (Harrison, 2004, pp. 30–2).

Conclusion

Development is the essence of a specifically *liberal* imperial urge. It embodies the experience of life that is culturally unfamiliar as provisional and incomplete, and consequently in need of external tutelage to induce self-completion. Governing through voluntaristic methods is held to be more effective and lasting than authoritarian or violent ones. Because development is always 'new and improved', it constantly reproduces this strategisation of power. However, while development acts in the name of people and their freedom, the experience of the unfamiliar as incomplete means that it denies itself the creative risk of conversing with people not already part of a scripted future. It is this 'impoverished conception of experience and communication, and not in its ideals of liberty, equality and community, that one should explain and even judge the long history of liberalism's support of the British Empire' (Mehta, 1999, p. 192). Even the tolerance that liberalism's impoverished experience of the unfamiliar supports is fickle and shallow. If the life concerned fails to make the right choices, tolerance can easily become intolerance. Unfortunately, the dominance of the security mentality today is reinforcing an increasingly narrow experience of life (Hörnqvist, 2004). The war on terrorism, for example, in over-riding civil liberties to protect mass consumer society, has curtailed rights to movement, association and expression. At the same time, development's petty sovereigns within the aid industry have reinvented themselves as a means of reducing conflict among the poor and alienated (Oxfam, 2003). This is development at a price. In helping to secure mass society and its need to live and consume beyond its means, the impoverished discourse of development condemns the non-insured to the permanent emergency of self-sufficiency. Rather than striving to find ever more effective means to manage this emergency, more attention should be focused on removing its causes (Agamben, 2001). This would require a new formula for sharing the world with others. Refusing to prejudge unfamiliar life as incomplete and therefore requiring development is a small but important beginning.

Notes

1. A version of this chapter was published in *Alternatives*, April–June 2007, 32, no. 2, pp. 225–46.
2. There is a non-imperial, or at least, non-developmental trend within Enlightenment thinking. Kant's understanding of perpetual peace, for example, allowed that 'no man, even though he is not morally good, is forced to be a good citizen' (Kant, 1983, p. 124). At the same time, Pitts (2003) and Mehta (1999) have re-evaluated the work of Bentham and Burke respectively in this light.
3. This relationship works not only in the international sphere, but the national as well. For example, in relation to the promotion of multiculturalism (Balibar, 1991; Barker, 1981; Duffield, 1984).

References

Agamben, G. (1998). *Homo Sacer: Sovereign Power and Bare Life*. Stanford: Stanford University Press.

Agamben, G. 20 September 2001. On Security and Terror. *Allgemeine Zeitung.*

Anderson, M. B. (1996). *Do No Harm: Supporting Local Capacities for Peace Through Aid*. Cambridge, MA: Local Capacities for Peace Project, The Collaborative for Development Action, Inc.

Arendt, H. (1994). *The Origins of Totalitarianism*. New York: Harcourt, Inc.

Balibar, E. (1991). Is There a 'Neo-Racism'? in *Race, Nation, Class: Ambiguous Identities* (eds) E. Balibar and I. Wallerstein, pp. 17–28. London: Verso.

Barker, M. (1981). *The New Racism: Conservatives and the Ideology of the Tribe*. London: Junction Books.

Benn, H. (2004). 'The Development Challenge in Crisis States.' Speech by the Rt. Hon. Hilary Benn MP, London: London School of Economics.

Biccum, A. R. (2005). Development and the 'New' Imperialism: A Reinvention of Colonial Discourse in DFID Promotional Literature. *Third World Quarterly* 26, no. 6, pp. 1005–20.

Blair, T. (3 October 2001). This is the Battle with Only One Outcome: Our Victory. *Guardian*, pp. 4–5.

Bloom, G. and H. Standing (2001). 'Pluralism and Marketisation in the Health Sector: Meeting Health Needs in Contexts of Social Change in Low and

Middle-Income Countries.' *IDS Working Paper 136*. Brighton: Institute of Development Studies, University of Sussex.

Boutros-Ghali, B. (1995). An Agenda For Peace: Preventive Diplomacy, Peacemaking and Peace-Keeping (17 June 1992), in *An Agenda for Peace: 1995* (ed.) B. Boutros-Ghali, pp. 39–72. New York: United Nations.

Brett, E. A. (1985). *The World Economy since the War: The Politics of Uneven Development*. London: Macmillan.

Butler, J. (2004). *Precarious Life: The Powers of Mourning and Violence*. London and New York: Verso.

Campbell, D., D. J. Clark and K. Manzo (2005). *Imaging Famine*. An exhibition at the Newsroom. London: Guardian and Observer Archive and Advisor Centre.

Coker, C. (2003). 'Empires in Conflict: The Growing Rift Between Europe and the United States'. *Whitehall Paper 58*, London: Royal United Services Institute.

Collier, P., L. Elliot, H. Hegre, A. Hoeffler, M. Reynal-Querol and N. Sambanis (2003). *Breaking the Conflict Trap: Civil War and Development Policy*. Washington and Oxford: World Bank and Oxford University Press.

Cooke, B. (2003). A New Continuity with Colonial Administration: Participation in Development Management. *Third World Quarterly* 24, no. 1, pp. 47–61.

Cooper, R. (2002). The Post-Modern State, in *Re-Ordering the World: The Long-Term Implications of 11 September,* (ed.) Mark Leonard, pp. 11–20. London: The Foreign Policy Centre.

Cowen, M. P. and R. W. Shenton (1996). *Doctrines of Development*. London and New York: Routledge.

CPRC (2005). *The Chronic Poverty Report 2004–05*, Chronic Poverty Research Centre, University of Manchester, Institute for Development and Policy Management.

DAC (2003). *A Development Co-operation Lens on Terrorism Prevention: Key Entry Points for Action*, Paris: OECD Development Assistance Committee (DAC).

Derlugian, G. M. (1996). The Social Cohesion of the States, in *The Age of Transition: Trajectory of the World-System, 1945–2025* (eds) T. K. Hopkins and I. Wallerstein, pp. 148–77. London: Zed Books.

Dillon, M. and J. Reid (2001). Global Liberal Governance: Biopolitics, Security and War. *Millennium* 30, no. 1, pp. 41–66.

Douzinas, C. (2003). Humanity, Military Humanism and the New Moral Order. *Economy and Society* 32, no. 2, pp. 159–83.

Duffield, M. (1984). New Racism…New Realism: Two Sides of the Same Coin. *Radical Philosophy*, no. 37, pp. 29–34.

Duffield, M. (2005). Getting Savages to Fight Barbarians: Development, Security and the Colonial Present. *Conflict, Security and Development* 5, no. 2, pp. 141–60.

Duffield, M. (2006). Racism, Migration and Development: The Will to Planetary Order. *Progress in Development Studies* 6, no. 1, pp. 68–79.

Duffield, M. (2007). *Development, Security and Unending War: Governing the World of Peoples*. Cambridge: Polity Press.

Duffield, M. and N. Waddell (2006). Securing Humans in a Dangerous World. *International Politics*, no. 43, pp. 1–23.

Easterly, W. (2002). The Cartel of Good Intentions: The Problem of Bureaucracy in Foreign Aid. *Journal of Policy Reform* 5, no. 4, pp. 223–50.

Elden, S. (2005). Territorial Integrity and the War on Terror. *Environment and Planning A*, no. 37, pp. 2083–2104.

Escobar, A. (1995). *Encountering Development: The Making and Unmaking of the Third World.* New Jersey: Princeton University Press.

Ferguson, N. (2003). *Empire: How Britain Made the Modern World.* London: Allen Lane/Penguin.

Foucault, M. (2003). *Society Must be Defended: Lectures at the College de France, 1975–76.* London: Allen Lane/Penguin.

Hall, C. (2002). *Civilising Subjects: Metropole and Colony in the English Imagination 1830–1867.* Cambridge: Polity Press.

Harrison, G. (2001). Post-Conditionality Politics and Administrative Reform: Reflections on the Case of Uganda and Tanzania. *Development and Change* 32, no. 4, pp. 657–79.

Harrison, G. (2004). *The World Bank and Africa: The Construction of Governance States.* London: Routledge.

Held, D., A. McGrew, D. Goldblast and J. Perraton (1999). *Global Transformations: Politics, Economics and Culture.* Cambridge: Polity Press.

Hobson, J. A. (1938). *Imperialism: A Study.* London: George Allen and Unwin Ltd.

Hochschild, A. (2002). *King Leopold's Ghost: A Story of Greed, Terror, and Heroism in Colonial Africa.* London: Pan Books.

HSC (2005). *The Human Security Report 2005. War and Peace in the 21st Century,* Human Security Centre, University of British Colombia.

Huntington, S. P. (1993). The Clash of Civilisations. *Foreign Affairs* 72, no. 3, pp. 22–50.

Hörnqvist, M. (2004). The Birth of Public Order Policy. *Race and Class* 46, no. 1, pp 30–52.

ICISS (2001). *The Responsibility to Protect: Report of the International Commission on Intervention and State Sovereignty,* Ottawa: International Development Research Centre.

Ignatieff, M. (2003). *Empire Lite: Nation-Building in Bosnia, Kosovo and Afghanistan.* London: Vintage.

Jackson, R. H. (1990). *Quasi-States: Sovereignty, International Relations and the Third World.* Cambridge: Cambridge University Press.

Jahn, B. (2005). Barbarian Thoughts: Imperialism in the Philosophy of John Stuart Mill. *Review of International Studies* no. 31, pp. 599–618.

Jones, M. (1965). *Two Ears of Corn: Oxfam in Action.* London: Hodder and Stoughton.

Kaldor, M. (1999). *New and Old Wars: Organised Violence in a Global Era.* Cambridge: Polity Press.

Kant, I. (1983). *Perpetual Peace and Other Essays.* Translator Ted Humphrey. Indianapolis: Hackett Publishing.

Kaplan, R. D. (1994). The Coming Anarchy: How Scarcity, Crime, Overpopulation, and Disease are Rapidly Destroying the Social Fabric of Our Planet. *Atlantic Monthly,* pp. 44–76.

Labour Party (1964). The New Britain. *1964 Labour Party Maniefesto.* London: Labour Party.

Leader, N. and P. Colenso (2005). Aid Instruments in Fragile States. *PRDE Working Paper 5,* Poverty Reduction in Difficult Environments (PRDE) Team. London: Department for International Development (DFID).

Lugard, Lord (1965). *The Dual Mandate in Tropical Africa.* London: Frank Cass.

Macrae, J. (2002). Analysis and Synthesis. *The New Humanitarians: A Review of Trends in Global Humanitarian Action – HPG Report 11* (ed.) J. Macrae, pp. 5–17. London: Humanitarian Policy Group, Overseas Development Institute.

Mehta, U. S. (1999). *Liberalism and Empire*. Chicago: University of Chicago Press.

Morawetz, D. (1977). *Twenty Five Years of Economic Development*. Washington: World Bank.

Morel, E. D. (1920). *The Black Man's Burden*. Manchester and London: The National Labour Press Ltd.

Myrdal, G. (1957). *Economic Theory and Underdeveloped Regions*. London: Gerald Duckworth.

OECD (1972). *Development Cooperation, 1972 Review*. Paris: Organisation for Economic Co-operation and Development.

Oxfam (2003). *Beyond the Headlines: An Agenda for Action to Protect Civilians in Neglected Conflicts*. Oxford: Oxfam GB.

Pender, J. (2005). Less Interests, More Influence: The Paradox of Poverty Reduction and the Redefinition of Development. Paper presented at *SAID Workshop*.

Pitts, J. (2003). Legislator of the world? A Rereading of Bentham on Colonies. *Political Theory* 31, no. 2, pp. 200–234.

Pupavac, V. (2001). Therapeutic Governance: Pyscho-Social Intervention and Trauma Risk Management. *Disasters* 25, no. 4, pp. 358–72.

Pupavac, V. (2005). Human Security and the Rise of Global Therapeutic Governance. *Conflict, Development and Security* 5, no. 2, pp. 161–82.

Schumacher, E. F. (1974). *Small is Beautiful: A Study of Economics as if People Mattered*. London: Abacus.

Smith, N. (2003). *American Empire: Roosevelt's Geographer and the Prelude to Globalisation*. Berkeley: University of California.

Strategy Unit (2005). Investing in Prevention: An International Strategy to Manage Risks of Instability and Improve Crisis Response. *A Strategy Unit Report to the Government*. London: Prime Minister's Strategy Unit, Cabinet Office.

Torres, M. M. and M. Anderson (2004). Fragile States: Defining Difficult Environments for Poverty Reduction. *PRDE Working Paper 1*, Poverty Reduction in Difficult Environments (PRDE) Team. London: Department for International Development.

UN (2004). A More Secure World: Our Shared Responsibility. *Report of the High-level Panel on Threats, Challenges and Change*. New York: United Nations, General Assembly (A/59/565).

UNDP (1996). *Human Development Report 1996*. New York: Oxford University Press on behalf of United Nations Development Programme.

Warner, D. (2003). The Responsibility to Protect and Irresponsible, Cynical Engagement. *Millennium: Journal of International Studies* 32, no. 1, pp. 109–21.

Weiss, T. G. (2004). The Sunset of Humanitarian Intervention? The Responsibility to Protect in a Unipolar Era. *Security Dialogue* 35, no. 2, 135–53.

Wheeler, N. J. (2000). *Saving Strangers: Humanitarian Intervention in International Society*. Oxford: Oxford University Press.

Wilson, H. (1953). *The War on World Poverty*. London: Victor Gollancz Ltd.

3
From Materialism to Non-materialism in International Development: Revisiting Rostow's *Stages of Growth* and Schumacher's *Small is Beautiful*

Vanessa Pupavac

'A bold new program'

US President Truman's 1949 Inaugural Speech famously outlined his Four Point Program for humanity, which proclaimed the creation of an international development programme as part of the post-war world order:

> we must embark on a bold new program for making the benefits of our scientific advances and industrial progress available for the improvement and growth of underdeveloped areas.

Truman's Four Point Program reiterated US President Roosevelt's 1941 Four Freedoms speech, which highlighted freedom from want:

> The third is freedom from want which, translated into universal terms, means economic understandings which will secure to every nation a healthy peacetime life for its inhabitants, everywhere in the world. (Franklin Delano Roosevelt, Annual Message to Congress, 6 January, 1941)

Their speeches are commonly cited in introductions to international development (Duffield, 2007; Escobar, 1995). Here I explore how the dominant international development models shifted from materialist to anti-materialist philosophies. This chapter's historical overview revisits two highly influential development texts: Walt Rostow's *Stages of Economic Growth* and E. F. Schumacher's *Small is Beautiful*, which shaped the direction of international development thinking. Rostow and Schumacher were contemporaries. Both had immigrant backgrounds and achieved high office in their respective countries – Rostow in the US, Schumacher in the UK (Milne, 2008; Wood, 1983). Both trained as economists, were involved in the reconstruction of Europe after the Second World War and became important government policy advisers in their respective countries. Rostow's text embodies a modernisation approach to international development, which dominated the first two decades of international development thinking. Schumacher's text embodies non-materialist, spiritual ideas, which has informed international development thinking in subsequent decades, especially in non-governmental development circles.

First, the chapter discusses Rostow's *Stages of Economic Growth* and his Cold War modernisation model. Second, the chapter discusses Western reservations towards the modernisation of developing countries. Third, the chapter discusses Schumacher's *Small is Beautiful* and the shift from modernisation theories to sustainable development theories, tracing Western cultural and colonial influences on sustainable development thinking. Fourth, the chapter highlights the recurring influence of anti-materialist ideas on international development thinking since the 1970s. Finally the chapter observes the economic rise of China and other emerging economies and the resurrection of modernisation strategies against the prevailing international, non-industrial development strategies.

Rostow's *Stages of Growth*

The field of international development emerged in the post-war context of national independence struggles and Cold War competition between the Western and Soviet blocs for influence in the newly independent states. Core concerns of Western policy-makers were firstly the destabilising impact of weak pre-industrial states on an international order based on national sovereignty and state capacity to guarantee their own security, and secondly securing the new states to the Western bloc. As Truman's speech outlined, humanity had a moral duty to address poverty, but poverty was also 'a threat to both' poorer nations and 'to more prosperous areas'. Indicatively, government adviser Rostow's famous treatise on *The Stages of Economic Growth* is subtitled *A Non-Communist Manifesto.*

Rostow's *Non-Communist Manifesto* put forward a capitalist modernisation model to counter a rival communist vision. The differences between Rostow's modernisation and Marxist models were obviously emphasised at the time. Rostow devotes a whole section of his work to criticising Marxist analysis of capitalism and imperialism, and to outlining how his model is distinct. However, examining his ideas from today's perspective, Rostow's counter-model appears to share much with the rival Marxist vision. Namely, Rostow offers an alternative *material* account to a Marxist *historical material* account, contrasting strikingly with the antipathy towards materialism that infuses present development philosophy. Rostow's *Stages of Growth* model sets out a progress of society from traditional forms to modern forms. He identifies a basic distinction between traditional and modern societies in terms of Enlightenment scientific knowledge and its application to improving the forces of production:

> A traditional society is one whose structure is developed within limited production functions, based on pre-Newtonian science and technology, and on pre-Newtonian attitudes towards the physical world. Newton is here used as a symbol for that watershed in history when men came widely to believe that the external world was subject to a few knowable laws, and was systematically capable of productive manipulation. [...] the central fact about the traditional society was that a ceiling existed on the level of attainable output per head. This ceiling resulted from the fact that the potentialities which flow from modern science and technology were either not available or not regularly and systematically applied. (Rostow, 1971, p. 4)

Rostow was confident about the potential for applying human scientific knowledge to improving society, and the superiority of modern society over traditional society. He associated traditional societies with hierarchical social and political structures, and considered they could only offer limited social justice:

> Generally speaking, these societies, because of the limitation on productivity, had to devote a very high proportion of their resources to agriculture; and flowing from the agricultural system there was an hierarchical social structure, with relatively narrow scope – but some

scope – for vertical mobility. Family and clan connexions played a large role in social organization. The value system of these societies was generally geared to what might be called a long-run fatalism; that is, the assumption that the range of possibilities open to one's grandchildren would be just about what it had been for one's grandparents. But this long-run fatalism by no means excluded the short-run option that, within a considerable range, it was possible and legitimate for the individual to strive to improve his lot, within his lifetime. (ibid., p. 5)

Rostow's model assumed that significant social improvement depended on economic transformation, 'economic progress is a necessary condition for some other purpose, judged to be good: be it national dignity, private profit, the general welfare, or a better life for the children' (ibid., p. 6). His assumption follows secular Enlightenment thinking and the dominant social progressive ideas of the nineteenth and twentieth centuries, including Marxism.

Rostow saw the stages of economic growth culminating into 'the age of high mass-consumption'. A mature economy, Rostow believed, allowed society to devote surplus resources to three core areas: the pursuit of external power and influence, social welfare and consumption:

When technological maturity is reached, and the nation has at its command a modernized and differentiated industrial machine, to what ends should it be put, and in what proportions: to increase social security, through the welfare state; to expand mass-consumption into the range of durable consumers' goods and services; to increase the nation's stature and power on the world scene; or to increase leisure? (ibid., p. 16)

Rostow considered that the US, Western Europe and Japan had already reached this stage of high mass consumption where the economy shifted 'towards durable consumers' goods and services' and 'real income per head rose to a point where a large number of persons gained a command over consumption which transcended basic food, shelter, and clothing' (ibid., p. 10). He thought that the Soviet Union was entering this stage or at least delaying entering this stage. The rival Soviet bloc was devoting resources to its military capability rather than domestic consumption. Rostow believed that it feared that a consumer culture would undermine its communist ideology, 'Communism is likely to wither in the age of high mass-consumption' (ibid., p. 133).

Having raised material living standards through economic expansion, Western societies were now turning to social redistribution policies, Rostow argued:

In addition to these economic changes, the society ceased to accept the further extension of modern technology as an overriding objective. It is in this post-maturity stage, for example, that, through the political process, Western societies have chosen to allocate increased resources to social welfare and security. The emergence of the welfare state is one manifestation of a society's moving beyond technical maturity; but it is also at this stage that resources tend increasingly to be directed to the production of consumers' durables and to the diffusion of services on a mass basis, if consumers' sovereignty reigns. The sewing-machine, the bicycle, and then the various electric-powered household gadgets were gradually diffused. Historically, however, the decisive element has been the cheap mass automobile with its quite revolutionary effects – social as well as economic – on the life and expectations of society. (ibid., p. 11)

So Rostow contended that higher goals could be realised within a developed capitalist economy against Marxist accounts, which believed that capitalist relations of production were exploitative and only facilitated uneven development and held back human potential.

Rostow believed that US society, having reached an age of high mass consumption, was moving beyond material growth concerns and developing post-material values, noting

their curious new obsession with family life, privacy, do-it-yourself, getting away on trailers, and in motor boats, writing impiously about the Organization Man. (ibid., p. 87)

Rostow makes the analogy with Thomas Mann's *Buddenbrooks*:

In Thomas Mann's novel of three generations, the first sought money; the second, born to money, sought social and civic position; the third, born to comfort and family prestige, looked to the life of music. The phrase is designed to suggest, then, the changing aspirations of generations, as they place a low value on what they take for granted and seek new forms of satisfaction. (ibid., p. 11)

Thus Rostow saw his critics' post-material values as the luxury of a post-consumption culture. He was anxious that these post-material values should not lead the West to neglect developing countries' material aspirations and that it had the will to mobilise resources 'to do the jobs which must be done' (ibid., p. 104). His Cold War political concerns were explicit:

> We must demonstrate that the underdeveloped nations – now the main focus of Communist hopes – can move successfully through the preconditions into a well established take-off within the orbit of the democratic world, resisting the blandishments and temptations of Communism. (ibid., p. 134)

The formidable tasks for combating communism's attractions to the developing world encompassed military security, industrial growth and welfare in India, Asia, the Middle East, Africa and Latin America (ibid., pp. 104–5). In reality, even in the heyday of modernisation strategies, developing countries struggled to find capital investment for industrialisation, except where they were of immediate strategic concern – such as Japan or South Korea.

Ambivalence towards the Age of High Mass Consumption

Rostow and other Western policy-makers were initially preoccupied with the conditions for economic take-off and sustained economic growth. However this concern was displaced by doubt as to whether developing countries should follow all of the stages of growth to a state of high mass consumption. First there were concerns about the problems of the leisure society. Rostow, too, alluded to the risk of 'secular spiritual stagnation' beyond consumption (ibid, p. 12). How would -society react to its new-found leisure?

> what to do when the increase in real income itself loses its charm? Babies, boredom, three-day week-ends, the moon, or the creation of new inner, human frontiers in substitution for the imperatives of scarcity? (ibid., p. 16)

The spectre of unemployment or underemployment among the mass of the population was a major preoccupation. Prominent economists such as John Maynard Keynes argued that the problem of production was one that humanity was overcoming and would not be a problem in the future (Keynes, 1952, p. 366). Economists speculated over the problem of advanced industrial societies having to adapt to leisure when machinery made large sections of the population redundant. Policies maintaining employment rather than increased production were recommended for the new circumstances in which the production of goods, it was argued, was becoming important for employment rather than for the goods themselves. In the words of the economic J. K. Galbraith, 'Production for the sake of the goods produced is no longer very urgent', however, 'production does remain important and urgent for its effects on economic security' (Galbraith, 1962, p. 165).

Concerns over modernisation strategies became more acute in the late 1960s, a decade marked by political assignations and civil riots.

Should developing countries follow the *Stages of Economic Growth*?

Even as modernisation theories were being codified, anxieties existed about the big international economic social experiment envisaged by modernisation models. Policy advisers, including Rostow as the most prominent advocate of modernisation, were concerned about political instability during the transition from a traditional society to a mature economy (Rostow, 1971, p. 90). Rostow's work already warned of the dangers of frustration and alienation, particularly the dangers of unemployment:

> Unemployment takes on a peculiar urgency, as a problem of policy, since the populations of these areas, notably their urban populations, live in a setting of international communications which makes their frustration, perhaps, more strongly felt than in comparable situations in the past. The gap between existing levels of consumption and those which might become possible – or which are thought to be possible – is extremely vivid; and a sense of the gap is spreading fast. (ibid., p. 141)

Furthermore there were implications for Western security interests. Rostow considered that military incentives propelled the decision to embrace economic industrial transformation and speculated whether those military incentives would pose a security threat to the Western powers:

> the whole southern half of the globe plus China is caught up actively in the stage of preconditions for take-off or in the take-off itself. They have a reasonably long way to go; but their foreseeable maturity

raises this question: shall we see, in a little while, a new sequence of political leaders enticed to aggression by their new-found technical maturity; or shall we see a global reconciliation of the human race. (ibid., p. 92)

Rostow was ambivalent about his stages of growth model, which entailed a 'world of diffusing power', that is, the diffusion of power away from the Western states (ibid., p. xiv). What would the rise of African and Asian military powers mean for the West and world order? Would this exacerbate an international arms race (ibid., p. 106)? His security concerns were underscored by the spectre of the atomic bomb and the potential for more countries to develop weapons of mass destruction:

man has pressed his control over his physical environment to the point where the destruction of organized life on the planet is technically possible, in a setting where the stages-of-growth move forward not only in the northern half of the globe, whose story dominates the history of the past two centuries, but in the southern half of the globe, and in China as well. (ibid., p. 122)

Cold War imperatives surmounted Rostow's reservations at decolonisation's height of the late 1950s. However the late 1960s witnessed a less confident political elite, rocked by political assassinations, civil riots and US losses in the Vietnam War. Economic growth strategies appeared to be failing to win hearts and minds both domestically and internationally.

Alarm over the social stability of Western societies in the 1960s encouraged the re-evaluation of modernisation strategies. It was feared that modernisation strategies were fostering social and political problems. Dudley Seers, Director of the influential Institute of Development Studies at the University of Sussex, warned in the late 1960s that 'it looks as if economic growth not merely may fail to solve social and political difficulties; certain types of growth can actually cause them' (Seers, 1979, p. 9). These debates had little impact on capital investment and technological innovation in Western domestic production. Economic growth strategies remained the orthodoxy for Western domestic economic policies. Indeed, the ideas of free-market economists like Milton Freedman became more influential in the 1980s while the influence of Keynesian theories declined. However, modernisation sceptics did influence how policy-makers thought about strategies for international development.

Employment was put forward as the goal of international development, (Galbraith, 1964, p. 9), rather than industrialisation per se, discouraging labour-saving technological investment and encouraging policies for labour retention. The importance of employment strategies was reinforced by the conclusions of US presidential commissions on the civil disorder and violence that rocked the US in the 1960s. Both the 1968 Kerner Commission and the 1969 National Commission on Violence suggested that the dissatisfactions behind riots had been intensified by too-high expectations of what society could do, and called for greater focus on employment. The problem of employment was taken up by international organisations, notably the International Labour Organization (ILO). The ILO published a series of reports and launched its World Employment Programme, which prioritised employment and shifted its policy away from capital-intensive to labour-intensive activities (ILO, 1969). The ILO recommended investment in labour rather than industrial technology, which would replace human labour, that is, the retention of labour-intensive work.

The policy of employment generation through retaining labour-intensive activities was initially still within a strategy of industrialisation but the weight of Western policy thinking was already retreating from the goal of industrialising the developing world by the late 1960s. Problems of insufficient capital, uneven development, mass urban poverty and widening economic disparities were becoming apparent, but these problems were no longer dismissed as temporary, remediable features of the early stages of industrialisation as experienced by Western societies. Instead these problems were discussed as dangerously unstable conditions susceptible to political radicalisation and posing risks to Western security concerns. Policy advisers voiced concerns that modernisation was contributing to political insecurity. In this vein, Samuel Huntington argued 'the higher the rate of change toward modernity the greater the political instability' (Huntington, 1968, p. 46). International policy was thus already shifting from industrialisation strategies and technological investment towards employment policies, even before radical development critiques proliferated in the 1970s.

Rostow's model had been developed as a response to communism. But the critiques of modernisation theories, like Schumacher's *Small is Beautiful*, which came to dominate international development policies in subsequent decades, embodied by NGOs, were not informed by Marxist historical materialist analysis. Instead, influential policy advisers were inspired by an antipathy towards modern industrial society rather than by Marxism, which sought to develop productive forces further than capitalism along with transforming social relations of production.

The doubts of Western official advisers were accompanied by broader social criticisms. Rostow's model argued that economic progress allowed states to choose between pursuing external power and influence, welfare or consumption. However, advanced industrial societies appeared to be choosing militarism rather than Rostow's 'more humane objectives' (Rostow, 1971, p. 74), whether the US prosecution of the Vietnam War or the Soviet invasions of Hungary in 1956 and Czechoslovakia in 1968. Civil unrest within Western societies revealed the alienating character and divisions of industrial society, from Belfast to Berkeley and Los Angeles to Paris. Rostow's close involvement in the US strategic bombing campaign in Vietnam – he has been described as one of its main architects – compromised the idea that his stages of growth model would lead to more humane policies (Milne, 2008). Meanwhile the 1973 oil crisis internationally rekindled Malthusian fears in Western policy circles over resources and created the spectre of developing countries holding Western states to ransom over raw materials.

Schumacher's *Small is Beautiful*

While Rostow's *Stages of Economic Growth* codified Western modernisation theories Schumacher's 1973 *Small is Beautiful* codified their rejection. Schumacher rejected industrialisation for the developing world, notwithstanding his two decades' experience in, and in defence of, the British coal industry (Wood, 1983). Schumacher's transformation from the chief economist of Britain's heavy coal industry to leading advocate of non-industrial development suggests elite alienation from mass industrial society.

Schumacher, like Rostow, developed his economic thinking against Marxist theories. Schumacher, while originally impressed by Marx's writing, intensely disliked his materialism, atheism and class hostility (ibid., pp. 293–4). Schumacher considered that publicly owned industries cultivated a public service ethos, but struggled to influence their own workforce, let alone wider society, against a culture of greed (ibid., p. 272). Over the decades Schumacher's philosophical influences shifted from economic and socialist writing to spiritual writings and figures like Gandhi and Ivan Illich (ibid., p. 349). Schumacher gradually became less worried about improving the material standard of living in industrial societies, than the character of culture (ibid, p. 283). Schumacher attacked working-class materialism and criticised aspirations to industrialise the developing world as cultivating the wrong values (ibid., p. 273).

Schumacher came to believe that the spread of prosperity was corrupting and sought a spiritual, non-materialist model of social improvement, seeing social happiness in terms of spiritual well-being (Schumacher, 1974, pp. 18, 23). His asceticism and denunciation of modern consumer society re-invoked the long Western cultural trope and religious teaching against the sinful city, discussed below. Schumacher mistrusted humanity unchecked by God and emphasised the prevalence of human depravity (ibid., p. 20; Wood, 1983, p. 264). Godless man, Schumacher believed, was a Machiavellian immoral figure driven by hubris, power and greed. Religious awe, respect for nature and humility had to be cultivated for social peace (Schumacher, 1974, 1977). Schumacher commended Buddhism for its anti-egoism (Wood, 1983, p. 343) and for seeing 'the essence of civilization not in the multiplication of wants but in the purification of human character' (Schumacher, 1974, p. 40).

Schumacher shared Malthusian ideas about population limits, and wanted to moderate human needs. But an even worse prospect for Schumacher was that humanity might be able to overcome natural limits and become limitless. If humanity escaped nature's limits, he feared, materialism would be allowed free rein (Wood, 1983, p. 304). Schumacher preferred technologically simple, local solutions, such as assisting villagers to build their own village pumps, to industrial mechanisation reducing labour (ibid., p. 315). His work on intermediate technology led him to make links with organisations like the Soil Association, highlighted above (ibid., p. 347). He worried that foreign aid was making people 'poorer by giving them Western tastes' (ibid., p. 314). He preferred non-material aid to material aid, arguing that 'A gift of knowledge is infinitely preferable to a gift of material things. [...] The gift of material goods makes people dependent, but the gift of knowledge makes them free' (Schumacher, 1974, p. 163).

Schumacher's ideas were adopted by international NGOs, whose development role was fostered following the demise of industrialisation as a goal of international development (Whitaker, 1983, p. 82). Western NGOs like Oxfam criticised international development thinking for conflating growth and development, and for seeing development primarily in material terms, without encompassing moral development (ibid., pp. 82–3, 220). The critique of a materialist, industrial development model has been repeated over the past 40 years. Often this rejection is framed by critics in terms of not imposing Western development thinking on developing countries. But the history of development politics does not follow this simple dichotomy.

Rejection of industrialisation as a goal by the international develop-ment sector continues the Western anti-industrial philosophy that can be traced through the past two centuries to the Romantic or evangelical critiques of capitalism and earlier. Indeed it has been argued that ideal-istic critiques within capitalist relations have been characteristic since capitalism's inception (Hochuli, 2008; Sayre and Lowy, 1984). The next section highlights romantic anti-modern ideas in Western culture.

Moral critiques of urban corruption

The history of sustainable development is often told as the struggle for non-Western development models against Western development mod-els. Yet this overlooks the strength of romantic anti-industrial ideas among Western elites and how Western policy was already retreating from industrialisation as a goal and how policy advisers like Schumacher were codifying these romantic anti-modern models against the demands of developing countries and mass political movements at the time.

There is a long Western cultural trope of the pastoral against the sin-ful city (Sennett, 2002, pp. 115–22). Some of the anxieties about the leisure society and urban disorder echo this tradition. Religious teach-ing suggested that leisure led to vice. When people were not occupied with their own survival, maintaining themselves and their families and fulfilling necessary social duties, then they risked giving way to their 'natural passions' (ibid., p. 116).

The philosopher Jean-Jacques Rousseau, drawing upon the Protestant tradition, believed that the city corrupted social manners:

> In a big city, full of scheming, idle people without religion or prin-ciple, whose imagination, depraved by sloth, inactivity, the love of pleasure, and great needs, engenders only monsters and inspires only crimes; in a big city, where *moeurs* and honor are nothing because each easily hiding his conduct from the public eye. (Rousseau, 1968, pp. 58–9 in Sennett, p. 118)

Major strands of modern Western culture, religion and philosophy defined themselves against industrialisation and urbanisation. Radical writings such as William Blake's poetry decried the misery and exploi-tation of the swelling numbers of urban labourers, including the ter-rible plight of children. But anti-emancipatory outlooks also expressed Romantic anti-industrial ideals. Just as Romantic writers turned to nature for solace from the miseries of the city, so the wealthy fled from urban squalor and social disturbance to the suburbs or the depopulated countryside. The abolitionist and evangelical William Wilberforce expressed such social fears. Wilberforce's widely discussed *A Practical View of Christianity* (1798) condemned a culture that asserted material self-interests. He feared that the spread of material prosperity downwards to the middle and lower classes would loosen social morals (Wilberforce, 1798, pp. 383, 410–12). His *Society for the Suppression of Vice and Encouragement of Religion*, alarmed at how industrialisation was swelling disorderly urban populations and fostering popular political agitation, supported draconian measures against trade unions and other political activism (Thompson, 1968, pp. 112–13, 141). Secular social critiques repeated antipathy towards modernity and commonly portrayed rural innocence destroyed by urban exploitation. The historian Thomas Carlyle, writing a few decades later, raged against a 'cash nexus' culture and men 'grown mechanical in head and in heart, as well as in hand' (Carlyle in Williams, 1961, p. 86).

Fearful of industrialisation's social consequences, various middle-class reformers were drawn to non-industrial rural social models. American and European nineteenth-century reformers' romantic reactions against industrial society anticipate the contemporary ideals of sustainable development. American writers like Bronson Alcott, Ralph Waldo Emerson, Nathaniel Hawthorne and Henry Thoreau were prominent proponents of seeking moral and social progress in return to a simple rural utopia against industrial society. Thoreau's mid-nineteenth-century *Walden* idealised a simple rural contemplative life (Thoreau, 2004). The British Victorian Arts and Crafts and Pre-Raphaelite movements looked back nostalgically to an idealised pre-modern Middle Ages in revulsion against modern urban society. They wanted to maintain rural labour and revive the handicrafts against the dominance of mechanised work (Williams, 1961, p. 37).

Romantic conservatism was restrained domestically in the face of the social demands from the working classes for much of the nineteenth and twentieth centuries. Romantic portrayals of organic, pre-industrial communities were treated sceptically. Writers like George Eliot, Elizabeth Gaskell and Thomas Hardy remained conscious of the difficulties experienced by the rural poor and the attractions of the town, despite the urban miseries they documented. Thomas Hardy's novels like *Tess of D'Urbervilles* have often been interpreted as tales of rural innocence corrupted by urban life. However Hardy parodied rural nostalgia. His poem *The Ruined Maid* humorously observed how a woman escaped from rural hardship and secured material security and an easier life for herself in the corrupting city:

'O 'Melia, my dear, this does everything crown!
Who could have supposed I should meet you in Town?

And whence such fair garments, such prosperi-ty?' –
'O didn't you know I'd been ruined?' said she.

– 'You left us in tatters, without shoes or socks,
Tired of digging potatoes, and spudding up docks;
And now you've gay bracelets and bright feathers three!' –
'Yes: that's how we dress when we're ruined,' said she.

(from Hardy, 1975, pp. 22–3)

Cultural writing has explored problems in the romantic inclina-tions of the social reformers from the beginning of the industrial era. Charlotte Brontë's *Shirley*, a novel related to the Luddite riots, illustrates how refined sensibilities may conflict with the population's material needs. I quote Brontë at length:

'I can line yonder barren Hollow with lines of cottages, and rows of cottage-gardens.'

'Robert! And root up the copse?'

'The copse shall be firewood ere five years elapse: the beautiful wild ravine shall be a smooth descent; the green natural terrace shall be a paved street: there shall be cottages in the dark ravine, and cottages on the lonely slopes: the rough pebbled track shall be an even, firm, broad, black, sooty road, bedded with the cinders from my mill: and my mill [...] shall fill its present yard.'

'Horrible! You will change our blue hill-country air into the Stilbro' smoke atmosphere.'

[...]

'Caroline, the houseless, the starving, the unemployed, shall come to Hollow's mill from far and near; and Joe Scott shall give them work, and Louis Moore, Esq., shall let them a tenement, and Mrs Gill shall mete them a portion till the first pay-day'. (Brontë, *Shirley*, 1974, pp. 597–8)

Here Brontë alluded to the heroine's romantic identification with a rus-tic idyll and her struggle to identify with the population's material needs for work and housing against their exploitation under expanding indus-trialisation. Yet the heroine herself cried out for paid employment and the greater autonomy it could give her (ibid., pp. 98–9, 204–5). Brontë presented here the recurring tension between the impulse to help and the power of a romantic anti-materialist critique. Sensitive souls may favour picturesque resolutions that answer their romantic imagination more than the aspirations of the people they champion.

The writer Louisa May Alcott, author of *Little Women* and daughter of the transcendentalist thinker Bronson Alcott, was attracted to the romantic identification with nature in contrast to the ills of contemporary society. However her *Transcendental Wild Oats* satirises her father's utopian Fruitlands project as Slump Apples (1975). Her satire wryly observes how the women end up doing the bulk of the community's work while the idealist male leaders are off lecturing about their wonderful community in comfortable city salons. Alcott observes the austerity, crop failures and meagre food rations provided by male anti-materialist idealism. She did not discount material needs and rejected her father's anti-materialism, for all the nobility she saw in his stance. Ultimately she saw women's emancipation as impossible in nature and saw industrialisation and technological goods as opening up possibilities for women, not least the development of domestic labour-saving goods, although her campaigning writing showed that she had no illusions about factory conditions or its low wages (Elbert, 1987, pp. 73–5, 104, 221).

The cultural critic Raymond Williams notes how the very distance of affluent urban dwellers from the realities of rural hardship facilitates their urban romanticising, which may hinder the development of policies to improve rural lives (Williams, 1973). In this vein Williams cites Hardy's essay on the *Dorsetshire Labourer* written a century ago, which objected to outsiders expecting rural communities 'to remain stagnant and old-fashioned for the pleasure of romantic spectators' instead of 'widening the range of their ideas, and gaining in freedom (cited in ibid., p. 203).

Furthermore romantic representations may disguise power relations and antipathy towards popular demands. Romantic preferences for simple rural folk may express ambiguity over working-class betterment, sometimes openly deploring them for vulgarity and philistine consumption. John Carey's *The Intellectuals and the Masses* has critically documented British intellectual prejudices against working people for their tinned food and cheap entertainment. Carey's study observes how when the masses are merged back into an innocent pastoral world they are redeemed, but also eliminated as subjects (Carey, 1992, pp. 44–5). The masses cannot be in a pre-industrial idyll. Thus romantic critiques may display, in writer George Eliot's words, 'sensibilities of taste' rather than 'humane sensibilities' (Eliot, 1995, p. 121–2).

Anti-industrial, anti-materialist ideas were not widely adopted by the nineteenth- and twentieth-century mass political movements which sought more social material provision from employment, housing, health care and financial welfare support. If social critics remained concerned about the population's moral improvement, they recognised the importance of its material improvements. Cultural studies challenged accounts romanticising the pre-industrial past (Williams, 1961, 1973). Richard Hoggart, who was Assistant Director-General of UNESCO from 1971 to 1975, is most remembered for his 1957 *The Uses of Literacy*, which sympathetically examined the impact of mass culture on the British working class. Hoggart was preoccupied in *The Uses of Literacy* about whether cultural progress was keeping up with material progress. Material progress did not guarantee cultural progress and might risk 'spiritual deterioration' through a 'mean form of materialism' (Hoggart, 1958, p. 322–3). He wanted society to think beyond 'a search for material goods' and reassess its goals around 'the need for higher satisfactions' (ibid.).

While material progress was not an end for Hoggart, it remained a crucial foundation opening up social possibilities for the working classes. Hoggart was keen to stress the importance of improved living standards for helping to realise higher moral aspirations, even as he worried about the state of cultural life: 'in many parts of life mass-production has brought good' although, 'culturally, the mass-produced bad makes it harder for the good to be recognized' (ibid., p. 174). Hoggart constantly cautioned against romanticising the past lives of the poor, 'no one could fail to be glad that most working-people are in almost all respects better off, have better living conditions, better health, a larger share of consumer goods, fuller educational opportunities, and so on' (ibid., p. 318). Hoggart emphasised how poverty wore people down and how his mother and grandmother 'would have had much less worrying lives had they brought up their families during the mid twentieth century. All their lives they needed, quite simply, many more of some essential goods and services than they had' (ibid., p. 172).

A lament for rural life against mass society persisted among the upper middle classes against mass urban society such as the earlier environmentalist Victor Bonham-Carter's *The English Village* and *The Survival of the English Countryside*, which deplored the commercialisation of farming and the demise of rural ways of life.

Romantic anti-modernity of development aid sector

In important respects, the NGO development sector evolved in reaction against industrial society. Its philosophy accords more with Bonham-Carter's aversion to modern industrialisation than with

Hoggart's affirmation of its benefits for ordinary people. It has been inclined to idealise authentic traditional peasant communities counterposed to an inauthentic, corrupting industrial society. Anti-industrial sentiments follow anthropological thinking, which informed colonial administration. Anthropology, of all the disciplines, has probably most exuded a romantic anti-modernity. Anthropological writings were at the forefront of challenging modernisation strategies. The US anthropologist Marshall Sahlins argued in his *Stone Age Economics* (1972), that traditional societies were the original affluent societies, reversing Rostow's stages of growth ladder. Anthropologists have long expressed alarm at how contact with modernity was destabilising the societies they researched.

Modernity's destabilising impact on traditional societies disturbed colonial administrators and shaped colonial thinking on development as it tried to deter nationalist movements (Duffield, 2007; Furedi, 1994). British colonial administrators were perhaps more obviously influenced by romantic anti-modern ideas than their French counterparts. British colonial advisers feared that the European presence undermined the traditional ways of life of subject populations (Furedi, 1994). They were concerned that coercive military rule, urbanisation and unregulated exploitative extraction industries would foster alienated, rootless, mobile 'deracinated' populations (Duffield, 2007, p. 173). Indirect rule or Native Administration was to mediate the disturbing European presence and reinforce the authority of rurally based tribal leaders against the influence of the emerging modern urbanised, politicised nationalist leaders. Native Administration was accompanied by education policies, seeking to limit modern influences, including knowledge of European languages. Colonial advisers recommended the promotion of primary schooling in native languages with a curriculum emphasising relevant skills training rather than European languages and academic attainment. And after national independence, the European cultural imagination continued to be attracted to romantic, idealised visions of simple traditional ways of living rather than nationalist modernising visions.

Indeed one of the draws of colonial service or the overseas aid sector for Bonham-Carter's readership was to escape from mass urban society (Lee, 1967). Post-independence aid work in the developing world offered the possibilities of retaining a world of servants and deference no longer possible at home to a former colonial class who found it difficult to reconcile themselves to post-war egalitarianism (Cannadine, 2001).

International aid work drew upon colonial administrative experience, as well as a younger generation of post-independence aid workers. Schumacher's *Small is Beautiful*'s emphasis on spiritual development and non-industrial technology fits with their romantic anti-modern vision. The younger generation of post-independence aid workers was inspired by a broadening of international solidarity. And yet there was an element, too, of the romantic escape from mundane, disappointed political activism at home to more glamorous, less accountable activism abroad when the post-1968 counter-culture rejected the industrial masses at home for the romantic ideal of the pre-modern rural peasant. Romantic anti-materialism consolidated in development circles as national struggles internationally and the working class domestically receded as political forces.

Romantic spectacle?

An original social concern risks becoming misanthropic when people in developing countries become subordinated to disenchanted moderns' romantic vision. Schumacher failed to consider how his philosophy might have a politically apologetic character, where local low-technology subsistence farming approaches became prescriptions for developing countries, de-legitimising material aspirations beyond basic needs, and legitimising much back-breaking manual work in the developing world that earlier development models had hoped to overcome. Schumacher condemned repetitive industrial labour, but his approach romanticised unmechanised rural labour and other non-industrial livelihoods, and failed to acknowledge their boring, repetitive aspects – agricultural 'shovelling, shovelling, shovelling', to borrow his words on industrial work (Wood, 1983, p. 273).

Consider Hardy again. His novel *Tess of the D'Urbervilles* describes the tyrannical demands of mechanised agricultural labour:

> Close under the eaves of the stack, and as yet barely visible, was the red tyrant that the women had come to serve – a timber-framed construction, with straps and wheels appertaining – the threshing machine, which whilst it was going, kept up a despotic demand upon the endurance of their muscles and nerves. (Hardy, 1957, p. 365)

However, Hardy equally describes the hardships of unmechanised labour in his writing. The exploitative social relations, not the machines as such, conditioned the experience. Again we can consider how agricultural machinery is discussed in *Little House on the Prairie*, the popular American classic of pioneer life. In the context of a family-run farm, the machine lightens the workload and helps secure the harvest in time.

Thus the machine is liberating rather than oppressive in *Little House on the Prairie.*

Simultaneously, non-industrial models and their 'Teach a man to fish' slogan assume that the majority of people in the developing world want to be only fisherman or farmers. How did Schumacher's model meet the ambitions of the potential Schumachers in the developing world, who aspired to a life outside agriculture? Schumacher did not have an adequate answer. Here, Alcott's portrait in *Transcendental Wild Oats* of the idealist philosophers lecturing in comfortable drawing rooms about the joys of simple agricultural living safely away from the realities of their experiment suffered by others springs to mind (Alcott, 1975). Schumacher's failure, like those of earlier moral reformers, was linked to his belief that the poor were spiritually superior to the affluent, ideas he shared with Mother Teresa, another influence on British humanitarianism. His non-material, spiritual model of well-being was, in addition, politically controversial where he praised separate development in South Africa (Wood, 1983, pp. 340–1).

Moreover the anti-mechanisation position of sustainable development philosophy appears to outdo its romantic utopian predecessors. William Morris, for one, was not against the use of labour-saving machines where the labour was back-breaking, repetitive and uninteresting. He wanted to free people from dull routine labour so they could spend more time on creative labour. However international development policies in the 1970s came to endorse low or medium technology as appropriate for developing countries without taking into account whether the labour in question was experienced as drudgery or not, and whether people's time could not be freed up to allow them to engage with more interesting creative work. The old saying 'the devil makes work for idle hands' runs through so much international development planning.

Demands of the New International Economic Order

Small is Beautiful's interest in basic needs was attractive to developing populations suffering poverty. But their basic needs concerns did not necessarily conform to Schumacher's development philosophy, whose ideas were rapidly absorbed into Western development NGO and research circles. The dominant critiques of modernisation in developing countries in the 1970s were underdevelopment and dependency theories. These influential theories, inspired by Marxist and anti-colonial ideas, targeted capitalism and imperialism, rather than industrialisation itself, as perpetuating international inequalities. They proposed alternative autonomous development models for developing countries outside the world economy dominated by Western states, and were interested in the paths of countries such as Cuba, or Chile under Salvador Allende.

Schumacher's denunciation of materialism appeared internationally when developing countries were flexing their new political authority and seeking to renegotiate their international economic position, such as in OPEC's successful renegotiation of oil prices with the West. A political vision limiting developing countries to basic needs represented a curb on these aspirations. The famous 1974 UN General Assembly Declaration on the Establishment of a New International Economic Order sponsored by Non-Aligned Movement states illustrated the divergent visions of Western development circles and developing countries in the 1970s. Developing countries had strongly criticised Western modernisation models and denounced inequitable terms of trade, but their criticisms did not amount to rejection of industrialisation per se. Indeed developing countries reasserted their aspirations for economic advancement in the 1970s, inspired by the OPEC countries' success in gaining more advantageous terms of trade in the sale of oil. The 1974 declaration, like so many UN declarations, had little practical effect in changing international economic relations. Nevertheless it articulated developing countries' key economic aspirations. Notably, the declaration specifically demanded support from developed countries for industrialisation and modern technology as part of 'accelerating the development of developing countries'. A whole section was devoted to industrialisation and the transfer of industrial technology, as this extract demonstrates:

III INDUSTRIALIZATION

All efforts should be made by the international community to take measures to encourage the industrialization of the developing countries, and to this end:

(a) The developed countries should respond favourably, within the framework of their official aid as well as international financial institutions, to the requests of developing countries for the financing of industrial projects;

(b) The developed countries should encourage investors to finance industrial production projects, particularly export-orientated production, in developing countries, in agreement with the latter and within the context of their laws and regulations;

(c) With a view to bringing about a new international economic structure which should increase the share of the developing countries in world industrial production, the developed countries and the agencies of the United Nations system, in cooperation with the developing countries, should contribute to setting up new industrial capacities including raw materials and commodity-transforming facilities as a matter of priority in the developing countries that produce those raw materials and commodities [...]. (UN, 1974)

Developing countries continued to emphasise the international economic structure, inequitable international trade relations, the role of the state, investment or international aid for industrialisation and technology transfer. Conversely the evolving basic-needs approach focused on local, small-scale approaches improving household non-wage income generation and simple community-level improvements such as village water pumps.

The shift away from industrialisation to basic needs implied the abandonment of the earlier aspiration that developing countries would catch up economically with the advanced industrialised countries. This abandonment had serious implications for the position of developing states within the international system, that is, the perpetuation of unequal capacities between states and the continuing potential for the advanced industrial states to dominate the developing world. Developing countries therefore voiced mistrust over the basic-needs concept after some initial support (Aspelagh, 1979, p. 404). Delegates from developing countries expressed hostility towards the implied perpetuation of an international division of labour and structural economic inequalities between the developed and developing worlds in their responses to the ILO's World Employment Programme (ILO, 1977, p. 13).

The desire to break the dependency of developing countries led to concerns over their industrial sectors being reliant on foreign investment and therefore subject to foreign domination, ownership and exploitation. Consequently non-industrial economic activities came to be stressed as being less dependent. Underdevelopment critiques subsequently merged with anti-industrialisation critiques and their earlier pro-industrialisation position is often forgotten.

Most development literature does not acknowledge developing the countries' hostility towards the shift from industrialisation to basic needs or how it fitted with the austerity measures imposed from the late 1970s. Rather, the literature persistently represents Western policies as seeking industrialisation while developing countries resisted industrialisation. The development literature's assumption is connected to how the literature attributes anti-industrialisation development thinking to the developing world rather than seeing its currents within Western policy circles. But as I have indicated, Western official development thinking had strong reservations about the industrialisation of developing countries, which encouraged its being dropped as a primary development goal.

Importantly Schumacher's development thinking went against one of the most significant mass political movements in the twentieth century – that of the majority in South Africa against apartheid. That his development philosophy allowed him to misunderstand the South African situation and naïvely endorse separate development (Wood, 1983, pp. 340–1), is not highlighted in the sustainable development literature. The anti-apartheid mass political movement was strongly influenced by Marxist ideas in the 1970s and 1980s (Lipton, 1986). Its dominant socialist model attacked capitalist exploitation but did not reject industrialisation, instead seeking to transform social, economic and political relations so that all of the population would own and enjoy the benefits of industrial production – machines replacing dull back-breaking work, producing cheaper goods and raising living standards. In the analysis of an anti-apartheid document:

> Behind all the different manifestations of apartheid stands the mighty economic machine of South African capitalism. This machine absorbs cheap black labour, puts it through the wheels of industry, mining and agriculture and then expels it to distant reservations for the unemployed until the system requires more labour. (Longford, 1986, p. 12)

Schumacher's politically naïve endorsement of the reservations revealed his distance from South African realities and anti-apartheid politics.

Consider further the British context in which Schumacher's philosophy appeared. Domestically, the 1970s in Britain were a decade of trade union militancy with workers demanding higher material living standards. Schumacher enjoyed good relations with the National Union of Mineworkers for his defence of the coal industry against oil and nuclear energy (Wood, 1983, pp. 289–90). But his anti-materialist philosophy clashed with British workers' material demands, expressed, for example, in the 1972 and 1974 miners' strikes. Moreover his ideas coincided with the breaking up of the post-war Keynesian welfare consensus started by the 1974 Labour government and continued by the 1980s Conservative government, which adopted policies incrementally attacking working-class organisations and living standards. Schumacher therefore went against contemporary social demands and embodied conservative, elite political perspectives.

Equally, the British aid sector's embrace of Schumacher's anti-materialist philosophy for both developing and industrial countries distanced itself from contemporary British working-class activism. Whitaker's history notes Oxfam's long concern about being a predominantly middle-class organisation lacking a solid basis in the working classes (Whitaker, 1983, p. 36). Oxfam failed to win over non-academic industrial Oxford (ibid., p. 20) and even as it saw itself as part of a global village – an indicatively pastoral analogy. Consider Oxfam's anti-materialist vision against the strong left-wing militancy associated with the Oxford Cowley car plant. Car workers were amongst the most militant and highest-paid industrial workers in Britain, including Cowley's approximately 22,000 workers in the early 1970s (Thornett, 1995). Government attacks on trade union militancy singled out Cowley's workers for disrupting the economy and exacerbating the economic crisis (Philo, 1995, pp. 3–20). Their official and unofficial strike action achieved significant wage increases and raised living standards, but their activism also encompassed international solidarity with political movements elsewhere from Chile to Vietnam (Thornett, 1995). Conversely, at Oxfam's headquarters a few miles away it was being discussed how its staff should embrace wage restraint and adopt simpler lifestyles as a model to the rest of British society (Duffield, 2007, pp. 63–4; Whitaker, 1983, pp. 30–2). Oxfam's *How the Rich Should Live* project envisaged eliminating poverty by reducing personal consumption in the industrial world (ibid.), a model at odds with local car workers' demands, but legitimising the squeeze on the population's living standards. Many families in the mid-1970s were experiencing a lowering of their real household income and rising costs of living through inflation (around 27 per cent in 1975), as well as redundancies or threats of them on a large scale (unemployment was around 12 per cent in 1975), which encouraged the official and unofficial strikes.

Oxfam's analysis of greed as the problem complemented the official position and the mainstream media, such as *The Times* articles, which attributed the ailing state of British industry to workers' excessive demands and industrial action. In this vein, Edward Heath stated in Parliament how 'priority has got to be given to investment as against claims on consumption and excessive wages' (in *The Times*, 25 April 1975). Retrospectively Oxfam's proposals for personal sacrifice effectively complemented official austerity measures, which were followed through in the 1980s with attacks on trade union militancy and imposed wage restraints. Ironically, Oxfam moved its headquarters in 2003 to a business park located on the site of the former car plant.

By the 1980s international development philosophy had abandoned the aspiration for universal prosperity, and had become orientated around selective poverty and normative goals. Substantial material transformation for the majority of the world's population was now off the agenda, although wealth creation (and impoverishment) obviously still went on in the international political economy. Wealth creation and international development were going their separate ways. So OPEC countries like Saudi Arabia followed a wealth creation and charity model, rather than universal political, social and economic material transformation, while South Africa's powerful movement for universal political, social and economic material transformation fragmented following the compromises with the old apartheid regime. Solutions to social problems became seen in South Africa, as elsewhere, in terms of individual improvement and empowerment within the existing capitalist world economy.

Development as non-material well-being

If we look at development policy after policy, whether sustainable development, participatory development, rights-based development, development as freedom, empowerment projects, etc. the striking thing is how questions of industrialisation and substantial material transformation have been displaced. Definitions of development and poverty are moving away from economic growth and income levels, as well as discussions of class. There is also a tendency to use ahistorical categories like rich and poor, rather than categories of social class. The more psychological concepts of well-being and social exclusion have displaced the material concepts of wealth and social inequality. In this vein Nobel Prize-winning economist Amartya Sen's *Development as Freedom* refers to 'poverty as a deprivation of basic capabilities, rather than merely as low income' (Sen, 2001, p. 20). Sen is one of the few development theorists still to mention industrialisation as part of development, but it is marginal to his development strategies. Sen's model essentially represents an attempt to improve people's personal capabilities and opportunities within the existing capital market relations and production methods, as opposed to transforming industrial capabilities and social relations in production. Sen's vision of a harmonious society of small entrepreneurs echoes Thomas More's *Utopia*.

The triumph of Schumacher's philosophy in international development thinking is evidenced in the World Bank's *Voices of the Poor* 2000
report. The World Bank's much heralded report – significantly for a
financial institution – proposed well-being rather than wealth as the
goal of development. Echoing Schumacher's philosophies, the report
declared how, '*Wealth and wellbeing are seen as different, and even contradictory*' (Narayan et al., 2000, p. 21). Repeatedly the report emphasised
the non-material needs of the poor, defining well-being and ill-being in
psychological terms, '*Wellbeing and illbeing are states of mind and being.
Wellbeing has a psychological and spiritual dimension as a mental state of
harmony, happiness and peace of mind*' (Narayan et al., 2000, p. 21, italics
in original). The report concluded that substantial material advancement was unnecessary to well-being and that small improvements made
a big difference to the poor. Yet careful analysis of the background documents suggests that the poor interviewed in the World Bank research
were more concerned about their material wants than the report represented (Pender, 2002).

At the same time as these empowerment models of development complement the successive Structural Adjustment Programs or the newer
pro-poor policies are premised on the expectation that the poor take
responsibility for securing their own livelihoods and welfare.

A romantic idealism runs through the various approaches, which maintain ambitious normative goals even as they have abandoned substantive material transformation. Consider the Millennium Development
Goals, which have severed the links between well-being, social justice
and material transformation in developing countries. Not one of the
goals relates to industrialisation, yet developing countries are expected
to realise post-industrial values of gender equality and education. The
2008 report highlights employment and infrastructure problems in the
developing world, but no mention is made of developing industries and
factories, roads and railways or electricity and power stations to support a national infrastructure able to provide employment and services.
It highlights health, gender and education, but makes no mention of
modern hospitals to treat the range of curable diseases, or agricultural
machinery to lighten rural labour for women and children and men,
and free up more time for education.

Low material horizons are repeated in recent campaigns like Make Poverty
History, which emphasises fairer trade and more aid rather than advancing the productive forces of society. Ironically, too, consciously radical critiques like post-colonial theories, alter-mondialism or anti-globalisation
thinking echo the recurring romantic anti-materialist critiques of modern

society (Hochuli, 2008; Malik, 2008; Sayre and Lowy, 1984). Radical critiques give legitimacy to international development's retreat from aspiring to universal prosperity and making substantial material improvements for the majority of the world's population. Too often the international development sector and broader alter-mondialism romanticise the lives of the rural poor, which Hoggart and Williams warned against (Hoggart, 1958, p. 172; Williams, 1961, p. 253). They condemn modern consumer society, neglecting how the major material improvements matter for the well-being and dignity of the working classes. People in the industrial world do less back-breaking work and overall spend less time working if education and retirement are taken into account. Moreover condemnations of consumerism may express elite sensibilities of taste against the rest of the population rather than humanitarian sensibilities, as Eliot also warned against (Eliot, 1995, pp. 121–2).

Ethical consumption

Emphasis on personal ethics has grown as progressive collective politics has declined and social change is understood essentially as the sum of individual actions. Much global advocacy relates to ethical consumption as a core aspect of ethical living and site of social action. Ethical consumption developed from the boycotts of South African goods, which became the dominant manifestation of political opposition to apartheid among Western liberals. A consumer approach emphasises redistributing consumption, rather than transforming production and redistribution to advance the living standards of all globally. Some paradoxes exist in consumption as a form of political social action and personal ethics (Butcher, 2003, 2007; Heartfield, 2008; Heath and Potter, 2005). Notably, those most likely to be concerned about ethical consumption are among wealthier, higher-consumption social groups (Heartfield, 2008). Shopping as social action fits, rather than necessarily opposes, a consumer outlook, which finds it difficult to conceive action beyond consumption. Moreover ethical consumption may represent a form of *conspicuous* ethical consumption (Heath and Potter, 2005). Affluent consumers may demonstrate their superior discernment to that of the masses through their organic diets, expensive foreign travel to novel destinations or specially sourced authentic fair-trade and ecological goods. Ethical attacks on mass consumerism echo uncomfortably earlier elite attacks on the masses, with moral sensibilities blurring with sensibilities of taste (Carey, 1992; Eliot, 1995).

Moral campaigns have historically been slow to transform the material conditions of the poor. The cause of climate change is now giving moral legitimacy to this reluctance. Ethical consumer campaigns challenge multinational corporations, but they are prepared to lower the material living standards of populations among industrialised populations, and contain the material aspirations of people in the developing world beyond basic needs. Following Schumacher, finding solutions to poverty and environmental problems that allow humanity to have higher consumption patterns globally appears morally repugnant, even if achievable. Aid organisations have tied solutions to climate change to their anti-materialist development philosophy. Christian Aid's recent reports on climate change invoke the global poor against the lifestyles of industrial countries and want to codify a framework that obliges industrial countries to 'adopt lower-consumption lifestyles' and developing countries to promote the basic needs of the poor (EcoEquity and Christian Aid, 2006, p. 2). Their basic-needs models consciously oppose the inhuman assumptions of earlier ecological writing, which brutally regarded famines and disasters as nature's way of dealing with overpopulation, but their anti-materialist models imply limiting social mobility rather than advancing the material position of the masses globally. Furthermore the potential to find solutions to the whole spectrum of environmental problems may be kept back by approaches focused on changing individual consumption.

Just as romantic sensibilities dislike mass consumption domestically so they fear developing populations' aspirations to material prosperity and modern consumer products. China's industrial expansion over the last decade has translated into some tangible material improvements for the population. As yet, the other rising economies, such as India, have inadequate infrastructures to support large-scale manufacturing industries, which would provide mass employment, and the rise of incomes has been limited to a narrower section of society than in China. However their rising incomes have been greeted with alarm. It appears that aspirations beyond basic needs are problematic. Revulsion is expressed in response to the Chinese or Indians adopting post-industrial countries' material standards of living, from cars to fridges to air conditioning. Romantic cultural preferences persist for an austere Buddhist China or an India of Gandhian spiritualism and self-denial against Nehru's modernising vision. Ethical consumption may ignore the costs for the masses domestically and globally, but if developing countries are not allowed to develop industrial means of production and are limited to basic technology and basic needs, they will continue to have little room for contingency. People will remain ever-vulnerable to emergencies and indefinitely entangled in dependent relationships with donor powers. Meanwhile environmentalism may legitimise new forms of protectionism, excluding competition from farmers in the developing countries in the name of the planet (Heartfield, 2008).

China and the return of economic growth

China's economic growth and new trade relations in Asia and Africa have the potential to shake the current international development consensus. China's new role has been greeted with some apprehension in Western official and NGO development circles because its approach challenges the sustainable development thinking and political and social conditionality they favour. As yet China has not elaborated an alternative international development philosophy to sustainable development, and has confined itself to trade and charity. This position may be contrasted to its advocacy of its own socialist modernisation models during the Cold War. China has not so far sought to absorb goals of material prosperity and social justice into its own international development model, although its new economic relations in the developing world rekindled aspirations and reopened some national development choices, at least until the global economic crisis emerged in 2008.

Ironically China's economic development model appears to be following Rostow's modernisation model, belying the romantic dichotomy of Western materialism and non-Western anti-materialism. China's economic development initiatives have primarily been bilateral, and based on trade and loans towards infrastructure projects. China has not explicitly codified an alternative international development model and promoted it in international institutions. Its thinking has been wary of international development models, one reason being its concern for national sovereignty and non-interference in the internal affairs of states, another its belief that national conditions are crucial to development and that there are limits to the applicability of external models. However, Chinese universities are introducing International Development courses open for foreign students to study China's economic development and development in general including potential scholarships and internships with international development organisations or Chinese government agencies.

It is not yet certain whether China will promote its own international development model or come to adopt Western sustainable development strategies. In certain respects its idea of the harmonious society parallels earlier Western anxieties over modernisation strategies and the socially destabilising impact of rapid economic growth. Its preoccupation with the idea of the harmonious society suggests that China will adopt a conservative development model. While the Chinese economic model focuses on material growth divorced from political-social democratic ideals, the international development model seeks to promote its ideals divorced from material transformation. Both approaches are problematic. The romantic anti-materialist model in international development legitimises the failure to improve people's lives materially. The Chinese national development model challenges Schumacher's anti-materialist idealism, but repeats the onesideness of Rostow's economic determinism. The current impasse between idealism and materialism in these onesided visions needs to be overcome. Where are the debates about how we could strive to universalise access to machinery to lessen drudgery, advanced medical care to treat curable diseases, better transport to allow people greater freedom of movement, etc? The fundamental interdependence between material advancement and political social advancement needs to be re-established as a starting point for progressive thinking and practice, which will substantially address people's aspirations for a better life for themselves and their children.

References

Alcott, Louisa May (1975). *Transcendental Wild Oats*. Boston, MA: Harvard Common Press.

Aspelagh, Robert (1979). Basic Needs and Peace Education. *Bulletin of Peace Proposals* 10, no. 4, pp. 403–6.

Brontë, Charlotte (1974). *Shirley*. Harmondsworth: Penguin.

Butcher, Jim (2003). *The Moralisation of Tourism: Sun, Sand ... and Saving the World*. London: Routledge.

Butcher, Jim (2007). *Ecotourism, NGOs and Development: A Critical Analysis*. London: Routledge.

Cannadine, David (2001). *Ornamentalism: How the British Saw Their Empire*. New York: Oxford University Press.

Carey, John (1992). *The Intellectuals and the Masses: Pride and Prejudice among the Literary Intelligentsia. 1880–1939*. London: Faber & Faber.

Christian Aid (2007). *Truly Inconvenient: Tackling Poverty and Climate Change At Once*. London: Christian Aid.

Duffield, Mark (2007). *Development, Security and Unending War*. Cambridge: Polity.

EcoEquity and Christian Aid (2006). *Greenhouse Development Rights*.

Escobar, Arturo (1995). *Encountering Development: The Making and Unmaking of the Third World*. Princeton, NJ: Princeton University Press.

Elbert, Sarah (1987). *A Hunger for Home: Louisa May Alcott's Place in American Culture*. New Brunswick, NJ: Rutgers University Press.

Eliot, George (1995). *Felix Holt, the Radical*. London: Penguin Books.

Furedi, Frank (1994). *Colonial Wars and the Politics of Third World Nationalism*. London: I.B.Tauris.

Furedi, Frank (1997). *Population and Development.* Cambridge: Polity.

Galbraith, J. K. (1962). *The Affluent Society.* Harmondsworth: Penguin Books,

Galbraith, J. K. (1964). *Economic Development.* Cambridge, MA: Harvard University Press.

Hardy, Thomas (1957). *Tess of the D'Urbervilles.* London: Macmillan.

Hardy, Thomas (1975). *Selected Shorter Poems of Thomas Hardy.* Basingstoke: Macmillan.

Heartfield James (2008). *Green Capitalism: Manufacturing Scarcity in an Age of Abundance.* London: OpenMute.

Heath, Joseph and Andrew Potter (2005). *The Rebel Sell: How the Counterculture Became Consumer Culture.* Chichester: Capstone.

Hochuli, Alex (2008). Is Contemporary Anti-consumerism a Form of Romantic Anti-capitalism?, Paper presented at LSE Postgraduate Forum, 1 October.

Hoggart, Richard (1958). *The Uses of Literacy.* Harmondsworth: Penguin.

Huntington, Samuel (1968). *Political Order in Changing Societies.* New Haven, CT: Yale University Press.

ILO (1969). *The World Employment Programme. Report of the Director General of the ILO to the International Labour Conference.* Geneva: ILO.

ILO (1977). *Meeting Basic Needs: Strategies for Eradicating Mass Poverty and Unemployment, Conclusions of the World Employment Conference 1976.* Geneva: ILO.

Kerner Commission (1968). National Advisory Commission on Civil Disorder, *Report of the National Advisory Commission on Civil Disorders.* Washington DC: Government Printing Office.

Keynes, John Maynard (1952). *Essays in Persuasion.* London: Rupert Hart-Davies.

Lee, J. M. (1967). *Colonial Development and Good Government.* Oxford: Clarendon Press.

Lipton, Merle (1986). *Capitalism and Apartheid. South Africa, 1910–1986.* Aldershot: Wildwood House.

Longford, Charles (1986). *South Africa: Black Blood on British Hands.* London: Junius.

Malik, Kenan (2008). *Stange Fruit: Why Both Sides are Wrong in the Race Debate.* Oneworld.

Make Poverty History http://www.makepovertyhistory.org/whiteband/index.shtml

Milne, David (2008). *America's Rasputin: Walt Rostow and the Vietnam War.* New York: Hill and Wang.

Narayan, Deepak, R. Chambers, M. Kaul Shah and P. Petesch (eds) (2000). *Voices of the Poor: Crying Out for Change.* Oxford: Oxford University Press for the World Bank.

National Commission on the Causes and Prevention of Violence (1969). *Report of the National Commission on the Causes and Prevention of Violence To Establish Justice, To Insure Domestic Tranquillity.* Washington D.C.: Government Printing Office.

Pender, John (2002). 'Empowering the Poorest? The World Bank and "The Voices of the Poor' ", in *Rethinking Human Rights: Critical Approaches to International Politics* (ed.) David Chandler. Basingstoke: Palgrave Macmillan.

Philo, Greg (1995). Glasgow Media Group, Volume 2, *Industry, Economy, War and Politics.* London: Routledge.

Pupavac, Vanessa (2005). Human Security and The Rise of Global Therapeutic Governance. *Conflict, Security & Development* 5, no. 2, pp. 161–81.

Rostow, W. W. (1971). *The Stages of Growth: A Non-Communist Manifesto*, 2nd edition. Cambridge: Cambridge University Press.

Rousseau, J. -J. (1968). *Politics and the Arts: The Letter to M. d'Alembert.* Ithaca, NY: Cornell University Press.

Sahlins, Marshall (1972). *Stone Age Economics.* Chicago: Aldine.

Sayre, Robert and Michael Lowy (1984). Figures of Romantic Anti-Capitalism. *New German Critique*, no. 32, pp. 42–92.

Schumacher, E. F. (1974). *Small is Beautiful: A Study of Economics as if People Mattered.* London: Blond & Briggs.

Schumacher, E. F. (1977). *A Guide for the Perplexed.* London: Jonathan Cape.

Seers, Dudley (1979). The Meaning of Development, in *Development Theory: Four Critical Studies* (ed.) David Lehmann, pp. 9–30. London: Frank Cass.

Sen, Amartya (2001). *Development as Freedom.* Oxford: Oxford University Press.

Sennett, Richard (2002). *The Fall of Public Man.* London: Penguin.

Thompson, E. P. (1968). *The Making of the English Working Class.* Harmondsworth: Penguin.

Thoreau, Henry (2004). *Walden.* Princeton, Oxford: Princeton University Press.

Thornett, Alan (1995). *Inside Cowley.* International Socialist Group. http://www.isg-fi.org.uk/spip.php?rubrique16

Times, The (1975). Government to Take over Leyland in £1,500m Investment plan. 25 April.

UN General Assembly (1974). *Declaration on the Establishment of a New Economic Order*, GA Resolutions 3202 (S-VI).

Whitaker, Ben (1983). *A Bridge of People: A Personal View of Oxfam's First Forty Years.* London: Heinemann.

Wilberforce, William (1798). *A Practical View of the Prevailing Religious System of Professed Christians, in the Higher and Middle Classes in This Country, Contrasted with Real Christianity*, 6th edition. London: Century Collections Online. Gale Group. http://galenet.galegroup.com/servlet/ECCO

Wilder, Laura Ingalls (2000). *Little House on the Prairie.* London: Egmont.

Williams, Raymond (1961). *Culture and Society 1780–1950.* Harmondsworth: Penguin.

Williams, Raymond (1973). *The Country and the City.* New York: Oxford University Press.

Wood, Barbara (1983). *E. F. Schumacher: His Life and Thought.* New York: Harper & Row. Available via E. F. Schumacher Society http://www.schumachersociety.org/Wood%20bio/index.html

4
Aid Policy, Civil Society and Ethnic Polarisation

Jens Stilhoff Sörensen

Introduction

The revival of the language of civil society in the 1980s, starting in Eastern Europe and subsequently in Anglo-Saxon and continental social science and public debate, came to exercise a profound influence on international aid policy in the 1990s. It received a central role in the reshaping of aid policy, which in line with the neoliberal turn of the 1980s, had come to de-emphasise the role of the state as an agent in development.

The neoliberal dogma of slimming states and allowing market forces to play the central role in economic development and investment opened up wider spheres of social and public life within the Western states, including their aid policies, to private initiative and subcontracting. Merging with other strands, such as 'participatory development' and 'sustainable development', this allowed for an increased role for NGOs, as both partners in and implementers of aid projects, in a variety of non-commercial issues.

Although not entirely novel, the practice of working with NGOs increased rapidly from the early 1990s onward. With the fall of bipolarism in 1989–91 a whole new area was opened up in Eastern Europe for capitalist expansion and a new arena was provided for Western aid policy. Moreover, a form of global geopolitical competition and an alternative state-centred socialist development paradigm had come to an end.

In the new post-communist states in Eastern Europe, NGOs were depicted as an emerging civil society structure upon which democratisation depended, and in post-conflict areas – as in the Balkans – they were seen as platforms of resistance to ethno-nationalist governments, as well as vehicles for inter-ethnic dialogue and reconciliation. This was the rationale for giving support to local NGOs, presented as civil society in the making, while various Western NGOs provided opportunities for penetration into receiving societies for aid projects that did not go to state institutions. Civil society was in this manner construed as an opposite to the state.

The general conceptualisation within the aid industry has been that civil society constitutes a cornerstone for democracy, and a public arena for fostering pluralism and liberal values. It posits civil society in opposition to the state, thereby relying heavily on an Anglo-Saxon version of the concept but filtered through the East European revival of the concept, where it had been formulated by dissidents in opposition to an authoritarian state.

In this chapter I shall suggest that there are considerable problems with such a conceptualisation of civil society, and thus problems with the policy of supporting NGOs as a means of promoting civil society, democratisation or reconciliation. Indeed, in certain regards such policies may contribute to fragmentation and polarisation in society, rather than integration and democratisation, especially in societies that are already polarised, such as those subject to post-conflict reconstruction. This chapter discusses this problem in relation to international support to civil society in Kosovo.

I will first discuss the concept civil society, briefly outline the policy of supporting civil society through NGOs and look at some key donor definitions of civil society and the rationale for supporting it. This leads me, in the third section, to raise further questions on the concept of civil society in relation to ethnicity, community and society, especially, how these concepts relate to the state, and which problems are generated for aid policy in post-conflict reconstruction. Then, in the fourth section, I move on to discuss the problem of support to civil society in Kosovo, first by outlining some characteristics of Kosovo society and its NGO sector, and second by looking at some current trends in ethnic mobilisation including mobilisation against the UN administration. In conclusion I shall suggest that although I draw on examples from Kosovo, with its own particularities, these issues represent a more general problem of civil society in relation to ethnicity, with lessons for other ethno-plural societies and post-conflict reconstruction missions.

Civil society: The concept reloaded

The term 'civil society' has a prominent place in European intellectual history and political and social theory, but since the traditions and contexts in which it has been used are so various the simple sharing of the term should not be confused with a sharing of conceptual meaning. An exercise in conceptual history may not even be particularly useful for a concept which in its contemporary usage is relatively new (cf. Trägårdh, 2008). Nevertheless, it can be claimed that the rich historical and intellectual heritage of the *term*, if not the content, has provided it with a positive value connotation upon which the term can partly 'free-ride', when applied within aid policy in order to mobilise support for this. For our purposes here it is useful to revisit at least one line of a broken path, which brings to the fore a contrast between an Anglo-Saxon perspective of a division of society into spheres, and a potentially opposing Hegelian tradition. Sadipta Kaviraj has noted that the concept, in both its ancient and modern varieties, typically needs a contrast, something that it stands in opposition to and is defined against. In the early modern period and in social contract theory it was the 'state of nature' from which man entered civil society through a social contract, while in modern conceptions civil society is defined in relation to the state (the liberal tradition), to the family, the community (or *Gemeinschaft*) or to the market (Kaviraj, 2001).

The term 'civil society', as such, goes back to antiquity (*societas civilis*) and was widely referred to in medieval and early modern legal and political thought. Until the early modern period the concept, or idea, of this term was roughly equivalent to a society governed by law, thus a 'political society' or what we would today call the state.[1] A series of departures, which lie at the roots of the modern conception, and the practice of dividing society into different spheres, may be traced to the seventeenth and eighteenth centuries: first to John Locke, who made a distinction between civil society and government, and then to the Scottish Enlightenment philosophers (especially John Ferguson and Adam Smith), who in the development of Political Economy came to include the free market in the concept of civil society.[2] For John Ferguson civil society was a 'natural society' (i.e., living in society is natural to man) of atomised individuals who are carriers of interest, both egoistic economic interest and 'disinterested interest', which is the basis upon which bonds form as well as break (Ferguson, 1767/1995). The departure taken in the Scottish Enlightenment, and with classical Political Economy, was analysed by Michel Foucault as crucial to a new way of thinking about government, whereby the economy was effectively separated from the realm of the sovereign, as consisting of 'natural' processes, and a sphere in which intervention would not merely be wrong, but indeed against

nature itself; according to classical Political Economy the governing
(or sovereign) had no hope of gaining knowledge upon which to base
decisions for intervention in this sphere with its complicated processes (Foucault, 2008). It is this epistemological position regarding
the economy to which the word 'invisible' in Adam Smith's 'invisible hand' was referring. According to Foucault, the idea of man as
a carrier of interest, *homo oeconomicus,* created a new subject for the
sovereign to relate to; in place of man as a carrier of 'rights', whose
relation to the sovereign could be thought of in judicial terms and on
the basis of natural law, emerged a man as carrier of interest and an
economic sphere which was governed by natural processes and over
which the sovereign had no privileged knowledge and in which he
must therefore not intervene.[3] This potential limitation of the sovereign generated a question of how to govern – in a space of sovereignty inhabited by economic subjects, with judicial rights and at the
same time as economic men – that could not be resolved by judicial
theory. It was possible only with the construction of a new domain
or field of reference – a new correlate of the art of government – and
this new ensemble of subjects with rights as well as economic actors,
was 'civil society' (ibid., ch. 12). Hence, civil society is here conceptualised as the correlate of a new way of governing and provides the
basis for rationalising the legal regulation of a self-limiting 'frugal' or
'economic' government (Burchell, 1991, p. 140).[4]

Friedrich Hegel reacted to these 'Scottish' developments and was
highly critical of their idea of a free market, which he considered a
threat to civil society. While Hegel accepted Adam Smith's idea that
individual self-interest, played out on the market, generated welfare
for the nation, he claimed that the market and civil society by necessity generated conflicts and tensions, which could only be mediated by
the state, which represented the universal public interest (Hegel, 1991;
cf. Trägårdh, 2008). Although Hegel introduced the idea of civil society as something between the family and the state, the latter was a
crucial reference point and vital to the concept, thereby rejecting the
autonomy of civil society from the state.[5] The contrast between Hegel
and the Scottish Enlightenment is in this regard a demarcation line for
the subsequent 'continental' and Anglo-Saxon traditions of the view
of the relationship between the state and the market. Here, the latter
(Anglo-Saxon) tends to view the state as a threat to the market and civil
society, whereas the former ('continental') views the state as a safeguard
against the private and particularistic interests generated within this
(non-state) sphere.

The idea of civil society was further developed in the Marxist tradition, and especially by Antonio Gramsci, but then the term became unfashionable and was largely absent from both social science and public debate for several decades, until revived in the late 1970s and 1980s by East European dissidents.[6] Here, it was placed in contrast to the authoritarian communist state. In the late 1980s it was revived within Anglo-Saxon and continental political theory and social science, sometimes with new terms (in German *'Zivilgesellschaft'* tends to be the novel concept, while *'bürgerliche Gesellschaft'* is the historical concept), and has since had a considerable renaissance. It should be noted that, in this renaissance, there has been a strong bias to the Anglo-Saxon conceptualisation of civil society vis-à-vis the state, both in the sense that it is embedded in an Anglo-American meta-narrative in which civil society is considered autonomous to the state – with its division of society into autonomous spheres – and with a conceptualisation of the economy as containing its 'natural laws' and essentially being ungovernable.[7] Although embraced by the left, the language of civil society is integral to liberalism, but it is not just liberal, it is neoliberal, and it is therefore no coincidence that it was revived with the turn to neoliberalism; it has been instrumental in shifting focus and masking other analytical frameworks for society, especially Marxist and Marxian perspectives that operate with the terminology of 'class'. The left can operate with the concept, for example on a Gramscian basis, and look to global networks of 'civil society' as a counterpoint to and mobilisation against neoliberal institutions and powerful multinationals, but it has – for the time being – essentially lost the battle over the formulation of the concept with regard to the aid industry. Thus, the term has travelled through rich layers of historical and cultural contexts, once being virtually equivalent to what we today would call the state, to being something 'other' than the state.[8]

The language of civil society became widely adopted within international aid policy in the 1990s. It was, however, rarely defined by the aid agencies until relatively recently. From policies enacted – and subsequent definitions to which we shall return below – it is evident that NGOs here play a considerable role, even if perhaps not directly equivalent to civil society. In many respects this has its logic, in that the donor agencies need a partner, an organisation or legal body, with which to sign a contract and to whom to transfer their funds.

Government donor funding of NGOs and subcontracting of projects is largely a phenomenon of the 1980s and 1990s, although it had existed before. Private organisations, and NGOs, had played a certain role as partners in international development since the Second World War, especially in US policy, and in the 1960s the US asked its allies to support NGOs as a means of broadening the support for development aid (Tvedt, 1998, pp. 48–49). The growth of the NGO sector was largely government sponsored and NGOs became and integral tool of policy, which they in turn supported in for example the Korean and Vietnam Wars (ibid., p. 48). However, until the 1970s there was a general consensus that the state had a crucial role as an agent in development (see introduction). The neoliberal impasse and definite break with Keynesian economics in the 1980s changed this. Along with private solutions to public services came an increased role for NGOs within the aid industry, too. The 1980s has been labelled the NGO decade, but there was an even wider proliferation of NGOs, and NGO subcontracting, during the 1990s (cf. Carothers and Ottaway, 2000). The pattern of NGO proliferation in the West was accompanied by the growth of NGOs in the developing countries as well. Trends from Africa, especially, during the 1980s received new momentum with the opening of Eastern Europe. Here, in line with earlier dissident concepts of civil society, and accompanied by democratisation and transition theories and subsequent neoliberal prescriptions for the 'transition states', the NGO sector became widely promoted as 'civil society' that was considered an essential component for democracy. In the disintegrating Yugoslav state, with its violent conflicts along ethnic lines, NGOs were promoted as a civic alternative to the ethno-nationalist political regimes. As embryonic embodiments of 'civil society' the NGOs were seen as carrying a mission for both democratisation and inter-ethnic dialogue and reconciliation.[9] Another target for donor support of 'civil society' was those print and electronic media considered to be 'independent'. Supporting free production and circulation of information, and civil society, became a central objective for many western donors, and separate budget posts were created for this purpose. Western NGOs thrived on these new budget posts and local NGOs mushroomed throughout the Balkans, as elsewhere in Eastern Europe. To quote some suggested estimates, the NGOs' share of the USAID budget rose from 13 to 50 per cent under the Clinton administration, and the funds transferred by northern NGOs increased at twice the rate of international aid as a whole (Tvedt, 1998, p. 1).

Eventually criticised for lacking definitions of the concept 'civil society', most of the key donors started to provide such definitions after 2000. The World Bank has provided its own term, 'civil society organisations', defining it as:

> ... the wide array of non-governmental and non-profit organizations that have a presence in public life, expressing the interests and values

of their members or others, based on ethical, cultural, political, scientific, religious or philanthropic considerations. Civil Society Organizations (CSOs) therefore refer to a wide of array of organizations: community groups, non-governmental organizations (NGOs), labor unions, indigenous groups, charitable organizations, faith-based organizations, professional associations and foundations.[10]

Here the idea of civil society is most explicitly linked to NGOs. However, some donors are more careful about making such a direct link. Thus, the British Department for International Development (DFID) explicitly warns about the tendency to reduce civil society to non-governmental organisations and instead offers the following definition:

> Civil society is located between the state, the private sector and the family or household, where society debates and negotiates matters of common concern and organises to regulate public affairs. It embraces:
>
> - Institutionalised groups: such as religious organisations, trades unions, business associations and co-operatives.
> - Local organisations: such as community associations, farmers' associations, local sports groups, non-governmental organisations and credit societies.
> - Social movements and networks.[11]

On its website the DFID makes some effort in suggesting the complexity of the concept, but – in line with the Anglo-Saxon tradition – the link to the state is still weak. The Swedish International Development Cooperation Agency (Sida) is quite explicit in eliminating the relationship between civil society and the state when it defines civil society as:

> An arena, separate from the state, the market and the individual household, in which people organise themselves and act together to promote their common interests.[12]

And in a further qualification it asserts:

> Under authoritarian regimes, or in devastated and fragmented societies in which there are conflicts between different armed groups and where the government apparatus is weak, it can be difficult to identify civil society. Nevertheless, with the above mentioned view of

civil society it is difficult to imagine a country in which there is no civil society at all, even if it may be fragmented and weak, or difficult for an outsider to detect.[13]

Here there is a notable absence of the state in relation to civil society. The state may be authoritarian, or it may be fragmented and experiencing violent conflict; nevertheless there is civil society to be found, it's only a matter or detecting it. One must assert that both the first and the last of the above definitions are very broad when suggesting that all non-state and non-market human collective activity is to be defined as civil society. Namely, the definition would work even where there is no state, thus allowing for example tribal gatherings, or say a terrorist network such as Al-Qaeda (separate from the state and the market, promoting the common interests of its members) to be grouped under the umbrella of civil society. The fact that a concept is loosely defined, open and all-embracing or not defined at all is not in and by itself a problem. Still, while fuzzy borders are part of language, the wish for clarification and delineation of at least certain key concepts, especially in academia, is often an essential tool for analysing the social and political. The problem with policy-maker definitions of civil society like the above is that they will be assumed to serve some purpose in policy, that is, to be instrumental. If the definition is so broad that it actually provides no guidance with regard to its objectives, in this case the funding of aid projects, the question arises what purpose it actually serves. In Sida's policy for civil society it is argued that civil society is neither good nor bad, and that many undemocratic groups and criminal networks such as the mafia, are part of society as well and cannot be easily excluded in an operational definition of civil society.[14] Hence, civil society *as such* is not what they support, but rather NGOs or activities on the basis of other criteria. Similarly, the World Bank and DFID do not follow their definitions as a working checklist for their support to individual projects. They support a range of projects, NGOs and media outlets, assessed both individually and on other criteria where the priorities may shift over the years, considered on the basis of for example human rights, gender awareness, geographical spread, attitude towards the West, etc. Together, they are then suggested to be part of civil society, which is considered essential for pluralism and democracy.

The crucial observation to be made here is, I suggest, that the role of the state in relation to civil society has been lost, and not just accidentally, but with some enthusiasm. Thus the language of civil society shows a remarkable conceptual journey from once referring to what we understand as the state, then gradually being repositioned and remobilised to include the market, finally to arrive at something quite different to either. This trajectory is not a mere curiosity, but a useful recapitulation of what can be made politically possible with the use of words. Or, to put it differently, it can be used to emphasise that *politics is language*. The revived language of civil society draws on positive value connotations and discursive fields within Western political philosophy and liberal theory, which are utilised in framing support for NGOs and private actors as an instrument for, and crucial element in, democratisation and liberal state-building. However, as an actual policy practice the result of this assumption is questionable. While the role of civil society, as such, in relation to democratisation has been questioned in a number of studies, there is an even larger space for questioning the role of *external support* to civil society in relation to democratisation.[15] Rob Jenkins has suggested that donor definitions are not capable of producing, in a coordinated way, the outcomes that assistance to civil society is designed to produce (Jenkins, 2001). Further, in studying the USAID in particular, he suggests that donors tend to apply different and contradictory conceptions tailored to different purposes; these may range from supporting groups in dislodging an authoritarian regime to providing a political sphere that can perform the roles assigned to it in liberal theory and neoliberal economic policy (ibid.). In particular the idea of support to civil society is connected to the conception of good governance, which he claims has an explicit bias towards neoliberal orthodoxy (ibid.).

The problem is even more pressing if we move specifically to the context of ethnically divided conflict zones or post-conflict societies. Does the model of subcontracting to NGOs, and stimulating the proliferation of NGOs in such aid-receiving societies, actually contribute to pluralism, democracy and reconciliation or social cohesion? Perhaps the question must be qualified with regard to a number of particular social, cultural and historical features of specific aid-receiving societies? For example, what is the relationship between civil society and ethnicity? How does above-mentioned policy practice play out in post-conflict reconstruction in an ethno-plural society characterised by identity politics? Will the result of such policy be pluralism or will it instead exacerbate fragmentation?

Ethnicity, community and society

Disconnecting the state, the family and the market from the concept of 'civil society' leaves the latter as a kind of by-product of all other forms of collective social action. In itself this is unproblematic, but when connected to a particular policy or strategy, where public money is spent and political programmes promoted, then a problem arises. It begs questions of *what kind* of collective social action the policy wishes to promote, on *what criteria* the *collective* is defined and indeed *what is social?* These questions relate to ethnicity, community and society. If a policy wishes to promote or support *civil society* as a means of fostering democracy, post-conflict reconciliation and liberal values generally, could such a 'civil society' be mono-ethnic? If so, can it be based on a single clan (in cases where this is relevant)?

If the society in question has experienced violent conflict between ethnic, religious, tribal or clan-based communities, such as those where post-conflict reconstruction missions are typically relevant, how may 'civil society' or 'civil society organisations' be supported without actually supporting platforms for self-organisation among the separate ethnic, communal or tribal communities, which have been involved in conflict? Does one support only inter-ethnic, inter-communal, etc. forms of organisation? If so, the problem is how to avoid this generating conflict with the rest of society and those pre-existing mono-ethnic, religious, clan-based, etc. structures of solidarity?

I would like to introduce here two further concepts that are related to the question of 'bonding' and 'bridging' in society; first the one of *social trust*, and second, the *Gemeinschaft and Gesellschaft* dichotomy.

The question of legitimacy is central for democracy and for the stability of institutions. Connected to this, and at a more fundamental level of cohesion or fragmentation of society, is the issue of *social trust*. The connection is obvious, although its nature is not. Legitimate and democratic institutions, it could be argued, may generate social trust, but at the same time a certain level of social trust is a necessary precondition in order to uphold – and integrate into – common institutions and democracy. They seem to be interconnected in a spiral, either directed towards the reproduction of social trust, legitimacy and democracy or leading to breakdown and social fragmentation. The question, especially in a post-conflict society, is how to set a spiral in motion in the positive direction, that is, to create social trust (and reconciliation), trust in institutions and democracy.

The relationships between democracy, civil society, social trust and economic prosperity have attracted increasing attention since the 1990s. The most influential work, opening this debate, is Robert Putnam's study of the effects of the regionalisation (and decentralisation) reform in Italy from 1970 onward (Putnam, 1993). Putnam concluded that it is the density of social networks, or civil society in terms of associations, which generates social trust between individuals in society. This, in turn, stimulates democratic efficiency as well as economic prosperity. Here, the influence on aid policy is obvious, since there is a seemingly clear empirical case for the role of civil society, in terms of associations and networks, in a number of objectives relevant to aid policy such as democratisation, reconciliation (social trust) and economic development. Putnam was able to compare regions in Italy and came to the conclusion that northern areas, and regions with medieval city republics, had a higher density or degree of 'civil society' (associations, networks), as well as social trust and more effective democratic institutions and higher economic prosperity. The problem for aid policy with regard to Putnam's work is that he explained these variations by referring to long historical traditions traced back to the medieval city republics. Putnam then conducted similar comparative work in the US and again emphasised the role of culture (Putnam, 2000). Within aid policy the former set of conclusions, that civil society – in terms of associations and networks – promotes social trust, democracy and prosperity, has taken root, while the latter conclusion, that there are deep historical and cultural reasons for this, has been largely ignored. The former can be promoted, or so it seems, but the latter cannot be reproduced. The influence of Putnam's work (even if not referred to) is evident in many aid-policy documents on civil society, such as Sida's policy for civil society.[16]

The Swedish political scientist Bo Rothstein has instead suggested that there must be some quite contemporary political considerations involved, and advocates the thesis that the high level of social trust in countries like Sweden may be explained by the institutions of the welfare state (Rothstein, 2003). His concern with Putnam's thesis is that it allows little space for contemporary reform and policy. The egalitarian-oriented institutions and welfare project, he claims, lie at the heart of the high level of social trust in Scandinavia. While Rothstein's thesis allows for a high potential for aid policy to influence the issue of social trust in aid-receiving societies, this is in fact not relevant under the present design of aid policy, since the latter has largely abandoned the project of building welfare institutions (and a social state) in favour of a neoliberal project in which privatisation, outsourcing and project management by private actors and NGOs tend to dominate.

This brings me to the second concept I would like to discuss, that of *Gemeinschaft* and *Gesellschaft*. This binary couple was introduced by Ferdinand Tönnies in the late nineteenth century to denote two contrasting images of social life (Tönnies, 1887/2001). While too complex to be quickly summarised, we should recall that *Gemeinschaft* was modelled on community life with family and friendship relations, prevalent in the village, while *Gesellschaft* was modelled on the impersonal relations in business life or in the city. Further, these concepts should be understood in terms of a 'puzzle picture', rather than as actual analytical descriptions of existing forms of society; in other words, a 'pure' *Gemeinschaft* or *Gesellschaft* exists only as a mental image, for in the real world elements of both coexist everywhere even though one may dominate (cf. Asplund, 1991). The translation into English has posed some problems and has gone from 'Community and Association', to 'Community and Society', and recently 'Community and Civil Society'.[17] Any of these translations may have complications, depending on what one is looking for. If *civil society* is understood in terms of contemporary aid discourse, then it does not translate well as *Gesellschaft*. However, if civil society is understood in the historical sense, as used by Adam Ferguson, with a strong connection to the state as a legal order but including the sphere of the market, then the translation is quite reasonable, and this is indeed how we should understand it.[18] As such, it differs considerably from the NGO-based idea of civil society in contemporary aid policy, which constitutes something *other* than *Gesellschaft*, and which perhaps is more akin to a form of *pseudo-Gemeinschaft*.

If civil society is supposed to promote, and be based on, pluralism and universal democratic principles, rather than ethnocratic or kinship-based institutions, then we have to look at the *Gesellschaft* analogy, which breaks away from traditional forms of organisation. In other words society has to be transformed from, and transgress, traditional loyalties, *Gemeinschaft*-like values, into a *Gesellschaft* (I allow myself a fairly liberal use of these terms here, aware of the different connotations they may have). Further, if civil society is expected to promote 'social trust', then it has to be a social trust that is accommodated in *Gesellschaft*. The question is *how* social trust is promoted and generated. It would be fairly meaningless to pose this question with reference to *Gemeinschaft* since that by its very definition and nature is based on friendship and familiarity![19] In *Gemeinschaft* we have to frame the meaning of 'social trust' differently, because although the people living in a *Gemeinschaft* do not need to trust everybody in it, they at least know with whom they are dealing. In *Gesellschaft*, by contrast, they relate to strangers and thereby the question of social trust has a different meaning. We may say that in *Gemeinschaft* there is a 'trust' in those one knows and is familiar with (even if it is a hated neighbour), whereas in *Gesellschaft* the relations to strangers places emphasis on the term 'social' (as opposed to 'communal'). In *Gesellschaft, social* trust implies that you have to place some confidence in the goodwill or plain common interest of your fellow citizen or fellow urban dweller. Thus, the question of how social trust can be generated only makes sense in *Gesellschaft,* since *Gemeinschaft is* trust, but of a different kind than that which can be generated in *Gesellschaft.* A village or a clan, where people can identify an individual with reference to a family or a village location, can be seen to correspond to the idea of a *Gemeinschaft.* The *Gesellschaft* analogy requires anonymous spheres and specific rules for relationships between individuals who are *mostly* or *principally* strangers to each other.

The crucial point to be made here is that the remoulding of a traditional society into one with universal, liberal (Western-style) values may, in fact, require a breaking down of traditional social institutions and networks, including the kind of social trust embedded in them, and may thereby generate social conflict. The alternative is that traditional networks and informal institutions are reproduced *within* a new formal institutional framework and that they become embedded in them and thereby shape them, which in turn makes those institutions less universal. Such a process might generate conflicts with the 'out'-groups, such as the 'ethnic other' or other 'clan-family networks'. Social trust is high *within* clans or ethnic groups which are in conflict with other clans or ethnic groups, and the problem is how to create social trust *between* them and thus reconciliation, how to transgress traditional loyalty networks and *extend* social trust beyond them. A requirement for the latter, and in order to create *trust in universal institutions,* may be the weakening of existing loyalty networks, which could otherwise be perceived as a threat to fair and non-corrupt institutions. The Western liberal ideal type requires an atomisation of traditional structures and an *individualisation* of society. The whole idea of *'one person one vote',* as well as the idea of *meritocracy,* is founded upon such an individualisation process. The requirement of such transgressions constitutes a dilemma, and the promotion of social and cultural change through contemporary aid policy, may thereby *generate* social conflicts as well as diffuse them.

We need to make one qualification to the discussion above. An ethnic community does not really constitute a *Gemeinschaft!* Ethnic identification is based on some idea of common traditions, history, heritage, language, religion or other identity marker, but it is not a *Gemeinschaft.* It is not a *Gesellschaft* either. This binary concept is only loosely connected to the question of ethnic or national identity, and you can have

Gesellschaft in a mono-ethnic society or *Gemeinschaft* in an ethno-plural village. These concepts were not at all developed with regard to questions of inter-culturalism or ethnic pluralism, but in the context of urbanisation and modernisation within an existing cultural community. The point to be made here is rather that in a highly polarised society, where conflict has been mobilised along ethnic lines and where the state is weak, ties of loyalty and social reliance are shaped by identity politics and lean towards more communal ties, or particular identity markers, thereby moving in a direction away from universal values or *Gesellschaft*.

In the debate over civil society versus institutions (as posed here by Putnam and Rothstein), and the question of how to promote social trust, the actual existing experience of social integration of separate ethnic or clan-based groups, is typically with institutions. Political Science literature is rich on such issues as institutional power sharing, and federalism is a classical solution to this problem (e.g., Lijphart, 1984). With regard to a policy for promoting social trust in civil society, while largely bypassing the state, the record is much weaker. Here, as discussed in the introduction, we should note that there has been a re-emphasis on the state in international aid and security policy following the war on terrorism and perceived threats with so called 'fragile states'. However, in this recurrence, the role of the state and the support to state structures are primarily limited to providing security and stability, for example by providing government, security and border-control structures. This is in contrast to the classical Keynesian-era idea of the state as a service provider and as an agent in social and economic development. Thus, I would maintain that we should consider this re-invoked emphasis on the state, and on institutions, as a minor adjustment in the neoliberal paradigm, where the private sphere and actors are still the main focus.

The reliance on and promotion of market forces and relations, and the accompanying limitations placed upon the state with regard to economic policy and development, carry the risk of leaving the state with few or no instruments for promoting integration and attracting loyalty and trust in its institutions. The problem is not only that development and economic policies are largely removed from the democratic process, but also that people are forced to retain and rely on alternative security and loyalty structures. In an underdeveloped and divided society, the free play of market forces may contribute to existing tensions and further fragmentation, and strengthen patron-client and nepotistic networks of favouritism, loyalty and security. In such a manner it may block allegiance to 'neutral' state institutions or alternatively shape these institutions along existing networks of nepotism and clientism. Such a shaping of institutions may be the trend anyway, it was certainly not unknown to institutions in the socialist or developmental state, but under conditions of programmes of development and welfare, where state institutions are more expansive, they can afford to be more inclusive, and crucial processes concerning development and welfare are brought under institutions that can be held accountable and subject to bargaining.

Several case studies show that support to civil society in post-conflict ethno-plural societies and, indeed, neoliberal aid policy in general have a weak track record in promoting reconciliation and democratisation. Before discussing Kosovo a brief look at Bosnia-Hercegovina (BiH) may be instructive, since it has both been studied more and received an additional five years of direct foreign control and involvement. Any comparison with BiH should take into account that the cultural distance between the ethnic groups in BiH is actually smaller than in Kosovo. Thirteen years after the Dayton Peace Agreement, and with a tremendous international engagement of aid, post-conflict reconstruction, state-building and support to civil society, there are still few signs of reconciliation, multi-ethnic integration and democratisation. Four years after the peace agreement, a study by David Chandler concluded that there was little evidence of any progress in terms of 'civil society development' or democratisation, and after ten years the general picture was equally dismal (Chandler, 1999, 2006; compare also Bose, 2006). A multi-disciplinary study undertaken for Sida in 2005 (i.e., ten years on) showed that there was no significant progress whatsoever in terms of reconciliation or social trust that could be recorded as a result of foreign assistance (Čukur, et al., 2005). The evaluation was conducted in relation to the direct material aid of Sida's integrated area programmes, and three separate studies involving surveys and anthropological fieldwork showed the same results. Although foreign assistance was effective in terms of the material conditions it produced, there was no sign of reconciliation or increased social trust between ethnic groups and the report concluded that the popular assumption that cohabitation will lead to interaction and subsequent integration is a false one (ibid., p. 131). Even with a fairly modest definition of reconciliation, the report stated that there was little or no sign of it:

> Since interaction is so rare one could hardly speak of social reintegration, and certainly not of reconciliation. (ibid., p. 126)

The report further concluded that although reconciliation is one of the aims with Sida's assistance, the evaluation in Bosnia confirms findings from studies in other parts of the world (ibid., p. 131).

This can be contrasted with the experience of post-conflict reconstruction and ethnic reconciliation in the 'developmental state' of Yugoslavia (and Bosnia) after 1945. Here, the socialist model of reconstruction was apparently quite effective in creating a framework for the various ethnic groups that had experienced inter-ethnic atrocities during the Second World War. Such a parallel should however take into consideration the very different historical conditions, including the geopolitical and bipolar order after 1945 and that a whole new framework for international political economy was created at that time. In this geopolitical and international political economic order, state- and nation-building were central to foreign policy and international aid policy, with the state considered a crucial agent in economic and social development.[20]

From parallel society to state structures: International support to civil society in Kosovo

The complexity of support to civil society in divided societies, and the problem of separating it as a sphere that can be promoted in order to stimulate liberal development across other spheres, is well illustrated by the experience of Kosovo. Throughout the 1990s, society in Kosovo was deeply divided along ethnic lines, with the formal structures dominated by Serbs, and a parallel (underground) Albanian society that was formed after 1990 and boycotted all (Serbian) state institutions.[21] The parallel Albanian structures covered a range of sectors such as social services, health, school, culture, media and sporting activities. They were financed by a 3 per cent tax among all Albanians, diaspora remittances, self-subsistence and international aid. Being subject to international sanctions along with Serbia, the parallel economy increasingly expanded, including activities in the black economy such as the drugs trade, which financed some smaller radical networks.[22] In addition many Albanians migrated for seasonal work.

The whole parallel society in Kosovo was dominated by a single party, or umbrella organisation, the Democratic League of Kosovo (LDK) under the leadership of Ibrahim Rugova. Under this rule the Albanians practiced a non-violence strategy of resistance, while hoping to receive international support and goodwill for their cause, which was independence. The strategy of non-violent resistance became increasingly challenged after 1995 when the Dayton Peace Agreement for BiH was signed. The issue of Kosovo was largely ignored in the Dayton process, and following the agreement sanctions on Serbia were relaxed and some European countries (notably Germany) started to repatriate Albanian refugees to Serbia. The Dayton Agreement generated strong reactions among the Albanians and a questioning of the strategy; for some, it seemed that the provocation of violence, as in BiH, was necessary in order to receive international attention and support for their cause. In 1997 the implosion of the neighbouring Albanian state led to increased access to arms. Gradually, in the second half of the 1990s, a more radical militant faction, the Kosovo Liberation Army (KLA), gained ground and challenged the authority of the LDK. Terror operations against police and Serbian civilians increased. Serbian counter-measures to combat the guerrillas meant that international attention was effectively gained. In the autumn of 1998 the US started to support the most radical fractions among Kosovo Albanians and the policy of Ibrahim Rugova and the LDK was effectively marginalised (cf. Magnusson, 1999; Sörensen, 2006).

Following the establishment of a protectorate in June 1999 the international administration began to support the build-up of state structures (provisional institutions for self-government). The policy and programme for economic recovery emphasised small and medium enterprises, the creation of a framework for a market economy and the rapid and widespread privatisation of socially owned enterprises (see Sörensen, 2009). The crucial political issue was the status of Kosovo – whether it would become independent or somehow remain as an autonomous region within the framework of Serbian sovereignty. In this context the process of privatisation became highly contested, and subject to international legal procedures; the Serbian minority considered privatisation to be pure theft and illegal under international law (cf. Sörensen, 2009, ch. 8). In addition to building state structures, and promoting a market economy, there was a continuous emphasis on developing civil society through NGOs. International donor agencies, such as USAID, emphasised the parallel Albanian structures of the 1990s as a foundation that could be developed into a 'vibrant' civil society, while elements of it would be the foundations for new state structures:

> Despite the lack of previous democratic and civil society experience, as a result of a long history of communist and Serbian dominated rule, Kosovar society provided itself with social, cultural and basic community services over the past ten years, through a largely voluntary civil society system.[23]

While both the OSCE and USAID referred to NGOs and 'civil society actors' as 'watchdogs' of government and of democracy, and the OSCE claimed that 'their empowerment will eventually counterbalance governmental institutions...'[24], USAID suggested that 'some of the more sophisticated NGOs may evolve into government institutions'.[25]

The NGO scene that today exists in Kosovo is a product of the 1990s, but it has undergone a considerable expansion and consolidation since the establishment of the protectorate in June 1999. It follows the same trend as the whole region of former Yugoslavia, where the expansion of the NGO sector in the 1990s was primarily the creation of an urban middle class. The new ethnic states rewarded supporters of the ruling party, and under a rapidly changing opportunity structure, parts of the politicised middle class, which was effectively squeezed in the social transformation in the new republics, could find a niche in NGOs (Sörensen, 1997). The cycle of expansion and consolidation is the same as in other parts of the former Yugoslavia, but the character of this new sphere of organisational bodies has an important feature, peculiar to, or at least stronger in, Kosovo. Throughout the 1990s, the main purpose of international (primarily bilateral) aid to NGOs in the post-Yugoslav states, especially Serbia, was to support 'anti-governmental' organisations that were critical of the ethnic nationalist regimes. In addition there was support to service-providing NGOs, working with relief, with children, psycho-social treatment and the like, but here, too, it was important that they were perceived as oppositional to, or at least largely outside the influence of, the governments. The rhetoric and conceptual logic behind this orientation was that the aid was 'building civil society', which would be the promoter of liberal democracy, peace and reconciliation.

However, in Kosovo, where the whole ethnic Albanian community stood in opposition not only to the Serbian regime, but to the Serbian state as well, the effect was to support an ethnic society against the Serbian state. Although some activity involved other ethnic communities in Kosovo (such as Serbs or Roma), the aid promoted organisational development within ethnic communities in an ethnically divided society and in effect provided an external source of funding to the parastate functions in Kosovo during the 1990s.[26]

Some organisations had an important role in the parallel structures of the 1990s, such as the (Catholic) Mother Theresa Society, with a history as charity organisation, but most of the present-day NGOs are the result of the increased access to funding from foreign donors, or were even directly created by foreigners.

The rapid expansion of the NGO sector in Kosovo indicates that these structures are quite disconnected from any 'organic' social development within the communities in Kosovo, and that they are a direct adaptation to the new financial opportunity structure provided by foreign intervention. From approximately 50 NGOs in Kosovo in 1999, the number increased to some 642 registered NGOs by July 2000, out of which some 400 were 'local' (Kosovo) organisations.[27] By 2004 the total number of NGOs registered to operate in Kosovo was more than 1000.[28] It has since increased to over 2800. Although many NGOs exist only on paper, the rapid expansion of this sector not only indicates that it largely is an external implant, but also shows how the NGO sector is not merely complementary for donor organisations, but indeed a prime instrument and channel for aid.

An example of an externally implanted NGO is the Kosovo Action Network (KAN), which was created in 1997 by an American, as a support group for students and NGOs.[29] The 'KAN' has worked in the fields of education, human rights and social issues, as well as art, and has received funding from various international donor agencies for projects on an annual basis, but has no core support. It gathered dozens of activists, mainly students from Prishtina, and in addition involved some international volunteers and organisations. The local branch in Kosovo started its work in 2003 and was the creation of foreign activists who subsequently involved locals. This is an extreme case of a foreign implant, and many NGOs have been formed through local initiatives in response to the new opportunities provided by foreign funds. The leader of KAN, coordinating activities in Prishtina, was Albin Kurti, a former student and translator for the KLA.

From 2005 Albin Kurti started to transform KAN into a broader nationalist movement, *Vetevendosje* ('Independence' or 'self-determination') with radical demands. The organisation, or movement, advocates that the Albanians should reject any negotiations with Serbs, reject status talks, move unilaterally towards independence and remove the UN Mission in Kosovo (UNMIK) from Kosovo by force if necessary.[30] In early 2006 graffiti with the word 'Vetevendosje' and 'End to UNMIK' started to appear on Serbian houses.

Together with KLA veterans, Vetevendosje opposed the UN decentralisation plans for Kosovo and protested against UN protection of Serbian orthodox religious monuments. In March 2006 'Vetevendosje' organised violence against the orthodox monastery of Decani and demonstrated against UNMIK. Similar incidents of ethnic violence occurred sporadically throughout 2006, as for example with the stoning of a Serb convoy in May near Prizren, which led the UNMIK police to intervene with the use of tear-gas. In spite of incidents of desecrated cemeteries, attacks on monasteries, explosions, stonings and some murders, UNMIK reported that this was not necessarily inter-ethnic violence although the Serbs perceived it as such.[31] The attacks on cultural sites were, however, condemned by the Council of Europe in June. On 16 June 2006 UNMIK decided to postpone the municipal elections, which were to be held in the autumn, until after the status negotiations or for up to a full year. With Serbian parliamentary elections coming up in January 2007, the UN Envoy Martti Ahtisaari decided to postpone his report on Kosovo's status in order not to influence elections in any negative direction. The continuous delays frustrated Albanian radicals and although there had been occasional Albanian attacks on the UN earlier, a peak was reached on 28 November, the Albanian Flag day, with demonstrations organised by Vetevendosje in front of the UNMIK headquarters in Prishtina. These turned into riots and the UN police had to intervene with the use of tear-gas.

In the aftermath of addressing these riots, and nationalist mobilisation, Albin Kurti was put on trial and placed under house arrest. Nevertheless, his career led him to earn a powerful position in articulating radical Albanian dissent with the international administration in Kosovo, as well as opposition to dialogue with Serbia. It should be noted that such mobilisation had taken place earlier, and that Vetevendosje only expresses its more recent accentuation. Frustration and dissent with the international administration grew after 2004, and in March 2004 there were widespread riots against Serbs in Kosovo, which resulted in some 20 deaths and hundreds of wounded, including some international officials.

A combination of factors contributed to the frustrated sentiments, including the reduction of international aid after 2003 and the dire social economic conditions, the stalemated issue of Kosovo's status and some widespread incidents of corruption within the UNMIK administration. After a series of critiques, the whole of UNMIK and international policies towards Kosovo were reviewed, resulting in policy adjustments and a restructuring of UNMIK during 2005. After these changes Vetevendosje took a leading role in an ethnic mobilisation, which gradually came to exercise corrosive effects on the legitimacy of the international administration in Kosovo. Since Kosovo's declaration of independence, on 17 March 2008, Vetevendosje has continued to advocate radical nationalist demands, and propagandised against the international administration. More recently, it has claimed that the EU mission of police and legal advisors, the EULEX, merely constitutes a continuation of external colonialism in Kosovo.

Concluding remarks

Conventional wisdom on democracy in ethno-plural societies emphasises the role of power sharing and vetoes for minorities on issues essential to identity and cultural affirmation.

In his by now classical studies on the theme, the Dutch political scientist Arend Lijphart compared dozens of political systems (states) and concluded that some form of consensus model and power sharing was necessary in ethno-plural societies, since the flexibility necessary for majoritarian models of democracy is lacking, especially in plural societies that are strongly divided along religious, ideological, linguistic, cultural and/or ethnic lines into de facto separate sub-societies with their own parties and interest groups (Lijphart, 1984, p. 22). Constitutions, state frameworks and institutional arrangements to address this problem have existed in both liberal democracies and non-liberal socialist states. This principle has been applied in such diverse states as Switzerland, Belgium, Lebanon and socialist Yugoslavia. The federal principle has been applied to address this issue. In a number of post-conflict reconstruction missions, from BiH to Iraq, this lesson has resulted in efforts to accommodate various ethnic, religious or tribal groups in the institutions of the state. In the difficult task of overcoming widespread ideological, inter-ethnic or inter-religious animosities within such societies, and resistance to state-building, there has been a reliance on fostering liberal-oriented values through the promotion of civil society. However, a conclusion offered from the discussion in this chapter is that observations such as those offered by Lijphart on the electoral system and institutional design in ethno-plural societies should be extended and amended to the non-state sphere. In already highly polarised and ethnically mobilised societies, or those otherwise polarised along particularistic interests related to crucial issues such as identity, support given to NGOs as an element of civil society may contribute to creating platforms for further polarisation. This is particularly delicate in cases where the state is weak or its role is withdrawn from being a service provider and agent in social and economic development.

There are two crucial observations, or problematisations, here. First, in post-conflict reconstruction the critical issue is integration into state structures and institutions, but in order for the state to gain legitimacy there must be real improvement in the life-chances of the various groups in the population, such as through service provision and employment. The state needs instruments to address ethnic integration, attract loyalty and gain legitimacy, and economic and developmental instruments may be crucial here. The tensions generated in an under-developed area by opening it up to market forces create an environment of insecurity that may block such a process, as well as create an environ-ment where reliance on alternative traditional structures is cemented or exacerbated. Second, the idea of a division of society into autonomous 'spheres', such as the 'market', the 'political system' and 'civil society, needs to be rethought.

Not only is there an inconsistency in the idea that 'civil society' and the 'market' should be separate spheres from the state, since the practice is to support civil society as a means of promoting better government, and since 'civil society' in some cases has been promoted as organisa-tions that could become part of state structures, but in addition there is a particularly problematic relationship between ethnicity, commu-nity and civil society that becomes urgent when the latter is adopted for instrumental purposes by aid donors in ethno-plural societies. Thinking of civil society as an autonomous sphere that provides checks and balances for government in an ethnically divided society where the state is subject to competition by ethnic groups constitutes a serious neglect of the forces of ethnic identity politics and the interconnections between state and society.

A rethinking of the relationship between state, market and civil soci-ety can be undertaken with reference to Hegel's concern that the state is a crucial safeguard against the particularistic interests of the market and in civil society. Promoting a state that is an active agent in social and economic development and a service provider for all ethnic communi-ties might be the alternative that could offer a window of opportunity for some loyalties and trust to be transferred to the state and its institu-tions instead of relying on alternative loyalty and security networks. Certainly this risks the problem of ethnic and clan-based nepotism and corruption, but the alternative is regeneration of the particularistic interests in the private sphere, where support to civil society carries the risk of contributing to the organisation of platforms for ethnic polarisa-tion and hence fragmentation. Institutions are at least accountable and can be subject to public scrutiny.

For all their dissimilarities there are parallels between such diverse regions as Kosovo, BiH and Iraq. To mention an example, in Iraq the US supported ethnic and religious-based groups, such as the Kurds and the Shi'a umbrella organisation SCIRI (later SIIC, with the aim of creating an

Islamic state), as well as individuals with quite personal agendas, such as Ahmed Chalabi, while dismantling all the state's unifying institutions, including the army and police (Ricks, 2006). Giving support to separate groups while dismantling the state created further self-organisation of non-state actors and exacerbated existing divisions. Again, there was an accompanying process of rapid privatisation and a generation of mass unemployment through the dismantling of the police and the army, and the closing of state industries. While there has been considerable support to NGOs and 'civil society', such existing civil society bodies as the trade unions, among which various ethnic groups have united against the adoption of the Oil Law and foreign economic exploitation, have been proclaimed illegal and received no assistance. Conditions in Iraq differ considerably from Kosovo, but in neither place is there a great willingness by the various communities to integrate into joint state institutions, and there is in both an excessive emphasis on private solutions, privatisation and non-governmentalisation. The record in the Balkans indicates that in the focus on private actors and NGOs, international aid policy fails to address the complexity of inter-ethnic and inter-community relations, which lie at the centre of conflict.

Notes

1. *Societas* was the Roman legal term for partnership, and *societas civilis* may be translated as a partnership under law. The classical definition was provided by Cicero.
2. This is quite rudimentary, and instrumental to this article; another tradition of dividing society and state emerged with Montesquieu and was concerned with limiting absolutist rule.
3. Here I follow Foucault (2008, especially ch. 12), but to be read in context of Foucault (2007 and 2008 *en bloc*).
4. This is obviously a considerable reformulation. With the earlier concept of a 'political society' the debate concerned such issues as the relationship, and various rights, between the sovereign and his subjects. Within this debate the idea of a 'social contract' came to play a significant role, first in the sense of being the foundation for a political society, that is, man living in the 'state of nature' entered 'civil society' through a social contract and thereby gave up some of his rights to the sovereign who would rule over him, and second, in the sense of explaining the origins of political society. In the republican tradition there was much debate over the virtues of citizenship; to be 'civil' meant to behave as a citizen and take part in political life. In the civic tradition, which challenged monarchical autocracy, the 'corruption' of the powerful was a vice typically associated with luxury and wealth (cf. Oz-Salzberger, 1995; more generally Pocock, 1975; Skinner, 1978). According to Foucault the conception of interests, or man as a bearer of interests that cannot be transferred to the sovereign through a 'social contract', as argued by David Hume and Jeremy Bentham, destroyed both social contract

theory in the Lockean sense and Blackstone's attempt to reconcile social contract theory with the principle of interest, and thereby created 'economic man' as a new subject of governance (Gordon, 1991; and generally Foucault, 2007, 2008). John Ferguson's essay on civil society is concerned with the place of civic virtue in the modern state. Here, where commerce and economic progress form a central issue, the 'stoic' idea that luxury and wealth are related to corruption of virtues must be renounced and instead he claims that man must conduct his affairs in civil society (essentially a republican idea). Crucially, for Ferguson 'civil society' is 'natural society', that it has always been there for man is by 'nature' political and in 'conducting the affairs of civil society' mankind comes to apply its best talents. The individual interest is what both forms bonds and creates cleavages in society and this is a natural process. With the Scottish Enlightenment civil society not only comes to include the market, but essentially there also comes a new view of governance, which renders the economy outside the realm of the sovereign.

5. Hegel considered it important that the urban professions and trades were organised into 'corporations' recognised by the state. Such corporations promoted collective responsibility and aims within civil society. This brings an institutional concretisation to the idea of civil society. Hegel established a much stronger link to the state, and the role of the state, in relation to civil society; the state had an important task in mitigating and balancing conflicts generated within civil society, for example by addressing *poverty*. Poverty was no natural phenomenon; it was a consequence of civil society and a 'social wrong' that the state had a task in policing (see Hegel, 1991).

6. Gramsci elaborated civil society as the arena for political struggle, which had to be completely transformed in order for socialism to come about. Here, Gramsci excluded the market but included the family, which was in direct contrast to Hegel's view of the family as a sphere with quite particular values that were non-existent in civil society as such (for example, motherly love and care).

7. There is a normative Anglo-American meta-narrative in which civil society is seen as absolutely autonomous and separate from the state (Somers, 1995a, 1995b; Trägårdh, 2008). It has its parallel in classical political economy, and in Anglo-American neoliberalism (as opposed to German neoliberalism, or *ordo-liberalism*) in which the economic sphere must be autonomous from the state (as discussed above; see Foucault, 2008).

8. Note that the term 'state' or '*lo stato*' only received its modern meaning in the sixteenth century; see, for example, Viroli, M (1994).

9. The author worked for the Swedish government and international organisations for a number of years in the mid-1990s and attended several donor coordination meetings where this rationale was widespread. Support to independent media and local civil society became a major policy objective among several donor countries and agencies, and was considered 'progressive' in the search for policy responses to the Balkan crisis. See also Ottaway and Carothers (2000).

10. The World Bank and Civil Society at: http://web.worldbank.org/WEBSITE/EXTERNAL/TOPICS/CSO/0,,contentMDK:200...

11. Cited from: www.dfid.gov.uk/aboutdfid/intheuk/workwithcs/sc-how-to-work-what.asp, pp. 1–2.

12. Sida's Policy for Civil Society, April 2004, p. 9.
13. Sida's Policy for Civil Society, April 2004, p. 10.
14. Sida's Policy for Civil Society, April 2004.
15. But experiences vary between cases; see for example the comparative case-studies collected in R. May and A. K. Milton (eds) (2005) *(Un)Civil Societies: Human Rights and Democratic Transition in Eastern Europe and Latin America.* University Press of America.
16. For example Sida's Policy for Civil Society, pp. 11–16.
17. F. Tönnies (1955) Community and Association (translated by Charles P. Loomis), London; F. Tönnies (1957) Community and Society (American Edition), East Lansing, Michigan; F. Tönnies (2001) Community and Civil Society (translated by Jose Harris and Margaret Hollis), Cambridge University Press. An excellent discussion in Swedish regarding the binary couple, including translation problems, has been provided by J. Asplund (1991).
18. Personal communication (through email) with the translator Jose Harris. Please note that I do *not* wish to criticise the translation, but merely highlight the problem with the discontinuity and different conception of the term 'civil society' in contemporary aid discourse. Again, positive connotations arising from the term are transported from a historical usage to which there is little reference.
19. Please note that this does *not imply* that *Gemeinschaft* should be free from conflicts, for certainly it is not (neither are families or friendships); it simply implies that social trust and familiarity are part of how the concept was elaborated by Ferdinand Tönnies, *in opposition to Gesellschaft.*
20. It could be suggested that this post-war reconstruction, following the Second World War, took place under non-democratic conditions, and that *firm rule* may have been the reason for success, but an international protectorate is also non-democratic (at least initially) and supposedly under firm rule by the international military presence.
21. For further details to the brief outline here see for example: S. Maliqi (1998); J. S. Sörensen (2009); H. Clark (2000); M. Vickers (1998).
22. Cf. J. S. Sörensen (2006), pp. 317–35.
23. USAID Kosovo NGO Sustainability Index 1999, p. 58: www.usaid.gov (accessed 25 July 2005).
24. OSCE Mission in Kosovo, Civil Society at: www.osce.org/kosovo/13376.html (accessed 25 July 2005); USAID Kosovo Civil Society Fact Sheet 'Civil Society and Government': www.usaid.gov/missions/kosovo/USAID_Kosovo_fact_sheets/civsoc_fact_she...' (accessed 25 July 2005).
25. USAID Kosovo NGO Sustainability Index 1999, p. 59: www.usaid.gov (accessed 25 July 2005).
26. The purpose here is *not* to criticise the fact that such organisations received aid, but to elucidate the actual processes at work and consequences flowing from the new type of aid-governance model and to highlight the problematic within it.
27. The Advocacy Project: www.advocacynet.org/news_view/news_68.html (accessed 25 July 2005).
28. See Freedom House, Nations in Transit 2004: Serbia and Montenegro with an addendum on Kosovo, p. 10: www.freedomhouse.org (accessed 25 July 2005); and http://unpan1.un.org/intradoc/groups/public/documents/NISPAcee/UNPAN016587.pdf (accessed 25 July 2005).

29. Interview with Kosovo Action Network, representatives Albin Kurti and Dardan Velija, in Prishtina on 13 May 2004. The following information on KAN is based on this interview.
30. A manifesto of the movement is available at: www.vetevendosje.org (accessed 17 November 2007). They also provide weekly electronic newsletters where the development of their claims can be followed.
31. UNSC Report S/2006/707, 1 September 2006.

References

Asplund, J. (1991). *Essä om Gemeinschaft and Gesellschaft*. Göteborg: Bokförlaget Korpen.

Bose, S. (2006). The Bosnian State a Decade after Dayton, in *Peacebuilding Without Politics: Ten Years of International State-Building in Bosnia* (ed.) D. Chandler. Routledge.

Burchell, G. (1991). Peculiar Interests: Civil Society and Governing 'The System of Natural Liberty', in *The Foucault Effect: Studies in Governmentality* (eds) G. Burchell, C. Gordon and P. Miller. The University of Chicago Press.

Carothers, T. and M. Ottaway (2000). Introduction: The Burgeoning World of Civil Society Aid, in *Funding Virtue: Civil Society and Democracy Promotion* (eds) M. Ottaway and T. Carothers, pp. 3–20. Washington, DC: Carnegie Endowment for International Peace.

Chandler, D. (1999). *Bosnia – Faking Democracy After Dayton*. Pluto Press.

Chandler, D. (2006). From Dayton to Europe, in *Peacebuilding Without Politics: Ten Years of International State-Building in Bosnia* (ed.) D. Chandler. Routledge.

Clark, H. (2000). *Civil Resistance in Kosovo*. Pluto Press.

Čukur, M. et al. (2005). Returning Home: An Evaluation of Sida's Integrated Area Programmes in Bosnia and Herzegovina, Sida Evaluation 05/18.

Ferguson, J. (1767/1995). *An Essay on the History of Civil Society*. Cambridge Texts in the History of Political Thought, Cambridge University Press.

Foucault, M. (2007). *Security, Territory, Population: Lectures at College de France 1977–78*. Palgrave Macmillan.

Foucault, M. (2008). *The Birth of Biopolitics: Lectures at College de France 1978–79*. Palgrave Macmillan.

Gordon, C. (1991). Governmental Rationality: An Introduction, in *The Foucault Effect: Studies in Governmentality* (eds) G. Burchell, C. Gordon and P. Miller. The University of Chicago Press.

Hegel, G. W. F. (1991). *Elements of the Philosophy of Right*. Cambridge Texts in the History of Political Thought, Cambridge University Press.

Jenkins, R. (2001). Mistaking 'Governance' for 'Politics': Foreign Aid, Democracy, and the Construction of Civil Society, in *Civil Society: History and Possibilities* (eds) S. Kaviraj and S. Khilnani. Cambridge University Press.

Kaviraj, S. (2001). In Search of Civil Society, in *Civil Society: History and Possibilities* (eds) S. Kaviraj and S. Khilnani. Cambridge University Press.

Lijphart, A. (1984). *Democracies – Patterns of Majoritarian Rule and Consensus Government*. Yale University Press.

Magnusson, K. (1999). *Rambouilletavtalet: texten, förhandlingarna, bakgrunden*. Current Issues No. 1, Centre for Multiethnic Research, Uppsala.

Maliqi, S. (1998). *Kosova: Separate Worlds*. Peje: Dukagjini.

Oz-Salzberger, F. (1995). Introduction to J. Ferguson *An Essay on the History of Civil Society* (ed.) F. Oz-Salzberger. Cambridge Texts in the History of Political Thought, Cambridge University Press.

Pocock, J. G. A. (1975). *The Machiavellian Moment*. Princeton University Press.

Putnam, R. (1993). *Making Democracy Work*. Princeton University Press.

Putnam, R. (2000). *Bowling Alone: The Collapse and Revival of American Community*. New York: Simon & Schüster.

Ricks, T. (2006). *Fiasco: The American Military Adventure in Iraq*. Penguin Books.

Rothstein, B. (2003). *Sociala fällor och tillitens problem*. Stockholm: SNS Förlag.

Skinner, Q. (1978). *The Foundations of Modern Political Thought*, 2 Vols. Cambridge University Press.

Somers, M. (1995a). What's Political or Cultural about Political Culture and the Public Sphere? Toward a Historical Sociology of Concept Formation. *Sociological Theory* 13, pp. 113–44.

Somers, M. (1995b). Narrating and Naturalizing Civil Society and Citizenship Theory: The Place of Political Culture and the Public Sphere. *Sociological Theory* 13, pp. 229–74.

Sörensen, J. S. (1997). Pluralism or Fragmentation. *War Report* May 1997, no. 51.

Sörensen, J. S. (2006). Shadow Economy, War and State-Building. *Journal of Contemporary European Studies* 14, no. 3, December.

Sörensen, J. S. (2009). *State Collapse and Reconstruction in the Periphery*. Berghahn Books.

Tönnies, F. (1887). *Gemeinschaft und Gesellschaft: Abhandlung des Communismus und des Socialismus als empirischer Culturformen*. Leipzig; recent English translation by J. Harris and M. Hollis (2001) *Community and Civil Society*. Cambridge Texts in the History of Political Thought, Cambridge University Press.

Trägårdh, L. (2008). Det civila samhällets karriär som vetenskapligt och plitiskt begrepp i Sverige. *Tidskrift för samfunnsforskning* no. 4.

Tvedt, T. (1998). *Angels of Mercy or Development Diplomats*. Africa World Press.

Vickers, M. (1998). *Between Serb and Albanian: A History of Kosovo*. Hurst & Company.

Viroli, M. (1994). *From Politics to Reason of State*. Cambridge University Press.

Part II
Asian Alternatives

5
Challenges or Complements for the West: Is there an 'Asian' Model of Aid Emerging?

Marie Söderberg

Introduction

Japan was the largest donor of Official Development Assistance (ODA)[1] in absolute terms during the 1990s and still is one of the largest donors. As the only Asian member of the Organisation for Economic Co-operation and Development (OECD)'s Development Assistance Committee (DAC) it is bound by many of the rules of this committee, which consists of donors with a Western, Christian background. Still, Japan has always been somewhat of an odd man out in this community of donors. The country has a belief in development through industrialisation and a concept of aid that is firmly integrated into a wider concept of economic cooperation. Japan's aid has consisted, to a much greater extent than that of other donors, of bilateral loans and the building of economic infrastructure in the form of roads, railways, ports and power plants. Recently a number of Asian former recipients of Japanese aid have become donors themselves. China, South Korea, Thailand and other Asian states are emerging as donors (some of them with an older tradition in the field). Their ways of giving aid, or cooperating with developing countries, as they prefer to call it, have been mediated by their own experience of development. There are certain common features among the Asian donors, such as an emphasis on loan aid and infrastructure. This chapter gives an overview and analysis of Japanese, Chinese, South Korean and Thai aid policies, and explores how such 'Asian alternatives' may constitute a challenge or a complement to Western mainstream international aid.

The experience of development of these Asian states is strongly connected with successful economic development in East Asia. During the past 50 years living standards for most of the population have been lifted high above the poverty level. Starting with Japan's fast economic growth and industrialisation in the 1950s and 1960s, the four tigers – South Korea, Singapore, Taiwan and Hong Kong – followed the same path. These were later followed by other East Asian countries such as Thailand, Malaysia and Indonesia, which also saw tremendous economic growth. Japan was deeply involved in this development. First of all Japan was seen as a model for the others and proof that Asian countries could climb the ladder of development, raise their living standards and become industrialised and economically prosperous. Second, Japanese trade and investment were abundant in all these countries. Third, Japan also provided huge amounts of foreign aid to Asian countries, which among other things helped build the infrastructure necessary for development. At the beginning of the 1990s Japan sponsored a major research project conducted by the World Bank to see if it was this Japanese model with a strong state and export-driven growth that was behind the successful development in Asia. There was no clear-cut result in the final project report, *The East Asian Miracle* (World Bank, 1993), which became the subject of intense debate among economists and scholars in development studies. The banking crises and the recession that Japan went into in the 1990s, the Asian financial crises of 1997 and changing conditions in a globalised world economy put an end to the discussion of a Japanese model for development.

Since the end of the Cold War, great changes have taken place in the field of aid. There is no longer a division into a communist East and a capitalist West, in which aid was to a great extent directed through the main powers in each group. For Japan, which because of its security treaty with the US was definitely part of the Western camp, the fall of the Berlin Wall meant a great change. The justification for the security treaty with the US – the threat from the Soviet Union – was disappearing. Suddenly it was not so clear whom to support. Japan started receiving requests for aid from a number of new countries, including those from the former eastern bloc. In Asia many of the former recipients of Japanese aid had started to do rather well and, even though there was an Asian crisis in 1997, many of the East Asian countries recovered fairly quickly and have seen their economies growing again during recent years. The Chinese economy in particular has undergone tremendous growth – of more than 10 per cent a year – during the last 25 years and has been a growth engine for the whole area. In Asia things have gone so well that recently a number of former recipients of aid have become donors themselves. China, South Korea, Thailand and other Asian states such as Malaysia and Singapore are emerging as donors (some with an older tradition in the field).[2] There are some striking similarities between Japanese aid, which all these countries have received, and the aid that other Asian donors are now extending. Having experienced Japanese aid, some of them modelled their own aid directly on the Japanese pattern.

In contrast to mainstream international aid, Asian donors have their own view of the concept. In Japan aid has always been seen as part of the wider concept of economic cooperation (*keizai kyō ryoku*), which besides aid also encompasses two other components – other official flows (OOF[3]) and private investment. Economic cooperation encompasses almost all activities considered helpful to economic development, without distinguishing between official and private, commercial and non-commercial funds. This conceptualisation can be traced to the idea of 'mutually beneficial economic assistance' (Jerve et al., 2008, p. 15).

Economic cooperation is not seen as something that is extended in one direction but as the word implies is a question of working together. In the same way China does not use the language of donor and recipient when giving aid, but talks about mutual benefit and win-win relations. President Hu Jintao, in his opening speech of the 2006 Forum on China-Africa Co-operation (FOCAC) summit, said that mutual support was the driving force behind growing China-Africa cooperation (Davies, 2007, p. 41). In Thailand's cooperation with Laos the term 'aid' is not used either, as this is said to have bad connotations: instead one speaks of cooperation (JBIC, 2007, p. 44).

While mapping development aid from Japan, South Korea, China and Thailand, this chapter will examine: (1) the historical context of the development aid, (2) the structural set-up of the aid distribution, (3) the characteristics of the aid and (4) recent policy developments concerning aid.

There are several difficulties in this field of study. One is to decide what is to be considered as development assistance and what is not. As Japan is a member of the DAC, its aid will be calculated according to the DAC standard classification of ODA. Official DAC statistics are available for which countries aid is extended to and in what fields. When it comes to the other Asian donors, information on what they are doing is very scarce, and there is no detailed collection of data or peer reviewing.

In the case of China, it might not be obvious what is aid and what are other types of credits, and sometimes there is a mixture of the two. Some information is not released at all. Classifications of financial resources may differ and there is a considerable lack of transparency. Regarding South Korea, the country gives roughly as much aid to North Korea as it gives to other countries, but as North Korea is considered part of the same country this is not seen as aid.

Thus we may not always be mapping comparable entities here. However, rather than exact categories and amounts, this study aims at the policy level. The structure for policy formulation and implementation will be mapped through the questions: 'What kind of aid?', 'For whom?', 'Under which conditions?', 'With what purpose?' The four countries' foreign aid patterns will then be compared to see if any specific Asian model can be deduced when compared with DAC aid in general. This is also difficult as there are as many DAC models of aid as there are member countries, and Japan is one of them. Therefore this comparison will be on a general DAC policy level. When numbers are used these will be DAC totals, although there may be variations between the individual members.

There are considerable differences in the size and scope of projects from different Asian donors. When the Chinese government announces a tripling of aid to Africa in the years 2006–2009, as well as the setting-up of a China-African development fund to encourage Chinese companies to invest in Africa, which will reach US$5 billion, its effect will be different from that of Thailand sending a team of doctors.

Although China signed the 2005 Paris Declaration on aid effectiveness, according to which there should be cooperation among donors in order to avoid duplication and increase effectiveness, most Chinese aid is channelled bilaterally without consultation with other donors. Fears have been raised among regular DAC members that the Chinese government's extension of aid to countries like Sudan could undermine mutually agreed rules for aid concerning issues like good governance and human rights.

Finally we ask what implications an Asian model (or Asian models) of aid might have both for the policy of Western donors and for the developing countries.

Japanese aid

Historical context

Japan's contribution of US$50,000 to the Colombo Plan in 1954 and the war reparations agreements with Burma in 1954, the Philippines in 1956 and Indonesia in 1958 are seen as the origin of Japan's aid programme. The war reparations were given for reconstruction after the Second

World War. They were tied to procurement from Japanese companies, thus also serving to promote exports from Japan (Söderberg, 1996, pp. 33–5). In 1957, the yen loans from the Export-Import Bank started going mainly to Asia, and besides meeting certain needs in the developing countries also served to establish Japanese industry in the area. Aid in the 1960s was mainly directed towards Asia and overwhelmingly served Japan's commercial purposes.

This pattern changed with the 1973 oil crisis when a huge aid package began for the Arab world in order to secure oil supplies. As a consequence of this crisis, a stable supply of natural resources became another ingredient of Japanese aid policy (Yasutomo, 1986). Trade was a prerequisite for obtaining resources and Japan, as a resource-poor country, recognised its interdependence with developing countries. To conduct trade, a certain amount of infrastructure was needed. This is one of the reasons for the huge amount of Japanese aid spent on infrastructure development in Asia. It was seen as a necessary cost for achieving a secure and peaceful world, as well as Japan's own economic development. Humanitarian considerations for aid did not appear with any weight until the late 1970s (Söderberg, 1996, pp. 33–5).

In 1977, the first of a number of aid-doubling plans was announced. The wish to be respected in the international community was another motive for these plans, which eventually turned Japan into a leading donor. Aid was seen as a way for Japan, which according to its constitution could not send its Self Defense Forces abroad, to contribute to international society and was sometimes explained in terms of burden-sharing (*yakuwari buntan*): Japan should take greater responsibilities in the field of aid to compensate for the US 'global security umbrella' (Islam, 1991). It was also a way of improving Japan's image in Asia, where Japanese businessmen had left far from favourable impressions of their country. This was the start of gift-giving diplomacy (*omiage gaikō*), which Japanese prime ministers touring Asia have since used extensively.

In 1989, Japan became the world's biggest donor of ODA in absolute terms and remained so until the end of the 1990s. Domestically, Japanese ODA was the subject of intense debate. There was a substantial number of researchers critical of the heavy emphasis on economic infrastructure, which they asserted profited only people in the developing countries who were already well off. Alternatively these projects were regarded as being of most benefit to Japanese companies. The infrastructure projects were regarded as detrimental to the environment and the government was criticised for giving aid without a face (Murai, 1989; Sumi, 1989). This, combined with the end of the Cold War and the requests for aid from new countries, led to the formulation of the ODA Charter (adopted in 1992). The charter called for environmental considerations and development to be pursued in tandem, for ODA not to be used for military purposes, for attention to be given to recipients' military expenditure as well as any production of weapons of mass destruction and for the promotion of democracy and the introduction of the principles of the market economy. With the charter came not only a commitment to certain values and goals in Japanese aid but also a turn away from a 'request-based' model of aid, with no intervention in internal affairs, to a 'consultative' one, where the Japanese government started formulating country strategies. In the 1990s, Japanese ODA, at least verbally, became more politicised and more environmentally conscious.

Structural set-up

During the 1970s and the early 1980s Japanese aid policy-making was usually fairly uncontroversial. There were few politicians who were knowledgeable about, and few private citizens or groups with a special interest in, the area. Aid was mainly handled by bureaucrats and the ODA budget was dealt with by the Diet annually without debate or deliberation on its content. Japan did not have one sole ministry or bureau responsible for aid but a number of different ones (Söderberg, 1996).

At the implementation level, several organisations were in charge of ODA. In the 1950s the Export-Import Bank began to be criticised for being too commercially oriented and too restrictive for many development projects. A new organisation, the Overseas Economic Cooperation Fund (OECF), was set up. In 1965 it made its first government loan as part of Japan's newly established relations with South Korea. The OECF became responsible for all aid loans. In 1999 the OECF merged with the old Export-Import Bank to form the Japan Bank of International Cooperation (JBIC), an institution that dealt with both aid loans and other official flows to developing countries as well as promoting the interest of Japanese companies.

The Japan International Co-operation Agency (JICA) was set up in 1974 to handle grant aid and technical cooperation. It came under the Ministry of Foreign Affairs (MOFA). There was constant fighting between JICA and the OECF (and later the JBIC), which sometimes had different ideas on best practice for aid. In all main recipient countries both institutions had their own separate offices. The reforms of Japan's general administrative system starting at the end of the 1990s also entailed some shift in the structural set-up and policy formulation of ODA. In 2006 an Overseas Economic Cooperation Council under the prime minister was formed and MOFA was put officially in charge of aid policy formulation as well as coordination (Ministry of Foreign Affairs, 2006). In 2008 the loan aid part of the JBIC merged with JICA into the 'New JICA', which would be responsible for implementation of all three types of Japanese aid (loans, grants and technical cooperation).

Characteristics

Although substantial in absolute terms, at over US$11 billion in 2006, in terms of a percentage of gross national income (GNI) Japan's ODA is less impressive. In 2006 it amounted to 0.25 per cent of GNI as compared to 0.31 as the average for the DAC countries (OECD, 2008, p. 137, table 1). Per capita ODA in Japan was US$98 in 2005–2006, as compared to US$119 on average for DAC members (OECD, 2008, p. 149, table 7).

One peculiarity of Japanese bilateral ODA as compared to that provided by many west European countries during the 1980s and 1990s was that it consisted to a large extent of bilateral loans. This meant that, although quantitatively the total amount of ODA was large, the quality (as measured by the share of total aid that consisted of grants) was rather low. The justification for this was often presented from a moral ideological viewpoint. This was to be help for self-help. If the donors knew that they had to repay the loans, they would be more careful with the money.

There were, however, also economic reasons for providing loans rather than grants. Japan did not want to increase the ODA part of the state budget at the same time as it was cutting down on other items such as education at home. This would not have been popular with domestic public opinion. Financing for loan aid could partly be found through sources other than the regular state budget, such as pensions and postal savings.

A second characteristic of Japanese aid used to be its heavy emphasis on Asia. In 1970 98 per cent of its ODA went to Asia; in 1980 the corresponding figure was 70 per cent and in 2000 54.8 per cent. With the rise in the living standards of the Asian countries and the fact that a number of countries have 'graduated' from the aid programmes, the figure has further decreased, to 37 per cent in 2005 (Ministry of Foreign Affairs, 2006, p. 68). Total ODA by Japan to East Asia between 1970 and 2004 amounted to approximately US$71.6 billion (in terms of net disbursement). This accounted for 54.4 per cent of the total from the DAC member countries (Ministry of Foreign Affairs, 2006, pp. 19–20).

Eighty-four per cent of outstanding Japanese loan aid is in Asia. The number one recipient on a cumulative basis is Indonesia. China has a much shorter history of receiving aid but was the largest recipient during much of the 1990s. Except for Iraq, which received a huge amount of aid from all DAC countries and was also the largest recipient of Japanese bilateral ODA in 2006, Indonesia and China were still the largest recipients (Table 5.1).

A third characteristic of Japanese aid, strongly connected with the emphasis on Asia (Table 5.2), is that the largest share of aid has gone not to the poorest countries but rather to Low Middle Income Countries (Table 5.3).

A fourth characteristic concerns the content of Japanese ODA, which has always emphasised economic infrastructure, that is building roads,

Table 5.1   The top ten recipients of Japanese gross ODA 2005–2006 (US$ million)

Country	Amount	Percentage of total
1. Iraq	2168	12.1
2. China	1529	8.6
3. Indonesia	1189	6.6
4. Nigeria	1107	6.2
5. Philippines	750	4.2
6. Vietnam	666	3.7
7. India	581	3.3
8. Thailand	476	2.7
9. Zambia	390	2.2
10. Sri Lanka	345	1.9

Source: OECD (2008), *Development Co-operation Report 2007*, Volume 9, No. 1, pp. 88, 211.

Table 5.2   Regional distribution of Japanese ODA (percentage of net disbursement) (compared to DAC total average)

Regions	1995–96	2000–2001	2005–2006
Sub-Saharan Africa	19.3 (33.9)	18.2 (33.4)	33.5 (42.8)
South and Central Asia	20.0 (13.7)	22.0 (16.5)	13.0 (11.7)
Other Asia and Oceania	39.5 (21.2)	41.1 (19.0)	24.4 (9.5)
Middle East and North Africa	7.3 (14.4)	6.0 (10.3)	21.5 (23.7)
Europe	1.2 (4.1)	1.9 (8.0)	1.5 (4.9)
Latin America/Caribbean	12.6 (12.6)	10.7 (12.8)	6.0 (7.4)

Source: OECD (2008), *Development Co-operation Report 2007*, Volume 9, No. 1, pp. 198–9.

Table 5.3 Distribution of Japanese ODA by income group (percentage of total aid)

Country	Least Developed Countries (LDCs)		Other Low Income Countries (LICs)		Low Middle Income Countries (LMICs)		Upper Middle Income Countries (UMICs)	
	1995–96	2005–2006	1995–96	2005–2006	1995–96	2005–2006	1995–96	2005–2006
Japan	22.0	27.4	21.7	25.9	53.4	44.3	3.0	2.3
DAC total (average)	33.5	32.7	20.8	24.7	40.5	39.2	5.1	3.9

Source: OECD (2008), *Development Co-operation Report 2007*, Volume 9, No. 1, p. 195.

Table 5.4 Japanese aid by major purpose in 2006 (%)

	Japan	DAC Total (Average)
Social and administrative infrastructure	22.6	34.9
Economic infrastructure	26.0	11.4
Production	8.5	4.8
Multi-sector	4	5.8
Programme assistance	1.4	3.1
Action related to debt	28.5	22.6
Humanitarian aid	2.4	6.9
Administrative expenses	5.0	4.1
Unspecified	1.5	6.4

Source: OECD (2008), *Development Co-operation Report 2007*, Volume 9, No. 1, pp. 182–3.

railways, harbours, airports, power plants and other infrastructure necessary for economic growth. Within the category of economic infrastructure, transport received the largest amount of ODA during the 1990s. Compared to other DAC donors Japan places a strong emphasis on economic infrastructure (Table 5.4).

Besides bilateral aid, a large share in percentage terms of Japanese aid is distributed multilaterally. With a heavy focus on Asia, the regional Asian Development Bank (ADB) is a case in point. Although the bank has many members it has always had a Japanese president and has been heavily influenced by Japanese development thinking (Saito and Kyoko, 2007, p. 15). The allocation of resources in the ADB is more influenced by donors' interests than is the case with the World Bank (Kilby, 2006, p. 26).

Recent trends

From the beginning of the twenty-first century, 'country assistance programmes' were to be formulated for major recipients. This was a change from the earlier policy of separating economics and politics and approving ODA on a request basis. In this way Japan's influence on how its aid money is used was strengthened. Since the end of the 1990s there has been a constant and continuous reduction of ODA. The amount allocated to ODA from the general budget in fiscal year 2006 (760 billion yen) meant a 35 per cent reduction calculated in yen over the last nine years (Ministry of Foreign Affairs, 2006, p. 6). With this has come a need to pursue more strategic and efficient implementation.

Global environmental issues and the widening gap between rich and poor countries were part of the background to the adoption of the UN Millennium Development Goals, according to which the proportion of the world's population living in poverty should be halved by 2015. The terrorist attacks in the US on 11 September 2001 raised awareness of the needs to fight terrorism and for peace-building, recognising that poverty in developing countries created a breeding ground for terrorism. Together, these developments led to a revision of the Japanese ODA Charter in 2003. The object of ODA from now on was 'to contribute to the peace and development of the international community, and thereby to help ensure Japan's own security and prosperity'.

As seen from the figures above, however, many Japanese ODA characteristics remain. Japan figures prominently in the new Aid for Trade initiative that was called for at the WTO's Hong Kong Ministerial Conference in 2005 in order to help less developed countries take advantage of trade openings and promote a more interconnected world economy. Aid for Trade has assumed a growing importance in most donors' programmes. Bilateral donors provide on average 31 per cent of their sector-allocable ODA to Aid for Trade. There are, however, big variations and Japan, driven by its sizeable economic infrastructure, provides as much as 61 per cent. Between 2002 and 2005, Asia received 51 per cent of total Aid for Trade (OECD, 2007, pp. 32–4).

South Korean aid

Historical context

The history of South Korea's modern aid programmes goes back to the 1960s when it was still a poor country and a recipient of ODA itself. In the early 1960s South Korea hosted trainees from developing countries with financial support initially from the US Agency for International Development (USAID), but soon also began to invite trainees itself and to dispatch Korean experts overseas as well as offering project-type technical cooperation. By the end of the 1960s the present programme of technical cooperation was mainly in place, although South Korea's gross national product (GNP) per capita in 1969 was only US$210 at current prices. Thus the decision to embark upon a policy of providing foreign aid at that time was not taken because the country had an abundance of resources. The reason was clearly political: South Korea had to gain an 'edge' over North Korea in a diplomatic competition (Kim, 2003, p. 15). The split of the nation and the end of the Korean War in 1953 led South Korea to formulate its national goals in line with Cold War policy. International recognition and national legitimacy as well as maintenance of a diplomatic 'edge' over North Korea were top priorities. Although the UN had recognised the South Korean government as the only legitimate government on the peninsula its legitimacy was continually denied by North Korea and major communist countries such as China and the Soviet Union. South Korea had also been denied UN membership through a veto in the Security Council by members that supported North Korea. During the 1960s South Korean aid was concentrated on Africa, where many countries were emerging from colonialism and South Korea was competing with North Korea in an attempt to win influence and friends. In 1960 South Korea's economic development took off. In 1965 diplomatic relations were established with Japan and South Korea received an economic cooperation programme of considerable size.

The 1970s were, however, a golden age for North Korean diplomacy when it played a leading role in the Non-Aligned Movement (NAM), which South Korean failed to join as a full member. The Nixon Doctrine, together with the partial withdrawal of US troops from South Korea, the fall of South Vietnam and the rapprochement in Sino-American relations, increased awareness of South Korea's security vulnerability. This led to a focus on improving relations with the non-aligned countries. Grant aid was one way of doing this (Kim, 2003, p. 18).

In the 1980s the South Korean economy improved considerably whereas that of North Korea deteriorated and there was no longer the same need to worry about rivalry with the North. The first significant aid programme with other motivations – economic benefit and the promotion of South Korean companies' business on the global market – was undertaken. These were also some of the motivations for the Development Study programme initiated in 1984. In the early 1990s South Korea became a member of the UN and established relations with the governments in both Beijing and Moscow. Its economy had been booming and in 1996 it joined the OECD as the second Asian member after Japan.

When South Korea started looking for a model for a future foreign aid programme during the 1990s it was not going to be the west European or American models that it turned to but the Japanese, of which South Korea had had most experience itself. Just as its own development had been inspired by the Japanese model of strongly state-led, export-driven economic growth, it was now to turn to Japan as a role model for aid.

Structural set-up

In 1987 South Korea created the Economic Development Cooperation Fund (EDCF) to provide bilateral concessional loans to developing countries. This was modelled directly on the Japanese OECF.[4] EDCF loans are extended through the Korean EXIM bank under the supervision of the Ministry of Finance (MOFE). These loans are almost completely tied to procurement from Korean firms and have primarily been used with commercial considerations in mind, just as the Japanese loans used to be.

Rather than aid, the wider concept of economic cooperation is also used in Korea. This refers to all outflows of financial resources to developing countries. The distinction between private (commercial) flows, other official flows (loans with softer conditions than regular loans but not soft enough to be considered as aid) and ODA (loans that have a grant element of at least 25 per cent) is not always clear and all three are considered equally important. As the ODA loans are tied, South Korean companies follow them to the developing countries, but once there they also make their own private investments. Besides helping the recipient country, South Korea's ODA loans are regarded as a way to improve South Korea's own economic growth (Kim 2003, pp. 46–7).

In 1991 another organisation, the Korean International Cooperation Agency (KOICA), was established as an implementing agency, again modelled on a Japanese organisation, the JICA. KOICA deals with grant aid and technical cooperation and is under supervision of the Ministry of Foreign Affairs and Trade (MOFAT). But there are also other ministries involved in technical cooperation, such as the Ministry of Education, the Ministry of Information and Communication, as well as institutions such as the Korean Development Institute (KDI). Where multilateral aid is concerned, MOFAT is responsible for contributions to international organisations such as the UN, and the MOFE is responsible for subscription to international development banks such as the International Development Association (IDA) or the ADB.

Characteristics of South Korean aid

A large part of the bilateral aid consists of loans, which so far have been tied to procurement from Korean companies. During 2007, for the first time, one project financed by untied aid was run on a trial basis.[5] Japan promoted the Japanese model of development in the 1980s, and in the same way South Korea's own experience with economic and social development is now often pointed out as a valuable asset for the country to share with developing countries (EDCF, 2006, p. 39). The foreign aid loans are of two types: those given to foreign governments, government agencies or other eligible organisations to support the economic development of developing countries, and loans to Korean corporations for overseas activities (Tables 5.5 and 5.6).

The priority sectors for KOICA in recent years have been health, education, disaster relief and reconstruction. These three sectors combined accounted for over 50 per cent of KOICA's budget in 2006 (Table 5.7).

As implied in the list of countries that received South Korean ODA (Table 5.6), as well as from ODA by income group (Table 5.8), it is not the less developed countries that are mostly targeted but rather lower middle income countries.

South Korea's ODA policy in the twenty-first century

Even though MOFAT has published ODA reports mentioning Korea's overall policy and the need to expand ODA, it has taken a rather passive attitude and ODA has mainly been seen as a tool for gaining diplomatic advantage. As the amounts involved have remained small, however, ODA has played a relatively minor role in overall foreign policy, and MOFAT has not had enough staff working with ODA (EDCF, 2006, pp. 61–2). Moreover the financial crisis of 1997 had a

Table 5.5 Net disbursement of Korea's ODA (US$ million)

	2001	2002	2003	2004	2005	2006
Bilateral ODA Total	171.5	206.8	245.2	330.8	463.3	376.1
Grants	53.0	66.7	145.5	212.1	318.0	259.0
Loans	118.6	140.1	99.7	118.7	145.3	117.1
Multilateral ODA	93.1	72.0	120.7	92.6	289.0	79.2
Total Net ODA	264.7	278.8	365.9	423.3	752.3	455.3
ODA/GNI (%)	0.06	0.06	0.06	0.06	0.10	0.05
ODA Commitment	350.7	368.8	432.2	780.5	771.7	892.0

Source: EDCF (2007) *Annual Report*.

Table 5.6 The top ten recipients of Korea's ODA in 2006 (net disbursement) (US$ million)

	Grant	Loan	Total	Share (%)
Iraq	57.1	–	57.1	15.2
Sri Lanka	7.4	15.3	22.7	6.0
Bangladesh	4.2	18.0	22.2	5.9
Indonesia	20.3	-1.4	18.9	5.0
Albania	–	16.9	16.9	4.5
Top 5	89	48.8	137.8	36.6
Kenya	1.1	14.4	15.5	4.1
Cambodia	7.4	6.5	13.8	3.7
Laos	5.4	8.2	13.6	3.6
Bosnia-Herzegovina	0.03	12.9	12.9	3.4
China	6.8	3.3	10.2	2.7
Top 10	109.7	94.1	203.8	54.1

Source: EDCF (2007) *Annual Report*.

Table 5.7 Sectoral distribution of South Korea's bilateral ODA (commitments) (US$ million)

	2005 Amount	2005 Share (%)	2006 Amount	2006 Share (%)
Social infrastructure and service	398.0	60.5	403.1	59.7
Economic infrastructure and service	138.1	21.0	170.9	25.3
Production sectors	50.3	7.6	33.5	5.0
Humanitarian aid	36.9	5.6	24.6	3.6
Administrative costs of donors	19.4	2.9	25.3	3.7
Support to NGOs	4.5	0.7	5.3	0.8
Others	10.6	1.6	12.7	1.9
Total	657.8	100.0	675.5	100.0

Source: EDCF (2007) *Annual Report*.

great impact on the Korean people's willingness to provide aid. The crisis made it difficult for people to feel economically secure. Many still regard their country as 'semi-developed', and there are still poor people in South Korea. Under these conditions there was no public support for increasing foreign aid.[6] Commercial considerations started to overtake diplomatic considerations where ODA was concerned and since 1990 there has been a gradual concentration of foreign aid towards the Asian region.

Table 5.8 South Korea's bilateral ODA by income group (net disbursement) (US$ million)

	2005 Amount	2005 Share (%)	2006 Amount	2006 Share (%)
Least-developed	115.1	24.8	92.1	24.5
Other low-income	52.9	11.4	48.3	12.8
Lower-middle-income	264.8	57.2	185.6	49.3
Upper-middle-income	4.8	1.0	5.2	1.4
Unallocated	25.6	5.5	44.7	11.9
Bilateral ODA (Total)	463.3	100	376.1	100

Source: EDCF (2007) *Annual Report*.

With the adoption of the UN Millennium Development Goals and the general consensus among developed countries that the level of development aid should be raised, South Korea adopted a new strategy for ODA. In November 2005 the Council of Ministers approved the ODA Reform Plan.[7] According to this South Korea will increase its ODA to 0.1 per cent of GNI by 2009 and 0.25 per cent by 2015 (EDCF, 2006, p. 39). In 2006 ODA was 0.05 per cent of GNI (OECD, 2007, p. 221). (The DAC average for 2005 was 0.33/GNI and the UN target for 2015 is 0.7 per cent of countries' GNI.)

According to the reform plan, South Korea should join DAC in 2010, an intention that was announced to the DAC in April 2007.[8] An International Development Cooperation Committee of 22 members has been set up. It is chaired by the prime minister and consists of 15 heads of ministries and representatives of academia, NGOs and private business. It meets four times a year but unofficial meetings are held in between.[9]

The reform plan contains three main objectives for South Korea's ODA: (1) to assist in poverty reduction in developing countries, (2) to assist the sustainable development of developing countries and (3) to improve conditions for the advancement of Korean interests in foreign countries. Of these the two first goals are in line with ODA norms while the third clearly represents national interests (Kim, p. 14).

At KOICA a major reorganisation has taken place and new geographical departments have been put into place, one for the Asia-Pacific region, a second for Africa and a third for South and Central America. Three-year country- and sector-specific programmes have been run. KOICA is in the process of slimming down the number of partner countries in

accordance with the principle of 'focused and selective implementation' (KOICA, 2005, p. 10). During the last three years a special fund for
reconstruction has made Iraq the largest recipient. This is an indication
that ODA still has a role to play as a tool for diplomatic considerations
such as the preservation of peace. Otherwise the recipients are mainly
Asian countries (see Table 5.6). According to the Korean initiative for
Africa, aid to Africa would be be tripled by 2008, although this was
starting from a low level.

Since the improvement in the South Korean economy during the
twenty-first century, and specifically since the tsunami disaster of
2004, public opinion has been more favourably inclined towards ODA.
It has also become popular to work at KOICA. Today it has a staff of 250
and there are around 100 applicants for every new position.[10] The fact
that a South Korean, Ban Ki-moon, is the Secretary-General of the UN
has also stimulated interest in development and international issues in
South Korea. But to most South Koreans humanitarian issues in North
Korea and future reunification are still the main issues. Aid to North
Korea amounts to almost the same as South Korea's total ODA. This
aid is dealt with by completely different channels than KOICA or the
EDCF, and the structural set-up indicates that it exists for quite different
purposes. In this case only one ministry, the Ministry of Unification,
is in charge.

Chinese aid

Today China has the double role of both recipient and donor of foreign aid. As a developing country itself, it has been accepting foreign
aid from DAC countries since its policy of opening up started in 1979.
Although the sums have been large, and for several years China was
at the top of the list of recipients from the DAC (except for the period
immediately after the massacre at Tiananmen Square in 1989, when
Western aid stopped), aid has never been a significant part of its economy and China cannot be considered to have been an aid-dependent
country. Among such countries the inflow of aid amounts to 20 per
cent of gross domestic product (GDP), whereas Chinese development
aid in 2003 amounted to some 0.1 per cent (Tjonneland et al., 2006,
p. 12). Today the PRC is again becoming a significant aid donor.

Historical context

There is a long record of Chinese aid to developing countries. After
1949, China quickly established diplomatic relations with many African

states. This was an ideological demonstration by Mao Zedong to show support for the fight against imperialism and colonialism. It was also a way to counter the diplomatic recognition of Taiwan (Centre for Chinese Studies, Stellenbosch University, 2007a, p. 1). China participated in the Bandung Conference in 1955 and the establishment of the Afro-Asian People's Solidarity Organisation (AAPSO). In 1956 China launched its first aid programme to Africa. A significant aim was to knit African and other developing countries into a Third World alliance with China to counterbalance the superpowers and the developed North (Tjonneland et al., 2006, p. 8). During the early 1960s China entered into relations with 14 newly independent African states. Zhou Enlai's visit to ten African countries in 1963–64 was part of the PRC's anti-Soviet policy and was a deliberately high-profile event to show a Chinese presence and interest in the continent (Taylor, 2006, pp. 23–5).

During the Cultural Revolution China's aid to Africa expanded. Among the most famous projects was the Tanzania–Zambia railway (1967–75), a turn-key project completed at a cost of US$600 million and with the help of 15,000 Chinese workers. This took place during a period of considerable domestic hardship in China itself and was a showcase for Mao of his policy of internationalism. One of the direct payoffs was the support of a large number of developing countries for the PRC's joining the UN, taking the seat in the Security Council that had been held by Taiwan until 1971. When China joined the UN, besides the African countries there were many others like Albania or Vietnam that were asking for its support, although China was quite a poor country itself.[11]

After taking control of the country's politics, from the early 1980s Deng Xiaoping introduced new guidelines for aid. His policy was 'Let China be a recipient and a donor at the same time' (*you jin you chu*). In contrast to Mao's rather generous aid (6 per cent of fiscal revenues in 1971), Deng's policy was one of 'giving moderately and receiving a lot'. In 1985 in a major policy speech Deng laid the foundation for the PRC's foreign policy during the coming years, stressing a concentration on economic development in order to become a modern and powerful socialist economy. Rapprochement with the US and Japan in the 1970s made China less isolated and aid was no longer important as a tool for winning new allies (He, 2006).

The Tiananmen Square incident of 1989 became a new turning point in Chinese relations with the developing world. Intense criticism and sanctions from governments in Western countries left China in the cold and damaged its economic development. In contrast to the West's involvement in what PRC leaders considered their internal affairs, some leaders of African countries expressed support for the Chinese government's handling of the situation (Taylor, 2006, pp. 62–5). The Chinese leadership recalled that Africa could be a useful support constituency, and relations again intensified. The shift was driven initially by a common stand against Western hegemony and the promotion of 'Western-centric' norms of human rights and liberal democracy, but has more recently been dominated by an economic rationale (Taylor, 2007, pp. 11–12).

Structural set-up

The State Council, the highest executive organ above ministerial level, decides on overall Chinese policy and the Chinese leaders often announce cooperation agreements with countries in connection with state visits.

There is no single main agency responsible for all foreign aid from China. A number of different ministries are involved depending on type of aid. The main body both in receiving and giving foreign aid is the Ministry of Commerce (MOFCOM), which has a special department for giving aid called the Department of Aid for Foreign Countries. This is roughly the same size as the department responsible for receiving aid.[12]

The department is responsible for compiling and executing annual foreign aid programmes and supervising the implementation of aid projects. This is done through the Economic and Commercial Counsellor's Offices of the Chinese embassies in the partner countries. However, as their presence is not large and their duties include not only aid but also economic cooperation in general, their capacity to monitor projects is rather limited.

MOFCOM is in charge of grant aid and government interest-free loans (Davies, 2007, pp. 43–5). The Ministry of Foreign Affairs also takes part in policy formulation and the Ministry of Finance is in charge of the budget. Annually they negotiate an aid budget with MOFCOM. The China Exim Bank is the lending bank for Chinese government concessional loans and has a special Concessional Loan Department. It evaluates loan aid projects and has a special list of companies (roughly 150) which are allowed to participate in tenders. Most of the companies are state-owned.

Besides the China Exim Bank there are a couple of other policy banks under the jurisdiction of the State Council that play an increasing role in the provision of financing for Chinese companies as part of China's 'going out strategy'. One of those is the China Development Bank (CDB), which has US$300 billion in assets, making it one of the largest finance institutions in the world (Davies, 2007, p. 45).

Characteristics

One of the difficulties in carrying out research into Chinese aid is that China has no standardised criteria for what is to be considered aid, as there is in the DAC. China does not use the language of donor and recipient. Aid is loosely defined and carried out within the framework of South-South cooperation, which also encompasses other types of cooperation such as commercial or semi-commercial cooperation. Nor is there public disclosure of the amounts of aid, although the budget for individual projects is sometimes disclosed.[13] One explanation for this might be that the Chinese authorities simply do not know themselves, as there are so many actors involved and that they in fact do not have a clear definition of what is to be considered aid.

Other explanations for the lack of transparency are: (1) that it might be sensitive for the recipients and that it is up to them if they want to disclose the amounts, (2) that it might be a sensitive matter to reveal whether one country is getting more than another and (3) that the Chinese public might not be supportive of giving foreign aid as poverty is still widespread in China (Davies, 2007, pp. 49–51).

One characteristic of Chinese aid is that as a general rule it is primarily bilateral. The Chinese government has demonstrated little inclination to become involved in multilateral development initiatives. Involvement in such arrangements is often also incompatible with the PRC's policy of non-intervention (Centre for Chinese Studies, Stellenbosch University, 2007b, pp. 78–9). Just as the Chinese government at home always wanted to be in charge of its own development policy and has never participated in round-table discussions or other meetings arranged by donors to China, in its own aid giving the government has, with few exceptions, not been interested in joining hands with groups of donors abroad.

A second characteristic is a general emphasis on various projects for the promotion of trade and foreign direct investment (FDI) opportunities for China, and, as one Chinese scholar put it, aid can sometimes be a prerequisite on such occasions.[14] In connection with this there is often strong emphasis on building economic infrastructure such as roads, railways, power plants and telecommunications.

A third characteristic is that aid has been closely linked to securing access to major natural resources such as oil or precious metals. Oil in particular is of vital importance for the continuation of China's own economic growth. Aid to Angola is a case in point. For Angola, which has now emerged as China's biggest supplier of oil, China announced two credit lines totalling US$4.4 billion for 'reconstruction and national development'. A significant portion of this is tied to the purchase of Chinese goods and services (Tjonneland et al., 2006, p. 13). Besides the oil industry, cooperation agreements have been signed in fields such as infrastructure, communications, agriculture, education and health care (Centre for Chinese Studies, Stellenbosch University, 2007b, pp. 18–19).

A fourth characteristic is a high element of tied aid through the provision of commodities and services as well as technical cooperation. It is Chinese products that are provided and Chinese doctors and construction workers who are sent abroad. Agriculture is one area where China has long traditions, and so is capacity-building in the social sector, especially that related to science, health and education. A large number of African technicians are now receiving training in China.

A further characteristic of Chinese aid is that it has involved a number of publicly visible features in the form of high-profile buildings such as stadiums, state houses and buildings housing parliaments. Such projects have a long tradition in Chinese support for Africa but have expanded significantly in recent years. At the FOCAC meeting in Beijing in 2006 President Hu Jintao pledged to build a conference centre for the African Union (Davies, 2007, p. 24).

Finally, Chinese aid is characterised by an almost complete absence of political conditionality, with the exception of support for the 'One China' principal. China's aid policy builds on the principle of 'non-interference in internal affairs'. There are usually no political strings attached to Chinese aid.

Recent trends

In connection with the Chinese economic policy of 'going out', which has been in place since 2000, there has been a steep increase in Chinese FDI abroad. According to the eleventh Chinese five-year plan (2006–2010) the country should invest US$60 billion abroad during this period. Most of the investment goes to Asia and the US, but in connection with this a steep increase of both FDI and aid in Africa in general is also occurring (for more information on this see He Wenping's chapter).

Another new trend for China is to give large amounts of humanitarian and emergency aid to crisis-hit countries, sometimes participating in concerted international efforts. Examples include aid to Afghanistan in 2003 and to tsunami-affected areas in 2005. In both cases, Chinese aid was above or close to US$100 million (He, 2006).

China has recently become more active in various international bodies, such as UN organisations and the World Bank, as well as the African Development Bank (Tjonneland et al., 2006, p. 12). A memorandum of understanding (MoU) has also been signed between the JBIC and the China Exim Bank.

Thai aid

Thailand's economy has advanced well and in 2003 former prime minister Thaksin Shinawatra in his speech 'Forward Engagement: The New Era of Thailand's Foreign Policy' announced that Thailand would take no more aid but would emerge as a donor instead. Today, Thailand, like China, is both a donor and a recipient of foreign aid.[15]

Historical context

The provision of ODA to Thailand was especially intense when its national economic and social development plans started to be implemented from 1960 and onwards. In the 1990s, when the Thai economy had gradually developed and Thailand's GNP was higher than US$1000 per capita per year, some donors, such as Japan, considered Thailand to be an advanced developing country with a high income; the grant aid that Japan provided to Thailand was terminated. The country still received ODA in the form of loans, and did not have any general policy for becoming a donor. Thailand has, however, long been a supporter of South-South cooperation and has promoted partnership cooperation on a cost-sharing basis. Its oldest ODA programme, the Thai International Cooperation Programme (TICP), was started in the 1960s (Ministry of Foreign Affairs of Thailand and UN Country Team, 2005).

During the last decade Thailand also pursued projects of so-called North-South-South cooperation on a cost-sharing basis with its development partners to assist less developed countries. Together with Japan, Canada, the United Nations Development Programme (UNDP) and the United Nations Children's Fund (UNICEF), Thailand has held various training courses, study visits and sub-regional programmes.[16]

Such programmes also existed at the beginning of the 1990s, although at that time Thailand was not sharing the cost but commissioning work as an educator for less developed countries.

After Thailand recovered from the Asian economic crisis in 2003, the decision was taken at the highest level that it should now become a donor. Then Prime Minister Thaksin announced a grand strategy, called the Forward Engagement policy, aiming to make Thailand a key regional player due to its strategic geographical location, its history and its current level of economic development. The aid policy was part of this strategy. The Forward Engagement policy has shaped the country's relations with its neighbours, in particular those in Indochina – Cambodia, Laos, Myanmar and Vietnam (CLMV). In his speech announcing the Forward Engagement policy, Thaksin saw Thailand as a donor cooperating with other donors such as Japan and Western countries, and taking responsibility to assist the LDCs in the neighbourhood by providing economic assistance.[17]

In the first place, it is in the regional area that Thailand sees its role as a prime mover helping its neighbours to reach a higher level of development. The issue is sometimes a touchy one, especially with Laos and Cambodia being sensitive to Thai influence in the region.[18]

Structural set-up

The Department of Technical and Economic Cooperation (DTEC), under the Office of the Prime Minister, was established in the 1960s to manage foreign aid – mostly technical assistance – which Thailand received from various donors. In 2002 it was dissolved following the bureaucratic reform bill announced that year, and its duties, responsibilities and officials were transferred to the Ministry of Foreign Affairs. In 2004, the Thailand International Cooperation Agency (TICA) was established as a new organisation under the Ministry of Foreign Affairs. TICA was to implement international development cooperation and many of the old officials from the DTEC were now transferred to it.

TICA has a vision of being a leading agency in the country.[19] Its main missions are the preparation, strategic planning and administration of the international technical cooperation. It administrates bilateral programmes, training programmes and various contributions.[20] But, depending on the type of project, there are also a number of other actors involved, such as the Ministry of Education, the Ministry of Public Health, the Ministry of Finance and the Ministry of Transportation.

A large part of Thai ODA, 73 per cent of the total, supports infrastructure development in Cambodia, Laos and Myanmar. Since 2005 this has been administered through the Neighbouring Countries Economic Development Cooperation Agency (NEDA). Concessionary loans are dealt with by the Ministry of Finance or the Export-Import Bank of Thailand.

Characteristics

Eighty-six per cent of Thailand's ODA goes to infrastructure projects. Most of this is to a number of road projects connecting Thailand to its neighbours. Thai contributions are also coordinated with the ADB and other developments partners' investment in this area (Ministry of Foreign Affairs of Thailand and UN Country Team, 2005, p. 16). The purpose of the new roads is not only to help the neighbours' economic growth but also to strengthen Thailand's own leadership in the area through increased trade. Roads are expected to increase labour mobility as well as the transit of goods. Currently Thailand has a problem with illegal labour immigration from neighbouring countries, and by providing better roads it also hopes to enable increased production in the border areas and thereby create jobs for the migrants. Higher living standards in the neighbouring countries would ease the pressure of migration as well as create new markets for Thai goods.

Better infrastructure in the region is also needed for the extraction of energy. Thailand has a powerful interest in the development of hydropower and the electricity sector along the Mekong River delta.

Most of the aid from Thailand takes the form of concessional loans. According to Thai figures, net ODA in 2003 amounted to US$167 million, of which US$147 million was concessional loans. As a percentage of GNI, this was 0.13 (Ministry of Foreign Affairs of Thailand and UN Country Team, 2005, p. 14). According to the OECD *Development Journal*, net disbursement of aid by Thailand in 2006 amounted to US$74 million, equivalent to 0.04 per cent of GNI (OECD, 2008, p. 221).

There are a number of regional cooperation frameworks such as the Ayeyawady-Chao Phraya-Mekong Economic Cooperation Strategy (ACMECS) initiated by Thailand to increase the competitiveness of Cambodia, Laos, Myanmar, Thailand and Vietnam. ACMEC'S programmes work in such areas as the facilitation of trade and investment, agriculture and industrial cooperation, transport linkages, tourism and the development of human resources.

According to a TICA document, the Thai government has adopted the concept of 'mutual benefits' and the demand-driven' approach to development cooperation in order to respond to the development challenges and needs of the targeted countries. The philosophy is 'to help them help themselves' and 'to stand on their own feet'. Most aid is tied to the procurement of Thai goods and services. In its technical assistance Thailand dispatches experts abroad. They consider themselves to have good capacity in HIV-related issues, tropical diseases, basic agriculture and basic education.

Recent trends

In the past, Thailand's bilateral programmes were mainly directed to its immediate neighbours. In recent years, the programme has been expanded to other developing countries such as East Timor, Sri Lanka and some African countries. The amounts involved are, however, still very small.

The emergence of Thailand as a donor was a policy for which former Prime Minister Thaksin pushed hard. Since the military coup in September 2006 and the fall of Thaksin there has been a certain wait-and-see attitude concerning foreign aid policy. In the December 2007 election a new government came to power, but since then political instability has continued and it is not yet clear how the government will develop its aid policy.

Is there an Asian model of aid?

Analysing the approaches of the four countries above it is obvious that there is no single 'Asian Model' but actually several. Each country has its own history, its own development experience, its own unique situation and its own motivations for engagement in development aid. The four Asian donors have signed the Millennium Development Goals as well as the Paris Declaration, as have the DAC members. There are, however, certain features which are common among the four and which deviate from the DAC members in general. There is a belief in a strong state, a weak role for NGOs in the planning and provision of aid and a considerably smaller element of conditionality, especially compared with the World Bank's approach.

Japan is a special case in the sense that it is both a DAC member and an Asian donor. It takes part in the formulation of DAC policy concerning aid and follows the regulations, but in other respects has its own beliefs and own model of aid. It has been the largest bilateral donor *to* the other Asian donor countries; in fact China and Thailand were both still on the top ten list of recipients of Japanese ODA in 2005–2006. This means that they have thorough experience of Japanese aid in their own development. At the same time, Japanese ODA has changed considerably over the years and is not the same today as it was when, for example, South Korea was a recipient.

The implementation of ODA in South Korea is heavily influenced by the old Japanese system – with one exception, aid to North Korea, which is driven by other considerations and is always channelled through the Ministry of Unification.

Among the four Asian donors there seems to be a common belief in development through industrialisation. Aid is often set within the framework of economic cooperation and is not seen separately from other economic activities such as private investment and other official flows. The three are usually seen as connected. In the Chinese case, where there are many state-owned companies operating in Africa, the borderline between private investment, official flows and aid becomes even more blurred.

In general there is a heavy reliance on loan aid. This is most often justified from an ideological standpoint – that it should be 'help for self-help' – but at the same time there is also an economic rationale behind it. Most of the aid loans are tied and intended to assist companies in the donor country as well. The exception is Japanese loans, which to a great extent are untied.[21]

Mutual benefit is a concept closely associated with Asian countries' aid. In China, which is a developing country itself, south-south co-operation rather than aid is the concept used and there is talk of a win-win situation. Thailand also uses the concept of cooperation rather than aid in dealings with its neighbours. In Japan as well, the principle of mutual benefit is strong. Sympathy is not merely for others' sake, as Japan's present prime minister Taro Aso said in a speech during his time as foreign minister in 2006, implying that development assistance was also linked to Japan's own stability and prosperity (Ministry of Foreign Affairs, 2006, Foreword). In South Korea, besides helping the recipient country, ODA loans are regarded as a way to improve the country's own economic growth.

All Asian donors spend a considerably larger part of their aid on economic infrastructure than do the DAC countries in general. Economic infrastructure is needed for trade and investment, and for economic growth. In general there is a strong belief in economic growth as a way to reduce poverty. Economic infrastructure is also needed to secure resources and energy, other prerequisites for economic growth. The mutual benefit concept applies. Trade, investment and natural resources are necessary for economic growth in the donor countries as well. China, besides needing trade, has an imperative to secure energy resources. This becomes clear from its choice of cooperation partners in Africa.

Both China and Japan have also sponsored a number of showcase projects such as grandiose government buildings or cultural centres in developing countries, a form of aid which is rare among DAC donors. Non-intervention in other countries' affairs is an explicitly stated

Table 5.9 Characteristics of Asian and DAC development assistance

Characteristics	Japan	South Korea	China	Thailand	Total DAC
Aid within the framework of economic cooperation	Yes	Yes	Yes	Yes	Not to the same extent
Mutually beneficial	Yes	Yes	Yes	Yes	No
Heavy reliance on bilateral loan aid	32%	Yes	Yes	Yes	7.4%
Untied	96%	Tied	Tied	Tied	95%
Economic infrastructure	24.3%	23%	Large share	Large share	11%
Showcase projects	Yes	Not common	Yes	Not common	Not common
Aid to LDCs	17%	24.8%	Very high	Very high	22%
Support of own companies	Yes	Yes	Yes	Yes	Not to a large extent
Bilateral versus multilateral	Both	Both	Mainly bilateral	Mainly bilateral	Both
Policy of non-intervention	no	Yes	Yes	yes	No
Transparency	High	High	Low	Low	High
Use of NGOs	0.01% of GNI	Low	Low	Low	0.04% of GNI

principle in China's case. It gives aid to countries like Sudan, which DAC countries avoid for the sake of human rights and because as a rule regimes of this type are not given assistance. Japan used to have a request-based ODA policy with a separation of politics and economics. This has, however, changed with the introduction of the ODA Charters, as well as the country assistance programmes. Japan now also supports the development of democracy and reliable institutions in developing countries. Besides the emphasis on economic growth and help for self-help among the Asian donors, they all have agriculture programmes, as well as giving a considerable amount of aid in the fields of education and health. This is especially true for Japan, which also assists with institution-building and provides huge amounts of aid related to environmental issues. Japan, China, South Korea and Thailand also provide emergency assistance.

That security considerations enter into the provision of aid is obvious from the fact that for both Japan and South Korea (the countries that have security treaties with the US) Iraq was their largest recipient of aid during 2006.

Very little of the aid from the four Asian countries studied here has as a general rule been channelled through NGOs. Compared to the West in general, there is a shortage of such organisations that are strong and independent and have experience of development issues.

Table 5.9 summarises the characteristics of the four countries' ODA policies and compares them with the approach of the DAC.

Challenges or a complement to mainstream aid?

Aid in the twenty-first century is radically different from what the process used to be during the Cold War. There are no longer Eastern and Western bloc countries and a number of regional powers are emerging. The Paris Declaration in 2005 made it clear that the recipients (now called the partner countries) should be more deeply in charge of their own development process. They should be in the lead themselves and the donors should harmonise their aid and cooperate more to avoid over-lapping and increase effectiveness. The UN Millennium Development Goals, signed by most countries, called for a sharp reduction of poverty in the world and in Africa in particular.

At the same time it is obvious that the economic flows are changing. Commercial flows and remittances overall have risen faster than aid. Aid itself, however, is also changing. Aid from non-DAC and non-OECD members is growing. In 2007 Chile, Estonia, Israel, Russia and

Slovenia were invited to open discussions on membership of the DAC. Discussions on 'enhanced engagement' with Brazil, China, India, Mexico and South Africa were also initiated.

Asia is often pointed out as a good example of successful development where poverty has been strongly reduced. What role can Asian donors or Asian models of aid then play in achieving the Millennium Development Goals? Japan, a long-standing member of the DAC has played a substantial role in influencing other DAC members' policy (at the same time as it has experienced substantial influence from other DAC members on its own aid policy). Aid for Trade[22] is a case in point and has assumed a growing importance in most donors' programmes. Many of the other Asian donors whose own economic development has been influenced by the Japanese model are now using similar approaches in their own aid policies. There is a strong belief in development through industrialisation and economic growth as a tool for poverty reduction. Aid in general is firmly based in the concept of economic cooperation. Mutual benefit is a key concept. Except in the case of Japan there is a great deal of tied aid, as the Asian donors want to gain something from their cooperation with poor countries. And they all see themselves as successful models for others to follow.

New South-South cooperation is being encouraged by the DAC. This means that aid from one developing country to another is regarded positively. The most challenging factor with Asian donors, just as for DAC donors, is probably accommodating a new or re-emerging donor the size of China. In Africa, Chinese aid – better termed economic cooperation, as it is combined with trade and investment – is on a large enough scale to make a difference. A key concern for DAC members is what Chinese engagement implies for their influence and leverage. China is not cooperating with other donors to any substantial degree and its aid lacks transparency. Its policy of non-intervention in domestic policies and its support of, for example, the regime in Sudan are quite contrary to DAC initiatives and are undermining their efforts to support good performance as well as democracy and sustainable institution-building. On the other hand, Beijing is also facing tension and frictions below the surface in its contacts with Africa. There have been anti-Chinese riots in several countries and in Zambia's election in 2006 the main opposition candidate based his campaign on a strong anti-China platform.

So what does all this imply for the developing countries? To some of them it has meant that they now have different cooperation partners to turn to. This goes especially for the resource-rich countries where certain donors will be more interested in cooperating than others. If they are refused by one donor, some of the developing countries might be able to get what they want from another. This will require some skill in managing their own development process, which not all governments in developing countries might possess. To some of the developing countries there will be several models available and a greater variety of development aid from which to choose.

Notes

1. ODA is defined as grants, technical assistance and loans to countries or territories on the DAC list of ODA recipients. It includes both bilateral assistance and that from multilateral agencies. It is aid provided by the official sector on concessional terms (i.e., with a grant element of at least 25 percent) that has the promotion of the economic development and welfare of developing countries as its goal. Grants, loans and credits for military purposes are excluded.

2. In other regions as well there are a number of 'new' donors such as Brazil, India and South Africa.

3. These are a different kind of subsidised official flows that are on terms below the market rate but the conditions of which are not concessional enough for them to qualify as ODA.

4. In Korean the name is an exact translation of the Japanese one but in the English translation 'overseas' has been dropped from the name, most probably to avoid confusion with the Japanese fund.

5. Interview with Sung-yong Um, Senior Deputy Director at the EDCF Planning Office, Seoul, April 2007.

6. Interview with Hyekyung Kim, Chairperson, Citizens' Coalition for Economic Justice, Seoul, April 2007.

7. The official name of the plan was The Master Plan for Reform of International Development Co-operation: A Strategy for the Korean Model of International Development Co-operation Toward a Global Leading Country.

8. Interview with Hyun-sik Chang, Managing Director, Office of Policy Planning, at KOICA, Seoul, April 2007.

9. Interview with Sung-yong Um, Senior Deputy Director at the EDCF Planning Office, Seoul, April 2007.

10. Interview with Hyun-sik Chang (ibid.).

11. Interview with Zhoun Hong, Institute of European Studies, Chinese Academy of Social Sciences (CASS), Beijing, October 2007.

12. Interview with Chunying Qian, Director, Department of Aid to Foreign Countries, MOFCOM, Beijing, October 2007.

13. When the author of this article asked at MOFCOM's Department of Aid to Foreign Countries (October 2007) about the amounts of aid to North Korea she was told that this was a state secret and could not be disclosed.

14. Interview with Xiaojing Zhang, Professor of Economics, Institute of Economics, Chinese Academy of Social Sciences, Beijing, October 2007.

15. See http://www.thaiembdc.org/pressctr/statement/pm/sifa031203.html (accessed April 2007).

16. TICA homepage, http://www.tica.thaigov.net/tica/index.jsp?sid=1&id=67& pid=1 (accessed 10 March 2007)
17. See   http://www.thaiembdc.org/pressctr/ststemnt/pm/sifa031203.html (accessed April 2007).
18. Interview with Banchong Amornchewin, Director of Planning and Monitoring Branch at TICA Bangkok, April 2007.
19. Ibid.
20. See http://www.tica.thaigov.net/tica/index.jsp?sid=1&id=71&pid=67 (accessed October 16 2008).
21. Japanese loan aid is still very large and to a certain extent the decrease is due to the methods of calculation whereby loans that are now being paid back are deducted from the amounts given.
22. See the 2005 Hong Kong WTO Ministerial Declaration, which called for the expansion of Aid for Trade to help developing countries.

References

Centre for Chinese Studies, Stellenbosch University (2007a). *China's Engagement of Africa: Preliminary Scoping of African Case studies*, a research report prepared for Rockefeller Foundation.
Centre for Chinese Studies, Stellenbosch University (2007b). *China's Interest and Activities in Africa's Construction and Infrastructure Sector*, a research report prepared for DFID China.
Davies, Penny (2007). *China and the End of Poverty in Africa: Towards Mutual Benefit?* Sundbyberg, Sweden: Diakonia.
EDCF (2006). *Annual Report*. Korea: Ministry of Finance and Economy, Export-Import Bank of Korea.
EDCF (2007). *Annual Report*. Korea: Ministry of Finance and Economy, Export-Import Bank of Korea.
He, Liping (2006). 'The Current Policy Discussion on China's Aid Policy and Organization', paper presented in Oslo at a conference organised by the Norwegian Ministry of Foreign Affairs, 5 December 2006.
Islam, Shafique (ed.) (1991). *Yen for Development: Japanese Foreign Aid and the Politics of Burden-sharing*. New York: Council of Foreign Relations Press.
JBIC (2007). *Kaihatsukinsoku Kenkyūjōho* (Journal of JBIC Institute), no. 35, October 2007.
Jerve, Alf Morten, Yasutami Shimomura and Annette Skovstedt Hansen (eds) (2008). *Aid Relationships in Asia, Exploring Ownership in Japanese and Nordic Aid*. Basingstoke and New York: Palgrave Macmillan.
Kilby, Christopher (2006). Donor Influences in Multilateral Development Banks: The Case of the Asian Development Bank, Vassar College Economic Working Paper # 70. Online. Available at http://irving.vassar.edu/VCEWP/VCEWP70.pdf (accessed 5 October 2008).
Kim, San-Tae (2003). *ODA Policy of the Republic of Korea: In the Context of its Evolving Diplomatic and Economic Policies*, KOICA Working Paper T 2003-9-41. Korea: Dong Hwa Printing.
Kim, Hyekyung (2006). How to Achieve Better Results, in *Korea Policy Review*, Volume II, John F. Kennedy School of Government, Harvard University.

KOICA (2005). *Cooperation for a Better World: Annual Report*. Korea.

Ministry of Foreign Affairs (2006). *Japan's Official Development Assistance*. Tokyo.

Ministry of Foreign Affairs (2007). Speech by Minister for Foreign Affairs Taro Aso ODA: Sympathy Is Not Merely for Others' Sake. Available at: http://www.mofa.go.jp/announce/fm/aso/speech0601-2.html (accessed 19 January 2006).

Ministry of Foreign Affairs of Thailand and UN Country Team (2005). *Global Partnership for Development, Thailand's Contribution to the Millennium Development Goal 8*. Thailand.

Murai, Yoshinori (1989). *Musekinin Enjo Taikoku Nihon*. Tokyo: JICC.

OECD (2007). DAC, *Development Cooperation Report 2007*, vol. 9, no. 1.

OECD (2008). *Development Co-operation Report 2007*, vol. 9, no. 1.

Saito, Tomoyo and Ishida Kyoko (Revised by Yuki Tanabe and Rupa Gupta) (2007). *ADB and Japan*. Philippines: NGO Forum on ADB. Online. Available at http://www.jacses.org/en/sdap/agm/adbandjapan.pdf (accessed 5 October 2008).

Sumi, Kazuo (1989). *ODA Enjo no Genjitsu*. Tokyo: Iwanami Shinshō.

Söderberg, Marie (1996). Japanese ODA: What Type for Whom and Why, in *The Business of Japanese Foreign Aid: Five Case Studies from Asia* (ed.) Marie Söderberg. London and New York: Routledge.

Taylor, Ian (2006). *China and Africa*. London and New York: Routledge.

Taylor, Ian (2007). Unpacking China's Resource Diplomacy in Africa, in *Current African Affairs*, no. 35. Uppsala, Sweden: Nordiska Afrikainstitutet.

Tjonneland, Elling N., Bjorn Brandtzaeg, Åshild Kolås and Garth Le Pere (2006). *China in Africa: Implication for Norwegian Foreign and Development Policies*. Norway: CMI.

World Bank (1993). *The East Asian Miracle, Economic Growth and Public Policy*. New York: Oxford University Press.

Yasutomo, Dennis (1986). The Manner of Giving: Strategic Aid and Japanese Foreign Policy. Lexington: Lexington Books.

6

China's Aid to Africa: Policy Evolution, Characteristics and Its Role

He Wenping

With the rapid development of China-Africa relations and especially the increasing development assistance that the Chinese government has provided for African countries, there is also an increasing interest and international coverage about China's aid policy on Africa. What is the policy and how has it developed? What kind of differences are there between China's aid policy and Western approaches? And in the end, how should we understand or evaluate the impact of China's aid on Africa? Over the past two years, I couldn't count how many times I have been asked about these issues, in conferences and interviews with Western scholars, diplomats and journalists as well as Ph.D. candidates. It is this strong demand that makes me think over the aid issue that we Chinese scholars have long neglected. In this chapter, I will try to answer the above questions from a historical and a comparative perspective.

Policy evolution: From politics to economics, from proletarian internationalism to mutual development

Even though China's aid in Africa has been an international focus only in recent years, China's aid in Africa itself, however, is not a recent story at all. As early as the 1950s, when the new-born People's Republic of China was itself still struggling with rebuilding the country after the decade-long anti-Japanese war and the civil conflict later, it began to offer a helping hand to countries in Asia, the Middle East and Africa.

In the early 1950s, when the People's Republic of China had not established any official contact with African countries, the majority of which were still fighting for their national independence from colonialism, the major recipients of Chinese aid were other socialist countries such as North Korea and Vietnam, Mongolia and Albania. After the Bandung Conference in 1955, with the establishment of official relations, China's aid expanded to African countries.

When we look through the whole period of China's aid provision in Africa, there are different ways to divide the half-century-long journey. According to different criteria (such as the change of the international situation or the readjustment of China's aid-providing system), Chinese scholars have divided the historical evolvement of China's foreign aid into different periods.[1] However, to analyse the evolution of China's aid from the angle of changes to its driving forces, I intend to divide the history only into two periods.

The first period (from 1956 to the late 1970s): Idealistic and politically driven

This period was characterised by a rich ideology and the reinforcement of political benefits. The driving force was to establish and strengthen diplomatic and political ties with African countries and to break through both the strategic domination from the former Soviet Union and the US and China's diplomatic isolation on the international stage.

In the 1950s and 1960s, the newly founded People's Republic of China was mainly faced with a security threat. With the Korea War in the north-east and the Vietnam War in the South, plus the split of the China-Soviet alliance, China's diplomatic space on the international stage was getting smaller than before and the nation's survival was the major concern for the top leaders.

China's foreign policy at that time was fully determined by the top leader's philosophy and world outlook. According to the late Chairman Mao Zedong's 'three worlds divided' theory, the former Soviet Union and the US are the First World, the Asian, African and the Latin American developing countries including China are the Third World, and the developed countries between the two are the Second World. He thought that only the countries and people of the Third World could be called the basic power in the struggle of against imperialism, colonialism and hegemonism. China should rely mainly on them and be united with them as direct allies (the Second World was the indirect ally). Mao pointed out clearly, 'In making friends in the world, we should put the stress on the Third World'. The struggle and victory achieved by the other Third World countries could weaken and destroy the colonial system of imperialism. 'This will divert the enemy's power and lighten the pressure on our shoulder'.[2] And then premier Zhou Enlai also pointed out as early as 1951 that after the victory of the October Revolution in Russia, there appeared in the world two camps antagonistic towards each other. Ever since then, the national liberation struggles by the colonial and semi-colonial countries were no longer part of the capitalist revolution but a part of the socialist revolution. Zhou went on, 'our task is to support and promote the development of the national liberation movement'.[3]

Guided by the above theory and thought, the Chinese government spared no efforts to support the struggles of the African peoples against imperialism and colonialism and for national liberation and independence in this period. For example, when Algerian Front de Liberation National was fighting against French colonialism in late 1950s, some French officials put forward an idea, saying the French could consider recognising China in exchange for China's stopping support to Algeria. Then Chinese deputy premier and foreign minister Chen Yi responded by saying, 'We could wait for the establishment of diplomatic ties with France. However, we will continue to support the Algerians' struggle for their independence until they achieve the final victory'.[4] During their armed struggle for independence, the Algerians also received some material aid and cash grants, valued at RMB70 million (US$28.4 million).[5] China also hailed Egypt's resumed sovereignty over the Suez Canal in 1956. In September 1956, Mao met with the Egyptian ambassador to China and said, 'Chinese people are firmly behind Egypt in its struggle to resume sovereignty over the Suez Canal. China is willing to do its best to help Egypt without attaching any conditions and to offer what you need within our power.'[6] In November 1956, the Chinese government provided a 20 million Swiss Francs (US$4.6 million) grant in cash to the Egyptian government to support their struggle over the Suez Canal.

In 1960, the Chinese government agreed to assist Guinea to build a match factory and a cigarette factory and these were the first development projects China helped in sub-Saharan Africa. In late 1961 and early 1962, China sent seven agricultural experts to Mali and helped the locals to plant sugar cane and tea successfully. In the late 1960s, China sent medical teams to Tanzania, Somalia, Congo, Mali and Guinea successively. In the 1960s, Mao frequently met with African leaders and the leaders of independence movements. According to his words, 'people who have achieved revolutionary victory should provide assistance to the people who are still struggling for liberation, and this is our international duty.[7]

Over the years, China has provided African 'freedom fighters' with aid in the form of material, military equipment and funds. And the military training of liberation organisations usually went through the Organization of African Unity (OAU) and several countries that had won independence earlier, such as Egypt, Morocco, Tanzania and Zambia.

According to the OAU Liberation Committee, during 1971 and 1972, 75 per cent of the military aid given to the OAU from outside Africa came from China. And many of these 'freedom fighters' later became important government figures, cabinet ministers and even heads of state.

Between December 1963 and June 1965, in order to strengthen Sino-African relations, late Premier Zhou Enlai paid three visits to Africa, putting forward the eight principles governing China's aid to foreign countries. They are:

1. The Chinese government has persistently been providing assistance to foreign countries according to the principle of equality and mutual benefit, never regarding the assistance as one-sided. The Chinese government maintains that assistance should be mutual;
2. While providing foreign aid, the Chinese government strictly respects the sovereignty of recipient countries, no strings are ever attached and no privileges required;
3. In order to relieve the burden of recipient countries, the Chinese government provides economic aid in the way of interest-free or low-interest loans, and the time limit of repayment could be delayed when it is needed;
4. The purpose of the Chinese government in providing foreign aid is not to make recipient countries dependent on China, but to help recipient countries gradually develop on the track of self-reliance and economic development independently;
5. For the projects constructed through China's foreign aid, the Chinese government does its best to achieve quick results through small investments. Thus, the governments of recipient countries could increase their income and accumulate money;
6. The Chinese government provides the best-quality equipment and material of its own manufacture at international market prices. If the material and equipment provided are not up to the agreed specifications and quality, the government undertakes to replace them;
7. While providing technical assistance, the Chinese government undertakes to teach recipients to master this kind of technology fully;
8. The experts who are dispatched by the Chinese government to help recipient countries carry out construction, should be paid as same as the experts of recipient countries. They are required to not ask for any special requirement or enjoy any special amenities.

It is very notable that, rather than directing the behaviour of the recipients, these principles disciplined only China itself in its efforts to provide aid. And since then, these principles have served as the core values for guiding China's aid to foreign countries including Africa.

Constrained by China's economic capabilities as well as the international set-up, the primary means of giving aid during this period was grants provided by the Chinese government. The building of 'Friendship Halls' and gymnasiums was the main form of assistance. China has constructed the Friendship Hall and the gymnasium in almost every African country that has established diplomatic ties with it. Although China itself was facing a very difficult economic situation and huge pressure from the imperialists, it provided tremendous support for African countries. Since 1956, China has rendered assistance to the best of her ability to African countries in a variety of aspects such as agriculture, infrastructure, forestry, animal husbandry, fishery, food processing, textiles and other light industries, energy, transportation, broadcasting and communication, water conservancy and the power industry, machinery, public buildings and housing, culture, education, health, arts and the handicrafts industry, etc.

Of all the projects, the best known was the TaZara (Tanzania-Zambia) Railway. After being turned down by the World Bank, the Soviet Union, the UK and Canada, Tanzania and Zambia quickly got an affirmative answer from China when they raised the request. Chairman Mao once said, 'we will help Africa to build this railway even though China itself doesn't build a railway'. Between October 1970 and July 1976, engineers and workers from China, Tanzania and Zambia worked in the extreme heat and cut through the thick jungles to build the 1860-km-long railway. The railway cost US$455 million and 64 Chinese engineers and workers sacrificed their lives. People call it the 'Freedom Railway', and it has contributed a lot to the regional economy and also played an important role in the national liberation movement, as well as in the struggle against apartheid in South Africa.

In the end, the politics-driven aid for Africa was paid back politically as well. According to a Chinese scholar, 'China's political prestige in Africa in 1960s was the very important political interest. Depending on the political prestige, China has gained support from African countries and broken imperialism's strategy of isolating China.[8] Indeed, African countries and people highly appreciate China's support and look on China as a most reliable friend. They support China's cause of safeguarding national sovereignty and realising reunification, condemning the US's interference in Taiwanese affairs. In the twenty-sixth UN Assembly in 1971, African countries played a very important role in the restoration of China's seat at the UN table. Among the 76 votes for China, 26 were from African countries, making one third of the total. Chairman Mao had said it was African friends who raised us into the UN.[9]

The second period (from the late 1970s to now): Pragmatic and economically driven

With the end of 'the Cultural Revolution' and Deng Xiaoping's assuming office in the late 1970s, China adopted its 'reform and opening-up' policy and the realisation of the 'Four Modernisations' (namely industry, agriculture, science and defence)' that were the focus of domestic concern and the government's priority. On the international front, at the end of the 1970s, with the normalisation of the relations with the Western countries, especially the improvement of Sino-US relations, China began to pursue a policy of non-alignment, and an independent and all-round peaceful strategy. To quote Deng Xiaoping: 'China will not play either the card of the US or the USSR, and also not allow others to play the card of China. The purpose of Chinese foreign policy is to strive for the world peace. Only under the prerequisite of the world peace can China concentrate on its modernisation and development, as well as constructing socialism with the Chinese characteristics.'[10] This illustrates that the guiding principle of China's diplomacy has been changing from idealism to pragmatic realism, from the unconditional internationalism to prioritising the national interest. To strive for and maintain the world peace and seek the national economic interest have become the main objectives for China's foreign policy.

In carrying forward large-scale modernisation, China found itself lacking capital and unable to provide African countries with as much economic assistance, including free aid, as before. China and Africa needed to establish a kind of economic cooperative relationship on the basis of equal and mutual benefit.

The Chinese government began to encourage enterprises from both sides to cooperate with each other on the principles of equality, mutual benefit and complementing each other with their own strengths. The mark of the policy shift was then Chinese premier Zhao Ziyang's visit to Africa in the early 1980s. From the end of 1982 to early 1983, Zhao Ziyang made a tour of 11 African countries.[11] During his visit, he proposed four principles for developing economic cooperation with African countries. These included *equality and mutual benefit; stress on practical results, diversity in forms and attainment of common development.* The four principles all focus on economic cooperation and derive from the deepening and development of the Eight Principles put forward by late premier Zhou Enlai in the 1960s. When then President Jiang Zemin paid a visit to Africa in 1996, he also put forward a Five-point Proposal that stressed the importance again of the aim 'to seek common development on the basis of mutual benefit with Africa'.

Under the guideline of the renewed principles, economic and technical cooperation between China and Africa has diversified and developed rapidly. For a long time, the free assistance provided to Africa has been one of important aspects in China's economic and trade relations with it, such as the big project TaZara Railway mentioned before. In the 1980s, since China itself needed huge resources for its domestic modernisation projects and focused on luring foreign capital from the developed world, it had limited resources to fund large-scale technical assistance projects in Africa. 'The emphasis was now placed on low profile co-operation projects requiring smaller investments and quicker returns that would enhance mutual self reliance and create mutual economic benefit.'[12] Therefore, apart from the old mode of assistance – giving loans – China started to engage in various new forms of cooperation such as contracting projects, labour cooperation, joint ventures, cooperative production and development and technological services.

In October 1995, China began to reform its form of foreign aid provision. The main component of the reform was the introduction of preferential loans mid-term and long-term low-interest loans with the government assistance provided through financial institutions designated by the Chinese government. The government offers an official subsidy to the financial institutions for the margin between the preferential rate (2 per cent) and the base rate publicised by the People's Bank of China. These preferential loans are mostly used for joint ventures by Chinese and local enterprises operating profitable, productive projects that meet local demands, for providing complete sets of equipment or mechanical and electrical products made in China and for some infrastructure and social welfare projects for which loan repayment is guaranteed. With the introduction of this policy, enterprises were mobilised to take part in the construction and management of foreign assistance projects. Up to the end of 2004, there were about 100 projects under the framework of the preferential loans.[13] The first preferential loan project was an oil exploitation programme in Sudan in 1996, followed by a forest development and timber-processing project in Equatorial Guinea and a textile factory in Tanzania in 1997. Meanwhile, China continued to provide the financial grant and humanitarian relief aid to the heavily indebted poor countries (HIPCs) and LDCs in Africa.

After all, from 1995 onward, as noted by Yahia M. Mahmoud, four issues have received high priority in China's economic cooperation strategy with Africa, namely, '(1) preferential loans to African enterprises [should be Chinese enterprises doing business in Africa], (2) promotion of cooperation between Chinese and African companies, (3) increment of the participation and project administration of Chinese banks and (4) combination of governmental efforts with those of enterprises from both sides.'[14] Compared to the simple way of providing foreign aid (grants only) and the highly centralised aid system in Beijing (the aid budget was solely provided and implemented by the Government) that existed prior to the 1990s, the manner of implementing aid has now become more diversified, from providing complete sets of projects to technical cooperative aid (agriculture and medical cooperation are the major two) as well as humanitarian aid, etc. With decentralisation and growing numbers of stakeholders in policy-making, provincial level authorities, banking institutions and enterprises are all involved in the process and are gradually increasing their responsibility and decision-making power in this area.

Since 2000, with the founding of the Forum on China-Africa Cooperation (FOCAC), the scope of China's aid to Africa has been further widened and diversified. Apart from providing complete sets of projects, which was the main form in the 1990s (above 60 per cent), technical cooperation, debt cancellation, cooperation on human resources development, dispatching of medical teams and youth volunteers, emergency humanitarian aid multilateral aid all contribute to the entire aid package programme. At the first FOCAC meeting in Beijing in October 2000, the Chinese government pledged to cancel African countries' 156 overdue debts totalling RMB10.5 billion (US$1.3 billion) in two years. The pledge was fulfilled ahead of schedule. At the second FOCAC meeting in Addis Ababa, Ethiopia, in December 2003, China granted some African countries tariff-free treatment for their exports to China, a huge increase in assistance for the African Human Resources Development Fund[15] and a boost to cooperation on tourism by encouraging more Chinese citizens to travel to Africa.[16] More importantly, parallel to the ministerial FOCAC meeting, the first China-Africa Business Conference was held, where over 500 Chinese and African entrepreneurs negotiated and signed 21 cooperation agreements with a total value of US$1 billion.

Three years later, at the opening ceremony of the China-Africa Summit and the third FOCAC meeting in Beijing in November 2006, President Hu Jinao announced China's eight-point proposal supporting African development, namely, (1) to double the 2006 level of assistance by 2009, (2) to provide US$5 billion in preferential loans and credits within the next three years, (3) to create a China-Africa Development

Fund of US$5 billion that can support Chinese companies investing in Africa, (4) to construct a conference centre for the African Union, (5) to write off the interest-free government loans of more than RMB10 billion (US$1.3 billion) overdue at the end of 2005, (6) to increase zero-tariff export items to China from 190 to over 440 from LDCs, (7) to set up three to five Sino-African trade and economic zones and (8) to train professionals for African countries and construct 30 local hospitals, 100 rural schools, etc.

As of the time of writing, all these promises are under implementation. For example, five trade and economic zones have been formally proclaimed and are in the process of construction, starting with Zambia, Mauritius, Egypt, Nigeria and Tanzania. In addition, a number of free trade zones or similar entities have been launched, some of them with support from Chinese provinces and municipalities. Moreover, at the annual meeting of the African Development Bank (ADB) hosted in Shanghai in 2007, it was announced that China would provide US$20 billion in infrastructure and trade financing for Africa over the next three years.[17] Following the meeting, the China-Africa Development Fund was officially established. Compared to the relevant state-owned banks, the approach that the fund is taking seems more commercial and profit-seeking. The fund will invest their money in chosen projects and be a shareholder only after thorough investigation and approval of the feasibility reports of the projects.

Over the past 50 years, China's foreign aid to Africa has amounted to RMB44.4 billion, accounting for 30 per cent of the total amount of RMB120.773 billion of China's foreign aid.[18] With the aid, China has helped to finish over 800 projects, including textile factories, hydro-power stations, stadiums, hospitals and schools. At the same time, direct Chinese investment in Africa has reached US$1.25 billion. Over 800 companies are currently operating in Africa, engaged in trade, manufacturing, natural resource exploitation, transportation, agriculture and agricultural processing.[19]

Policy characteristics: The poor help the poor

Although to become a developed country is the goal, China is still a developing country at the moment. Its aid to other developing countries, including in Africa, is kind of mutual assistance among friends and falls into the category of South-South cooperation. It's a kind of 'poor helps the poor' assistance, a developing country helping other developing countries. Meanwhile, the nature of being a developing country decides that the sum of China's aid to other developing countries is limited and cannot be compared with that of Western developed countries.

There are a number of major characteristics of China's aid policy to Africa that may differ from Western approaches. The main characteristics are the following:

'No political strings attached' and 'non-interference' aid policy. China's aid policy is firmly anchored in the principle of there being 'no strings attached' and 'non-interference' in internal affairs. As mentioned in the previous section, this policy has its roots in its shared history and culture with African countries. Both China and African countries are historically colonial or semi-colonial countries, as well as developing countries and recipient countries for a long time. Moreover, China and Africa both attached great importance to 'dignity' and 'sovereignty' when they sacrificed a lot to fight back against colonialism. As an African adage says, 'the receiving hands are always below the giving hands'. The African recipient countries don't want to sacrifice their sovereignty and dignity in acquiring loans and aid. To a great extent, sovereignty is the last frontier of dignity. Given the painful historical experience of Western interference, plus China's objective of preventing the West from interfering in her domestic issues, such as Taiwan and Tibet, as well as the success story of China's own economic development based on 'crossing the river by groping for rocks' (to seek the development path that suitable for its own national conditions with no interference from the outsiders), China is careful not to interfere in African countries' internal affairs, expressing respect and a strong belief that African countries by themselves will sooner or later find their own development path, one suitable for their own national conditions. As stated by the Chinese premier Wen Jiabao, the Chinese government believes 'that African countries have the right and capability to solve their own problems'.[20] In other words, even from a philosophical perspective, China has always believed that, after all, things in one country can only be done by its own people since they alone are familiar with the realities and know what is needed.[21]

In this sense, China carefully avoids using the word 'donations' to describe the assistance provided to African countries. Rather than the language of donor and recipient, China strongly prefers to present its activities in terms of two-way exchanges and two-sided cooperation. The aim with aid should be mutual benefit rather than one-way assistance, and not on one-way donations, as if to a beggar. As a British scholar noticed, Western agencies regularly present Africa as the poorest continent in the world, and as the continent least likely to reach the Millennium Development Goals. An interesting comparison is that *China's African Policy* does not even contain the word 'poverty', while it contains multiple references to economic cooperation.[22] While the West applies such rhetoric as 'civil war', 'poverty', 'disease', 'corruption' and 'underdevelopment', the Chinese use such words as 'peaceful coexistence', 'common development', 'win-win', 'friendship', 'sincerity', 'mutual respect' and 'mutual benefit'. These beautiful rhetorical words should not just be understood as elegant or diplomatic language, but as showing a kind of new mentality characterised by equality and mutual respect that is quite different from the traditional Western donors' mentality filled with patriarchal behaviour. And this approach and mentality seem to have charmed and boosted the confidence of African leaders and help implement things in an efficient way.

For example, in an article published in the *Financial Times*, Senegal's President Abdoulaye Wade wrote, 'China is doing a much better job than western capitalists of responding to market demands in Africa', 'China's approach to our needs is simply better adapted than the slow and sometimes patronizing post-colonial approach of European investors, donor organizations and non-governmental organizations' and 'Western complaints about China's slow pace in adopting democratic reform cannot obscure the fact that the Chinese are more competitive, less bureaucratic and more adept at business in Africa than their critics.' He went on to describe the high level of efficiency by saying, 'I have found that a contract that would take five years to discuss, negotiate and sign with the World Bank takes three months when we have dealt with Chinese authorities. I am a firm believer in good governance and the rule of law. But when bureaucracy and senseless red tape impede our ability to act – and when poverty persists while international functionaries drag their feet – African leaders have an obligation to opt for swifter solutions. I achieved more in my one hour meeting with President Hu Jintao in an executive suite at my hotel in Berlin during the recent G8 meeting in Heiligendamm than I did during the entire, orchestrated meeting of world leaders at the summit – where African leaders were told little more than that G8 nations would respect existing commitments.'[23]

In fact, when we trace the history of China's aid in Africa, we will find that the 'non-interference' policy itself gradually has been undergoing some slight changes. In the 1970s and 1980s, when Chinese experts undertook the technical cooperation for maintaining those 'turn-key projects' in African countries such as TaZara railway, they abided by the 'non-interference' policy in a very strict way by concentrating only on 'technical guidance' and avoided participating in the management of the project, which they regarded as 'internal affairs'. However, the Chinese experts later considered that 'technical guidance' alone was not sufficient to bring the new productive capacity of the projects into full play, and that participating in management was a necessary condition for running the projects in a sustainable way. Today, the 'non-interference' policy, of course, has long transcended the 'management' concept trap, but still faces new challenges such as how to respond to the human rights issue and bad governance in the recipient countries.

Frankly speaking, in the era of globalisation, it is a little bit challenging to make a clear demarcation for or to set criteria on 'internal affairs' and to what extent and under which conditions they should be 'interfered' in by the outside powers. Nowadays, some people say that the 'one China policy' (i.e., recognising that there is only one China in the world that is represented by the People's Republic of China and that Taiwan is part of it) is a sort of 'strings attached' policy for China's aid provision. However, China regards the Taiwan issue as a most crucial sovereignty issue and as part of its internal affairs and reasons that it does not amount to interfering in African countries' ability to make their own choices for economic and political development.

Moreover, the opinion and stance coming from African countries are more relevant and important for China's policy-making. It was said when a Chinese delegation visited a farm that was established with Chinese aid in Tanzania in August 1994, that the Tanzanian side still believed that management power involved 'sovereignty' and could not be changed. As for joint ventures, the Chinese side could have only minority shares.[24] In addition, a member of Djibouti's ruling party approvingly noted that China shows 'esteem of our sovereignty and freedom. That's why we African people always keep a friendly feeling toward China.'[25] In this sense, the making and maintaining of a 'no political strings attached' aid policy is a two-way street since it also involves relationships with recipient countries, and their opinions, to some extent, have more leverage than those of the West.

Emphasising bilateral aid projects rather than multilateral. Most of China's aid is provided bilaterally and it has evolved relatively independently from the traditional donor community. China has set up embassies in nearly all the African countries except the four that still recognise Taiwan. Since 1956, China's aid has been conducted in a bilateral way. Even though it began to join the multilateral aid system when it re-entered the UN in 1971, its major channel for delivering aid is still in bilateral.

In terms of the organisational and institutional arrangement of China's foreign aid, the most important ministry in the Chinese government is the Ministry of Commerce (MOC). Generally speaking, its task includes preparing and organising inter-governmental economic negotiations and meetings of mixed commissions and signing multilateral and bilateral economic agreements on behalf of the government, administering foreign aid and formulating aid plans for each recipient country, and organiing the implementation of aid projects and technical cooperation. Within the MOC, there are three departments related to African issues, but these focus on different areas. The Department of West Asia and African Affairs (DWAA) provides policy advice on Africa to top policy-makers and encourages investment as well as trade with Africa by distributing information on the investment environment in Africa to Chinese firms. The Department of Foreign Economic Cooperation (DFEC) is responsible for regulating all Chinese companies involved overseas.[26]

The Department of Foreign Aid (DFA) plays the central role in regulating and administering China's aid projects. Within the department, it has set up 13 divisions and one office with the main responsibilities being the following: (1) drafting and implementation of policies on foreign aid, drafting of laws and regulations on foreign aid and rules in the department portfolio, and research on and promotion of the reforms in foreign aid; (2) formulation of plans on foreign aid and organisation of their implementation, drafting of plans on aid to specific countries and design of the aid projects; (3) responsibility for the negotiations on aid between governments, signing of aid memorandums, dealing with the inter-governmental aid affairs and the handover of the aid projects to the recipient countries, and responsibility for the aid loan redemption and debt restructuring; (4) making assessments of the qualifications of bidding enterprises for future participation in the projects, organization of the bidding for foreign aid projects, designing the task and objectives of these projects and monitoring their implementation; (5) responsibility for formulating and reporting on the foreign aid fund budgeting and final accounting, and the associated statistical work; (6) responsibility for the expenditure of foreign aid funds, monitoring and managing the foreign aid preferential loans and the foreign aid joint ventures and cooperation fund projects, and solving disputes between governments; (7) providing supervision on the work of the International Economic Cooperation Affairs Bureau.[27]

Apart from above departments at home, the MOC also has set up an agency in many of its embassies abroad called the Economic Counsellor's Office of the Embassy of China. These offices are in charge of implementing the aid projects in the host countries and maintaining contacts with Chinese firms there, as well as for providing updated economic information on host countries to the MOC. Although the MOC takes major responsibilities for the aid issue, other related departments in the Chinese government are also involved in the various aspects of foreign aid work, such as the ministries of Foreign Affairs and Finance, China's Import and Export Bank (Exim Bank) and the ministries of Science and Technology, Education, Agriculture, of Health, etc.

There are four main reasons why China prefers bilateral aid. (1) Historical habit and enriched experience in doing so. The history of the establishment and development of Sino-African relations shows that bilateral relations have been build step by step and country by country, from the very first one, Egypt (China-Egypt diplomatic ties were established in 1956), to the late post-apartheid South Africa (in early 1998, China and South Africa established formal diplomatic relations). China supported a number of African countries in fighting for national independence and economic development. (2) The 'poor helps the poor model' doesn't belong to the OECD/DAC club (the Organization for Economic Co-operation and Development and its Development Assistance Committee). Compared to Western countries, China has been influenced relatively little by the 'donor community' and is accumulating its experience and building up its expertise through learning by doing. And China does not use the donor-recipient mind-set or even language. More importantly, there is a strong African opinion saying they don't want to see that China becomes a part of international donor system or becoming a member of the traditional donor club, the DAC. (3) The bilateral way is more efficient than the multilateral way. Since China's foreign assistance is usually provided in the form of projects, rather than cash, these can be implemented quickly after the relevant agreements have been signed between the governments. (4) The African Union (AU) and the New Partnership for Africa's Development (NEPAD) are relatively new initiatives and African integration is still in the process of being developed. Apart from joining the DAC, another way of taking the multilateral approach would be to strengthen the ties with AU/NEPAD as well as the sub-regional African organisations such as the Southern African Development Community (SADC) and the Economic Community Of West African States (ECOWAS). However, when we talk about Sino-African relations, we must be fully aware that this is a relationship between a country with a population of 1.3 billion and a continent with 53 countries. Without the development of African integration itself, it will be difficult to improve multilateral cooperation dramatically.

However, with the increase in China's aid to Africa, the development of Africa's regional integration, as well as the increasing demand and pressure from the traditional multilateral donor club, there are also signs that China is moving towards more collaboration with international institutions. In fact, as early as 1983, China began to work with UN under the framework of Technical Cooperation among Developing Countries (TCDC) to carry out multilateral technical cooperation with other developing countries. China now is a signatory to the 2005 Paris Declaration on Aid Effectiveness (even though as a recipient state) and a shareholder of the African Development Bank. In May 2007, the China Exim Bank signed a MoU with the World Bank on collaboration between the two institutions in African development, especially in infrastructure. China has recently also pledged to increase its contribution to the World Health Organization, World Food Programme, UN Industrial Development Organization and many regional and international development banks; it can be expected that cooperation with multilateral organisations will be stressed and expanded in future. In terms of multilateral cooperation with the AU/NEPAD, the establishment of FOCAC in 2000 should be regarded as another important step forward for building a mechanism for collective dialogue.

In fact, China has a dual role and great potential for becoming a driver of aid effectiveness in multilateral cooperation. On the one hand, China itself has been one of largest recipient countries in the system and knows exactly how to engage with donor countries. In the meantime, 'China's own reform process showed key elements of national ownership for development, it can provide advice to other developing countries, and be a convening power for the global debate on aid effectiveness'.[28] On the other hand, with China's economic development and increasing foreign assistance, it is also becoming a 'donor' (although not using that word) or aid-providing country. While China is accumulating experience through learning by doing, there is also a great desire to develop international collaboration and to learn from international experience.

Strong focus on 'hardware projects' such as physical infrastructure construction rather than 'software projects' like research and capacity-building. Infrastructure is the foundation for national economic development and reflects the level and potential of a country's national economic development. More importantly, it also has a direct bearing on a country's attraction for foreign investment and is a key lever for the environment of investment. It is widely known that underdeveloped infrastructure is a major bottleneck hindering Africa's economic development. The primitive state of the transportation industry and horrible road conditions not only keep the cost of trade between and within African nations very high but also choke the flow of foreign investment to the continent. An insufficient and unstable power supply is another common drawback for African nations and even South Africa – the continent's economic powerhouse which enjoyed a full, cheap supply of electricity – has begun feeling the pain of power shortages in recent years.

'Build roads and profits will come rolling in.' It is from its own success in reform, opening up and economic development that China has learned the importance, necessity and great business potential of investing in Africa's infrastructural development. So, on the one hand, Africa is in urgent need of better facilities across the board but not financially capable of paying for them as it stares at a funding gap of at least $20 billion a year. On the other hand, with China's 'going-out strategy' and its internationally competitive construction industry, there is a strong inter-complementary nature of economic cooperation between China and Africa, and China could suit Africa's need perfectly in this regard.

While Western countries focus on 'software' such as capacity-building, China puts more investment into 'hardware', such as roads, railways and other tangible infrastructure projects that bring direct and visible benefit to the host country. The China ExIM Bank, founded in 1994, has played an important role in providing financial support for such infrastructure projects. By September 2006, there were 259 projects financed by the China Exim Bank in 36 African countries, 79 per cent of which were committed to infrastructure development, such as railways (Benguela and Port Sudan), dams (Merowe in Sudan, Bui in Ghana and Mphanda Nkuwa in Zambia), thermal power plants (Nigeria and Sudan), oil facilities (Nigeria), and copper mines (Congo and Zambia). Most of these loans were issued as buyers' credit with low interest (2 per cent) to Chinese companies and are not classified as bilateral assistance by the OECD/DAC.[29]

On 11 July 2008, the World Bank published a report entitled *Building Bridges: China's Growing Role as Infrastructure Financier for Sub-Saharan Africa*. Unlike other reports, books and articles about Sino-African relations produced by various international institutions and European or American think tanks of different stripes in recent years, the latest World Bank report is focused on two aspects: (1) Africa's infrastructure sector, where China is playing an enormous role, and (2) an in-depth analysis of the sector, reaching the objective and positive conclusion that it is a fact that China has been serving Africa's economic growth as a proactive driving force.

The World Bank report maintains that China has constructed many bridges, railways and roads in sub-Saharan Africa, where natural conditions are harsh to say the least. The total value of Chinese financial commitments to African infrastructure projects rose from less than US$1 billion per year in 2001–2003 to around US$1.5 billion per year in 2004–2005, reached at least US$7 billion in 2006, then tailed off to US$4.5 billion in 2007. Among an array of infrastructure developments, hydropower plants and railways are two key areas of China's investment. With a total investment of $3.3 billion already in place, the ten hydropower plants currently under construction can add 6000 megawatts of electricity to the sub-Saharan region, raising its power supply capacity by 30 per cent. Meanwhile, the 1350 km of existing railways China is renovating and 1600 km of new track will be a significant addition to the 50,000-km railway network in sub-Saharan Africa.[30]

There is no doubt that these investments have greatly improved Africa's infrastructure, as well as the overall investment environment, and boosted economic development on the continent.

Furthermore, it is also interesting to note, when the Western media talks about China's cooperation model of 'infrastructure in exchange for resources' or 'China is plundering Africa's natural resources', the figures and statement given by the World Bank report show that only 7 per cent of China's investment in African infrastructure is connected to the excavation of natural resources and that the Chinese oil company arrived in Africa to explore and produce oil much later than many of its Western multinational counterparts did, and its investment in Africa's oil industry is less than 10 per cent of what others have invested there.[31]

In recent years, China's aid also gradually entered in 'software' areas, such as human resources training and technical and management cooperation. China will increase its aid expenditure in technical cooperation, especially personnel training, education exchange and medical services so as to make further contributions to the capacity-building of the recipient countries.

In fact, with its rapidly growing economy, China has begun to cultivate the attraction of its language, culture, political values and diplomacy around the world. In Africa, these efforts have come in mainly two forms: bringing Africans to China and sending Chinese to Africa – exchanges which strive to share China's experience in national development. To this end, China has promised to up its efforts in human resources training for Africa. Invitations have been extended to a variety of African specialists (party and government cadres, economic management personnel, middle- and high-ranking military officers and professional technical personnel) to visit China for opportunities to learn both professional and technical skills, as well as to get an up-close and personal feel for China's development experience. China also dispatches many Chinese experts to African countries to give lectures at universities, visit medical facilities and hospitals and advise farmers on agricultural production techniques.

The Chinese government has also robustly promoted the development of Chinese language instruction overseas over the past few years. By the end of March 2007, 11 Confucius Institutes in Africa had been set up in seven African countries: Egypt, Zimbabwe, Kenya, Nigeria, South Africa, Rwanda and Madagascar.[32] Africans have shown enthusiasm for learning Mandarin. By the end of June 2005, roughly 8000 students in Africa were studying Chinese and 120 schools in 16 African countries included Chinese language in their curricula.[33] Furthermore, Chinese government scholarship quotas for African students to study in China will increase from the current 2000 to 4000 persons in the next three years.[34] China is boosting cultural exchanges to improve ties between people in China and Africa, especially between the younger generations.[35]

As for utilisation of the aid, the Chinese government usually chooses not to provide funds to the recipient country directly, but through government-to-government economic and technical cooperation, and construction projects are directly implemented by Chinese enterprises and organisations. The mode of providing aid in the form of projects implemented by Chinese firms might not be conducive to building local capacity, but can avoid corruption in the host countries as there is no direct funding involved.

The role of aid: Achievements and challenges

In general, China's aid to Africa has generated effective results and helped China's involvement in Africa. However, it is also facing new challenges at the moment and future.

Role and achievement

The positive role of China's aid in Africa can be understood at least from two points, namely, promoting African economic growth and contributing to debt relief for African countries.

Up to May 2006, China spent RMB44.4 billion (US$5.69 billion) in assisting African countries (account for 30 per cent of all China's foreign

aid) with over 800 projects, including textile factories, hydropower stations, stadiums, hospitals and schools. Most of these are infrastructure
projects that considerably benefit local communities in African countries. In terms of the projects accomplished and handed over, Ethiopia,
Sudan, Tanzania, Zambia, Mali, Egypt and Algeria, to name just a few,
are among the top recipient countries on the continent.

As a matter of fact, Chinese aid and investment in, and economic
cooperation with, African nations have contributed significantly to the
strong rebound of the African economy in recent years. The Chinese
economy's rapid growth has helped to raise the prices of primary
products on the world market, which, in turn, increases the foreign
exchange income of the African countries engaged in exporting primary products. It improves their foreign trade climate and strengthens
their payment capabilities. Since the middle of the 1990s, the African
economy has been growing at a rate of 5–6 per cent annually. And
this is partly the result of the rapid price rise of raw materials and
the increasing demand for raw materials by China and other emerging
markets in Asia. In terms of investment, capital flows are now outpac-
ing aid for the first time in Africa's history. And China is diversifying
the monopoly of investors in Africa and contributes a lot to the encouraging development trend. For example, once war-torn Angola has been
enjoying double-digit economic growth in recent years because China
helped build the country's infrastructure. It also made large investments in the country. In 2006, the Angolan economy grew at a rate as
high as 17 per cent.

Furthermore, since China's provision of aid has a stronger focus on
projects and is managed in a bilateral way, it normally acts more quickly,
and with shorter procedures. Sierra Leone's ambassador to Beijing, Sahr
Johnny, once said, 'The Chinese are doing more than the G8 to make
poverty history in Africa', and 'If a G8 country had wanted to rebuild
the stadium, we'd still be holding meetings! The Chinese just come and
do it. They don't hold meetings about environmental impact assessment, human right, bad governance and good governance. I'm not saying they are right, just that Chinese investment is succeeding because
they don't set high benchmarks.'[36]

China's aid in Africa has also promoted bilateral trade dramatically.
The bilateral trade volume rose from US$12.11 million in the 1950s to
US$10.5 billion in 2000, US$29.4 billion in 2004, nearly US$40 billion
in 2005 and over US$70 billion in 2007. In recent years, China has
increased imports from African countries and thus maintained a trade
deficit with them, enabling these countries to earn a large amount of

foreign exchange. For example, since China removed import tariffs on 454 separate categories from the 32 least developed countries in July 2007, some $450 million worth of duty free trade has entered the Chinese market from Africa.[37] According to a Chinese expert utilising a calculation in common use, the contribution of China-Africa trade to African economic growth has reached around 20 per cent in recent years.[38] As president Museveni of Uganda pointed out: 'Aid by itself cannot change the society, only trade can promote durable economic increase and the development of the society'.[39]

In terms of debt relief, although China is a minor creditor country compared with Western creditor nations and monetary institutions – and at the same time a debtor developing nation itself – the country still makes efforts to help resolve the African debt issue. In 2000, at the first ministerial meeting of FOCAC, China declared it would cancel debts from African countries amounting to a total of RMB10 billion (US$1.28 billion). A debt relief mechanism was formed in 2000, which consisted of ministries of Commerce and Finance, the Central Bank and other banks concerned with aid affairs. By the time of writing, China has written off total debts of RMB16.6 billion (US$2.13 billion) for 44 recipient countries of HIPCs and LDCs, 31 of which are African countries, for which there is a total write-off of RMB10.9 billion (US$1.40 billion). Another debt cancellation of RMB10 billion (US$1.28 billion) for African countries is under negotiation and arrangement. The write-offs in total will amount to 60 per cent of all debt obligations to China.

Moreover, China began to send medical teams to Africa since 1963. To date, China has dispatched total 15,000 medical personnel. At the time of writing, there are 35 medical teams working in 34 African countries. The number of persons in human resources training has reached 12,000, having soared in recent decades. All of these have contributed a lot to African economic development, social progress and Sino-African friendships.

Challenges and developing trends

1. 'No strings attached' versus 'conditionality', and 'non-interference' versus 'interference'. With China's increasing aid to Africa, conflict between China's 'no strings attached' and 'non-interference model and the Western donors' aid conditionality is likely to occur. China will face more pressure and more criticism from the West, in such terms as 'rogue aid' or 'free-rider'. In fact, the Chinese government and the Chinese people should be fully aware that the goodwill strategies on paper will face challenges in the process of implementation. Nowadays, there are a lot of concerns not only from the West but also from Africa about China's perceived impact on political systems and economic development in Africa.

Elsewhere, I have analysed these bottlenecks in China-Africa relations and argued ways forward to deal with these challenges in the future (He, 2008).[40] I agree that the 'non-interference' policy today is facing new challenges such as how to respond to the human rights issue and poor governance in some African countries. Moreover, since Chinese aid also goes to so-called 'failed states'. such as Sudan and Zimbabwe (the two have been constantly mentioned), that normally have domestic conflict and problems of governance, Chinese aid and investment there are naturally becoming increasingly vulnerable to local conflicts and instability. The news of kidnappings and even killings (one occurred in Sudan, in late October 2008, with five Chinese workers dead, three injured and one who remains missing) towards Chinese workers and engineers working in Sudan, Ethiopia, Niger and Nigeria have generated great security concerns for both the Chinese companies involved and the high-level leadership.

In fact, the Chinese government has also realised the increasing economic danger in investing in these countries. For example, in March 2007, the National Development and Reform Commission, China's main economic planning agency, released a public document saying that Sudan had been removed from the latest list of countries with preferred trade status. This also means that Beijing will no longer provide financial incentives to Chinese companies to invest in Sudan.[41] Even in terms of political and image risks, I do believe that the Chinese government has also been made aware somehow by constant reminders in the Western media and the emerging debate among Chinese scholars themselves. Take the Darfur issue as an example, how to seek a balance between the traditional principle of 'non-interference' with the requests and needs of international society is no doubt a real challenge for China's African diplomacy. Through the appointment of a special envoy to Darfur and increasing humanitarian assistance to the region, as well as persuading the Sudanese government to cooperate with the international community, it is encouraging to see that the Chinese official policy has showed more and more flexibility and pragmatism so far.

2. *How to engage 'old' and 'new' donors and improve aid effectiveness and harmonisation.* The question of how to harmonise aid programmes and improve aid effectiveness no doubt constitutes a big challenge facing all

aid providers including 'old' and 'new', as well as recipient countries themselves.

Through years of experience, the 'old donors', such as the DAC donors, have developed a set of norms, rules and procedures that constitute the aid donor regime, which, unfortunately, is not yet familiar to 'new donors'. It is interesting to note that the 'old donors' themselves took the exactly same aid model – such as tied aid, a focus on infrastructure and a preference for channelling aid via projects rather than cash – for which they now shun and reproach the 'new donors' today. Thus, for 'old donors', it is very reasonable to say that the old aid model doesn't work well, because we experienced the failure. For 'new donors', however, it seems very logical to respond that the failure itself wasn't caused by the model, but by the West's patriarchal behaviour and the Euro-centred mind-set. Since the departure point now is different – South-South cooperation versus donor-recipient relations – even the same means could lead to different results. Moreover, they argue that it is the failure of the aid policy of the 'old donors' itself during the past half century that disqualifies them from directing others.

In fact, mutual accusations, and such labels as 'rogue aid' or 'hypo-critical donor', are meaningless. Even though the rhetoric of 'aid' has been addressed with anti-poverty and fighting HIV-AIDs, etc. in reality, 'aid' has never been 'pure' and has always been political. In that sense, avoiding conflict between the 'old' and 'new' donors requires a two-way street mind-set and practice. On the one hand, China's foreign aid should change to a more transparent form and seek collaboration with other donors. Whenever aid or investment projects are being planned, the issues of local labour and environmental protection measures should be taken into consideration. Moreover, multiple consultations should take place, not only with a few African elites, but also with a wide range of stakeholders such as African civil society, media, ethnic and religious organisations and even opposition leaderships. The more opinions that are heard, the wiser the moves taken. It was not surprising to see that while he was in Namibia in February 2007 President Hu Jintao took a half day off from his heavy schedule when he paid visit to several African countries, to meet with Chinese entrepreneurs doing business in the region, and urged them to respect investment rules and labour issues, and broaden their engagement with the local community.

On the other hand, OECD donors should also understand more about China's aid model from the angle of history and culture, and could make sure they avoid politicisation, and instead seek active partner-ships with key aid institutions in China. Perhaps, the 'old' donors also could learn something from the 'new' donors. However, it would be better and more practical for the next step of international dialogue to focus more on cooperation on specific issues, rather than concepts and principles or trying to change each other's mind-sets in the short term. As a DFID China Workshop Report pointed out, 'international cooperation also will be a process of learning, but of learning from practical rather than theoretical experience'.[42] Moreover, more attention should be paid to the needs of recipient countries. There is an African opinion saying with respect to the DAC 'model' and the need to ensure that African voices are heard in the discussions about how China can cooperate with the DAC.

After all, to some extent, the differences between the two aid models also reflect the differences of two philosophies and ways of thinking. The Chinese philosophy, and way of thinking, is to pay more attention to the result (that's why the famous saying of 'no matter if it is a white cat or black cat, it will be a good cat as long as it catches the mouse' given by the late leader Deng Xiaoping has become a totem in modern China). To the Western way of thinking, the norms and procedures seem more crucial than the result. Hence, there is a need to do more homework and bring multidisciplines into the process of engagement of the two aid models.

3. More work needs to be done to upgrade China's aid managing/monitoring system and expert training. Unlike OECD (DAC) countries, China doesn't yet have an equivalent independent aid agency in charge of development assistance issues. Sometimes there are conflicts between the ministries or departments that bear responsibilities for aid issues. There is a need to consider establishing one in order to coordinate the aid programme, which is beyond the current capacity of the Ministry of Commerce (MOC) and the Economic Counsellor's Offices in the Chinese Embassies abroad. They are facing shortages of personal and lack of experience and professional knowledge in dealing with the huge foreign aid programmes. As Prof. Zha Daojiong from Peking University emphasised in the DFID China Workshop in March 2008, the way China implements its aid programme may be different from the OECD experience, but is in line with domestic experience, so few people would recognise that there were problems. Moreover, few people in China know about the aid programme, which is a very small part of the activities of MOC.[43]

Supervision and management of the capital flow and progress of all aid projects underway should be strengthened to avoid misuse and embezzlement of capital. In the past, the majority of Chinese aid projects were called 'turn-key projects. Once they were finished, they were handed over to the locals completely and there was no follow-up system to monitor and evaluate their maintenance and effectiveness. This state of affairs certainly lowered the combined social and economic effect of the aid itself and there is a need for more consistent results for Chinese aid in the future.

There is also an urgent need to train up experts in foreign aid, including the researchers and the administrative staff dealing with the organisation, management, implementation and monitoring of the aid projects. Research into foreign aid is still quite limited and has lagged far behind China's aid activities in Africa. China does need to increase its expertise on foreign aid, learn from past experiences and build capacities in its institutions that manage aid. It is not sufficient to build up expertise only through 'learning by doing'. It is quite encouraging to see that the Chinese Academy of Social Sciences (CASS), the biggest think tank for the Chinese government, is about to announce the creation of a development policy institute and is expressing an interest in working together with international institutions. To a great extent, capacity-building in China (not only in Africa), including joint studies and workshops, could help to improve mutual understanding dramatically, and this in return will serving as a stepping-stone for other practical cooperation in development aid.

Notes

1. There are at least three kinds of demarcations by period. One scholar has divided China's aid history into three phases, namely, a first phase (1950–78), a second phase (1979–94) and a third phase (1995–now); another scholar has further divided the history of China's aid into five phases: an initial phase (1950–63), a development phase (1964–70), a boom and set-back phase (1971–78), and adjustment and initial reform phase (1979–94) and a further reform phase (1995–now); and a third dividing scheme is phase I (1950–74), phase II (1974–90) and phase III (1991–now). For detail, see Li, Xiaoyun, *Chinese Foreign Aid to Africa*, online: http://www.iprcc.org.cn/ppt/2008-05-13/1210662570.pdf.
2. *Mao Zedong's Selected Works on diplomacy*, 1994, p. 408.
3. *Selected Works of Zhou Enlai on Foreign Affairs*, 1990, cited from Ai, Ping, From Proletarian Internationalism to Mutual Development: China's Cooperation with Tanzania, 1965–95, chapter 5 in Goran Hyden and Rwekaza Mukandala (eds), 1999, p. 162.
4. Xinhua Biweekly publication, no. 11, 1960, p. 53, cited from Gu, Zhangyi, New Pattern of Contemporary Relations between China and Africa, in *China and Africa* (ed.) The Center for African Studies of Peking University.

5. Ai, Ping, From Proletarian Internationalism to Mutual Development: China's Cooperation with Tanzania, 1965–95, 1999, p. 166.
6. *People's Daily*, 18 September 1956.
7. *People's Daily*, 9 August 1963.
8. Yan, Xuetong, 1997, p. 38
9. Chen, Dunde, 1999, p. 378.
10. *Deng Xiaoping's Selected Works*, 1994, p. 57.
11. The 11 African countries are: Egypt, Algeria, Morocco, Guinea, Gabon, Zaire, Congo, Zambia, Zimbabwe, Tanzania and Kenya.
12. Chris Alden and Ana Cristina Alves, 2008, p. 53.
13. Wang, Chen-An, 2004.
14. Yahia M. Mahmoud, 2007, pp. 114–15.
15. A 33 per cent increase in the fund will allow China to hold 300 training courses in three years for some 10,000 African professionals in various fields as well as to raise the number of scholarships that China offers for African exchange students.
16. Apart from the original travel destinations of Egypt, South Africa and Morocco, China has decided to grant a further eight African countries Approved Destination Status: Mauritius, Ethiopia, Tunisia, Zimbabwe, Kenya, Zambia, Tanzania and the Seychelles.
17. Penny Davies, 2007, p. 49.
18. Li, Xiaoyun, 2008.
19. Jia Qinlin, head of the Chinese Political Consultative Conference, speech at the opening ceremony of the China-Kenyan Economic and Trade Co-operation Forum in Nairobi on 24 April 2007.
20. *Xinhua*, 18 June 2006.
21. Ai, Ping, 1999, p. 194.
22. Kenneth King, 2006.
23. Abdoulaye Wade, 2008.
24. Ai, Ping, 1999, p. 183.
25. African officials affirm China's aid for development in Africa, *Xinhua*, 15 June 2006.
26. See Bates Gill and James Reilly, 2007, pp. 42–3.
27. See Li, Xiaoyun, 2008.
28. DFID China Workshop Report, 2008.
29. OECD, 2007.
30. The World Bank Report, 2008.
31. Ibid.
32. *People's Daily* (overseas edition), 7 April 2007.
33. Minister of Education, Zhou Ji's speech at the Sino-African Education Minister Forum, 27 November 2005.
34. President Hu Jintao's speech at the opening of the third China Africa Cooperation Forum and Chinese and African leaders' summit on 4 November 2006.
35. The invitation was made during a speech delivered to all African young people at Pretoria University in South Africa. Hu Jintao: China Invites 500 African Youths to Visit China in Three Years, Chinanews.com, 7 February 2007. Available at: http://news.sohu.com/20070207/n248108503.shtml.
36. Lindsey Hilsum, 2005, p. 239.

37. Wei Jiang, 2007.
38. President of the Chinese Political Consultative Conference (CPCC) Jia Qingling's speech at the opening ceremony of the China-Kenya Economic and Trade cooperation Forum in Nairobi, Kenya on 24 April 2007 during his visit to Kenya. See (Beijing) *People's Daily* (Overseas Edition), 26 April 2007.
39. *The Ethiopian Herald*, 3 December 2004.
40. He Wenping, 2008.
41. See Richard McGregor, 2007.
42. DFID China Workshop Report, 2008.
43. Ibid.

References

Alden, Chris (2007). *China in Africa*. London and New York: Zed Books.
Alden, Chris and Ana Cristina Alves (2008). History and Identity in the Construction of China's Africa Policy. *Review of African Political Economy* 35, no. 115.
Ampiah, Kweku and Sanusha Naidu (eds) (2008). *Crouching Tiger, Hidden Dragon? Africa and China*. Scottsville: University of KwaZulu-Natal Press.
Center for African Studies in Peking University (2000). *China and Africa*. Beijing: Peking University Press.
Centre for Chinese Studies, University of Stellenbosch (2006). *China's Interest and Activity in Africa's Construction and Infrastructure Sectors*.
Chen, Dunde (1999). *Exploring Journey: Zhou Enlai Flew to Africa*. Beijing: World Affairs Press.
Davies, Martyn, Hannah Edinger, Nastasya Tay and Sanusha Naidu (2008). *How China Delivers Development Assistance to Africa*. Centre for Chinese Studies, University of Stellenbosch.
Davies, Penny (2007). *China and the End of Poverty in Africa: Towards Mutual Benefit?* Sundbyberg: Diakonia.
DFID China Workshop Report (2008). *Managing Aid effectively: Lessons for China?* Beijing: DFID.
Deng Xiaoping's Selected Works (1994). Volume 3, Beijing: The People's Press.
Fues, Thomas, Sven Grimm and Denise Laufer (2006). China's Africa Policy: Opportunity and Challenges for European Development Cooperation. *German Development Institute Briefing Paper*, no. 4.
Gill, Bates and James Reilly (2007). The Tenuous Hold of China Inc. in Africa. *The Washington Quarterly* 30, no. 3, pp. 37–52.
Gu, Jing, John Humphrey and Dirk Messner (2007). Global Governance and Developing Countries: The Implications of the Rise of China. *German Development Institute Discussion Paper*, no. 18, Bonn.
He, Wenping (2008). China's Perspective on Contemporary China-Africa Relations, in *China Returns to Africa: A Rising Power and a Continent Embrace* (eds) Chris Alden, Daniel Large and Ricardo Soares Oliveira. London: Hurst & Company.
Hilsum, Lindsey (2005). We Love China. *GRANTA* 92.

Hoeymissen, Sara Van (2008). Aid within the China-Africa Partnership: Emergence of an Alternative to the NEPAD Development Paradigm? *China Aktuell*, no. 3, pp. 102–30.

Hyden, Goran and Rwekaza Mukandala (eds) (1999). *Agencies in Foreign Aid: Comparing China, Sweden and the United States in Tanzania*. Macmillan Press Ltd.

Huse, Martine Dahle and Stephen L. Muyakwa (2008). *China in Africa: Lending, Policy Space and Governance*. Norwegian Campaign for Debt Cancellation and Norwegian Council for Africa.

Jiang, Wei (2007). Projects with Africa Going On Well. *China Daily*, 14 November, Beijing.

King, Kenneth (2006). China's Partnership with Africa. *International Politics Quarterly*, Peking University, no. 4, pp. 10–20.

Li, Xiaoyun (2008). Chinese Foreign Aid to Africa. Online. Available at: http://www.iprcc.org.cn/ppt/2008-05-13/1210662570.pdf.

Mahmoud, Yahia M. (2007). *Chinese Development Assistance and West African Agriculture: A Shifting Approach to Foreign Aid?* Sweden: Lund University.

Mao Zedong's Selected Works on Diplomacy (1994). Beijing: The Central Documentary Press.

McCormick, Dorothy (2008). China and India as Africa's New Donors: The Impact of Aid on Development. *Review of African Political Economy* 35, no. 115, pp. 73–92.

McGregor, Richard (2007). Iran, Sudan, Nigeria, off China Incentive List. *Financial Times*, 2 March.

OECD (2007). *Is China Actually Helping Improve Debt Sustainability in Africa?* OECD.

People's Daily (1963). Mao's Talk with Visiting African Friends, 9 August.

People's Daily (Overseas Edition) (2007). Warmly Congratulating the Establishment of the Headquarters of Confucius Institute, 7 April.

Stähle, Stefan (2008). Towards China's Integration into the Aid Donor Architecture: Learning from Chinese Participation in International Regimes. *China Aktuell*, no. 3, pp. 130–65.

Taylor, Ian (1998). China's Foreign Policy towards Africa in the 1990s. *Journal of Modern African Studies* 36, no. 3, pp. 443–60.

Taylor, Ian (2006). *China and Africa: Engagement and Compromise*. London and New York: Routledge.

Taylor, Ian (2009). *China's New Role in Africa*. Boulder, CO and London: Lynne Rienner.

Tjønneland, Elling N., Bjørn Brandtzæg, Åshild Kolås and Garth le Pere (2006). *China in Africa – Implications for Norwegian Foreign and Development Policies*. Bergen: Chr. Michelsen Institute (CMI).

Wade, Abdoulaye (2008). Time for the West to Practice What It Preaches, *Financial Times*, 24 January.

Wang, Chen-An (2004). The Outline of Foreign Assistance Projects and the Operation of Preferential Loans and Fund for Joint Ventures. *Foreign Trade Review*, no. 13, Beijing.

World Bank Report (2008). *Building Bridges: China's Growing Role as Infrastructure Financier for Sub-Saharan Africa*.

Xinhua News (2006). Premier Wen Hails Sino-African Ties of Cooperation, 18 June.

Yan, Xuetong (1997). *Analysis of China's National Interest*. Tianjing, China: Tianjing People's Press.

Zhou Enlai's Selected Works on Foreign Affairs (1990). Beijing: The Central Documentary Press.

Zhou, Hong (ed.) (2002). *Foreign Aid and International Relations*. Beijing: Chinese Academy of Social Sciences Press.

7
Chinese and African Views on Chinese Aid and Trade in Africa

Johan Lagerkvist

> It is important to give encouragement and support to all countries in taking development paths suited to their national conditions and exploring development models conducive to their national development and poverty eradication efforts. Respect for the right of people of all countries to independently choose development paths and models should serve as a basis and precondition for democracy. (Prime minister Wen Jiabao in his statement to the United Nations, 25 September 2008)[1]

Wen Jiabao's statement to the United Nations reflects two principles adhered to and defended by Chinese leaders for decades. First, sovereignty is a next to a holy principle not to be compromised by China or any other state. Second, as China is a developing country it advocates that national context, such as cultural traditions and political conditions, makes it difficult to apply a universal development model everywhere.

Chinese views on development, human rights, security and poverty reduction will become increasingly important as China continues to integrate with the world economy and the international community and gains more weight in international affairs. There is also a need to understand what 'aid with Chinese characteristics' means. One of the big issues for international relations in the twenty-first century is if China's economic integration might lead to alignment with international, or perhaps even Western, norms and beliefs. If so, some of the long-standing principles mentioned above, outlined by the incumbent premier, are bound to evolve into something new. In any event, it is important to take into account present Chinese aid policies and their evolution when the issue of an emerging new aid paradigm is addressed. If there has in recent years been an increasing merger between aid and security policy and a structural change in operations with non-state actors, such as non-governmental organisations (NGOs), China is largely exempt from that development. China shuns working with foreign NGOs operating overseas, as much as it prefers civil society organisations inside the People's Republic to function as so-called government organised NGOs (GONGOs).

The over-arching question on which this paper seeks to shed light is if the 'no strings attached' policy guiding the increasing volume of Chinese aid constitutes a challenge to Western aid paradigms, be they old or new. Is there such a thing as an emerging Chinese model of 'effective governance' – guided by a South-South vision of mutuality, equality and reciprocity at work – to be contrasted against Western notions of good governance that have, in different ways, since the 1990s been incorporated into the Western and therefore by default also the global discourse on foreign aid? Is there a dark Chinese hand at play working with unaccountable Third World dictators, endorsing 'bad governance', because China fears democratisation per se as, the development economist Paul Collier has argued (2007, p. 183)?

In order to answer these questions, the first more benign and the second more sinister, this paper sets out to analyse how some of China's 'Africa watchers', representatives of NGOs and state officials in Zambia and Tanzania comprehend Sino-African relations, and how they foresee economic development, development assistance and democratisation processes in Africa.[2] The 'Chinese views' are interpreted through textual analysis and represent those of an elite academic stratum in Chinese society, informed and aware of China's increasing role and impact in Africa. Naturally, there are many other Chinese points of view voiced in mass media outlets or the Internet, e.g. about Chinese business opportunities or the dangers for Chinese nationals in doing businesses in conflict-ridden countries such as Sudan or Nigeria. The choice to study these particular texts was made because they have an influence on official discourse and offer such independent analysis as exists in China on these issues. The 'African views' are analysed through in-depth interviews conducted in Zambia and Tanzania in July and August 2008. Although not exhaustive or sufficient to give a consummate and final answer to the above research questions, the analysis of the views of these Chinese and African scholars, NGO representatives and bureaucrats is useful for narrowing down the spectrum of potential answers. To find out what the Chinese view(s) amount to is especially pertinent, as in the global discussion on China's new and ambitious engagement with Africa, Chinese voices have seldom been heard or even actively sought.[3] The Chinese voices here described and analysed do not always represent the government's position, although at times they echo its statements and analysis on development in Third World countries. Moreover, arguably there are other important, and even more hidden, voices such as the CEOs of state-owned companies or banks investing in, for instance, the oil fields of Sudan or the copper-belt region of northern Zambia. These persons are also more influential and better connected to senior decision-makers in the foreign policy-making process than academicians. They even have access to information and time spent in the field, something that most of China's academic Africa watchers lack. Nonetheless, what the latter write and say reflects the concern and debate about China's growing importance and role in Africa.

China's new role and ODA in Africa

The increasing weight of China in international affairs is growing. It is felt almost everywhere through its strong balance of trade and the growing market presence of Chinese goods and services.

The trade volume between China and Africa has in recent years grown rapidly. By 2007, China ranked as Africa's second-highest trading partner, behind the US, and ahead of France and the UK. By 2003, trade between China and Africa was US$18.5 billion and by 2007, the Sino-African trading volume amounted to US$73 billion. By the end of 2005, the accumulated Chinese direct investment in Africa had reached US$12.5 billion and the number of Chinese companies investing in Africa was more than 800.

They are involved in trade, manufacturing, resource exploitation, traffic and transportation, comprehensive agricultural development and other areas (Zhan, 2006). Up until the end of 2005, the accumulated value of contracting projects and labour cooperation was US$412.5 billion. Zhan Shiming, a researcher with the Department of African Studies at the Chinese Academy of Social Sciences calculated that, in 2005, 82,000 Chinese were engaged in contracting projects and labour cooperation in Africa.

An ambitious diplomatic effort conducted worldwide, not least in African countries, has recently caught the attention of foreign observers awed by the cunning Chinese soft power strategy (Kurlantzick, 2007). Indeed, active diplomacy is paying off, or rather as Chinese spokespersons with the Ministry of Foreign Affairs would have it, mutual interest exists. Since the late 1990s the African continent has attracted much Chinese attention. President Hu Jintao has travelled extensively in Africa since he took office in 2003, as have other high-ranking Chinese leaders. The FOCAC meetings (Forum on China-Africa Cooperation) between China and African nations, which started in 2001, have created an organisational infrastructure through which Sino-African cooperation and future development are negotiated. In November 2006, the heads of states of 48 African countries participated in a uniquely large and focused Sino-African FOCAC summit in Beijing. Today, Chinese investment, loans and official development assistance (ODA) are growing at a tremendous pace in almost all African countries. China is not the only Asian donor, though, as Japanese aid diplomacy has been around for decades, too. Now it seems that Japan is adopting the Chinese way of delivering ODA. As argued by Zambian economist Yusuf Dodia: 'it is interesting to see how Japan is actually following China's more project-specific model, instead of as before, going together with a donor club consortium.'[4] India is also emerging as an important investor and donor country to be reckoned with, making use of Indian diaspora networks in eastern and southern Africa. Africa may, although in different ways, for these Asian states represent a place where their global ambitions are given expression at the same time as their economic needs are being fulfilled.

ODA constitutes a means to other ends beyond the goals of poverty alleviation and economic growth. According to the UN *Millennium Project Report* (UN, 2006), development aid has the potential to help countries to achieve the UN Millennium Development Goals. Thus, the contributions of emerging new donor countries, such as China and India, become increasingly important. In this context, it is imperative to assess the arena of international aid provision – how different programmes overlap, complement or contradict each other. The playing field is obviously changing as the newly emerging donors become more significant sources of financing for developing countries. It is therefore important to analyse the way in which these new donors will change and challenge the established positions of traditional donors. As the UN *Millennium Project Report* identifies, the current development aid system of the world is likely to suffer from incoherence and be 'in need of a much more focused approach' (2006), an already complicated issue may become even more difficult and politicised if a harmonisation between aid policies, Eastern and Western, cannot be achieved.

It is, however, difficult to make comparisons between the aid programmes of emerging donors, as China's ODA is almost like a 'black box'. The government of China does not disclose how much aid it gives to foreign countries on an annual basis, or to which countries and in what form, loans or grants, it does so (Davies, 2007, p. 47; Tjönneland et al., 2006, p. 10). The opaque nature of Chinese foreign aid results from the conflation between cooperation in general and 'real aid; therefore, observers have to decipher the official statements from Chinese officials to the best of their ability (Alden, 2008, p. 22).

This is reflected in arguments made by African NGOs. Muyatwa Sitali, officer in charge of the debt, aid and trade programme at the Jesuit Centre for Theological Reflection in Lusaka complained: 'In my view of it, Chinese aid is not different from others, the problem is not whether it is good or bad, rather, the problem is about the lack of transparency. The Zambian government, the embassy of China do not give anyone access to the relevant documents.'[5]

This problem of Chinese aid being opaque is not just a conundrum for outsiders. Chinese scholars have a hard time figuring out what the aggregate sum of China's ODA might be, too. Moreover, on the issue of the quality or efficiency of aid, a Chinese scholar has stated that only rough evaluations of the benefits of aid are made, and no systematic methodology is employed in so doing (Davies, 2007, p. 64). According to the Chinese scholar Zhan Shiming, in the past 50 years, China's provision of foreign aid to Africa has amounted to RMB 444 billion (US$5.6 billion) and more than 900 infrastructure and social projects have been carried out (Zhan, 2006). Today, China gives African countries the largest share of its budget for development assistance: 44 percent, that is, US$1.8 billion (Alden, 2008, p. 22).

From studying the different levels of effectiveness of Chinese agricultural aid projects carried out in Gambia, Sierra Leone and Liberia during the 1960s and 1970s, Deborah Brautigam (1998, p. 3) argued the limited value of viewing aid as an element of foreign policy in analysing foreign aid. Instead she believed that domestic politics in both the donor country and the aid-receiving countries analysed as a whole explain better how particular projects and programmes are designed and implemented, and why only some are sustained over time. As Brautigam correctly argued, very little on-the-ground knowledge exists about Chinese foreign aid as very few researchers have conducted fieldwork about it on African soil (ibid., p. 5). Furthermore, as Chinese assistance, aid and trade with Africa have increased tremendously since Brautigam wrote her book in 1998, and continue to do so, there is a great need to start to evaluate the experiences of Chinese assistance. According to Penny Davies, who has interviewed Chinese government officials and scholars about how they define what aid effectiveness means for China, the common answer was that Chinese aid 'is effective as it is concrete'.

The implicit argument was that Chinese aid is providing Africa with concrete things they can use – infrastructure like buildings and roads (Davies, 2007, p. 63). Yusuf Dodia described it well from the local perspective: 'like little bees they come in and do an infrastructure project'. And according to Lee Habasonda of the NGO the Southern African Centre for the Constructive Resolution of Disputes (SACCORD), it is all quite simple: 'The beauty of Chinese aid is that it is project specific, you see visible results that we do not see from the West. In this way, these short-term projects buy into the loyalties of local leaders and civil society. In the short term it might be useful and effective, in the long term, however, we cannot be sure.'[6]

Thus, although it is difficult to measure its effectiveness, some African NGO leaders are beginning to raise questions about the sustainability or long-term effectiveness of Chinese aid. Chinese scholars are often quite proud of China's practical and project-specific approach to aid, which means that Chinese aid looks more effective, with concrete and visible results, than that of OECD countries Some of them argue, too, that Western aid has become an industry infested with bureaucratic politics and a waste of resources spent on expensive consultants (Davies, 2007, p. 64).

The Beijing Consensus

Development assistance is merely one of the many tools of the Chinese strategy for Africa, institutionalised in 2000 with the establishment of FOCAC. Several Western NGOs and African civil society groupings are concerned about China's cultivation of ties with corrupt leaders of African states. But apprehension about increasing Chinese engagement is also shown in statements made by political leaders such as the former president of South Africa, Thabo Mbeki, and Michael Sata, leader of the largest opposition parties in Zambia.[7] Both representatives of NGOs and officials in Zambia and Tanzania have discussed at length the increasing competition between locals and petty traders from China in outdoor and indoor markets in small and large cities. As Florence Turuka, an official with the Ministry of Trade in Tanzania bluntly stated, 'Then there are the small traders who are opening shops. We want them to come in on a bigger scale in terms of investment than this petty trading. I do not know if the Chinese government cares, perhaps it reduces tension back home? But for us this creates concern.'[8]

There is, however, some evidence that suggests that the Chinese government is sensitive to how it is perceived and judged by ordinary Africans. Xu Weizhong, of the Foreign Ministry's think tank, CICIR, for example, argues that China faces three big challenges in transforming Sino-African relations. First, elite diplomacy must expand into mass diplomacy. Second, official diplomacy must expand into popular diplomacy. Third, bilateral diplomacy must expand into multilateral diplomacy (Xu, 2007, p. 320). Another Chinese Africanist, Liu Hongwu, of the Chinese Academy of Social Sciences, wants to cool down the euphoria and exuberance that followed in the wake of the Sino-African summit in November 2006:

> The nature and content of Sino-African relations now turn into a new form of relationship; from politics to economy. It will give rise to the wholesale expansion and advancement of the contents, forms, and scope of bilateral relations. It must be said that the process of this new form of bilateral relations between China and Africa, now emerging, has just got started. Therefore, it is also too early to predict how the new characteristics it possesses may in reality produce complexities impacting both sides. The fact is that the contemporary understanding and knowledge of one another, is in general rather sweeping or on the surface. (Liu, 2007, p. 13)

Also sobering was a recent report from an academic conference in Beijing, where it was reported that both the central government and Chinese companies investing overseas should 'appropriately handle emerging problems in Sino-African cooperation, like trade frictions etcetera'. It is, however, almost impossible for the Chinese Ministry of Foreign Affairs to exercise any monitoring of the thousands of Chinese companies and entrepreneurs operating on African soil (Gill et al., 2006, p. 12). In line with Xu Weizhong's call for a Chinese diplomacy that targets ordinary Africans, too, through popular diplomacy, the participants in a conference on Sino-African relations also judged it necessary to intensify the level of publicity work in Africa, in order to strengthen the exchange and contacts between the peoples of China and Africa (Zhan, 2006).

The issue of conditionality of aid, based on the so-called Washington consensus, is tested against China's emerging role as a major donor and financial investor linked to what has been termed the 'Beijing Consensus' (Ramos, 2004). Irrespective of ideological positions, it has been conventional wisdom to regard Beijing's aid model of 'no strings attached', as expressed in the government's policy paper 'China's African Policy',[9] as a way to exert pressure on European governments, the World Bank and the International Monetary Fund (IMF) to lower their tough conditions and standards and instead find more acceptable international standards that the whole world can unite around, even if not necessarily acceptable to Western liberal democratic countries. As a matter of fact, Chinese aid projects have been competing with the World Bank in a number of countries. In Angola, the Chinese utterly defeated the bank on a large aid package (Naim, 2007). Florence Turuka outlined the difference with China in the following words: 'with the World Bank, it takes ages to agree on anything. The bank has its priorities and it is not a straightforward thing.' When African elites describe the bank's working practices in this way, it is no wonder that the new Director of the World Bank, Robert Zoellick, strives hard to have joint discussions with China about how to find ways to cooperate on the African continent. In the West, there is a growing awareness that cooperation between Western and Chinese donor organisations is crucial to avoid competition that may be less than beneficial for long-term African interests. The EU has started to engage China in joint aid talks. At the time of writing, however, few discussions on this topic have been held between China and Western countries (Tjönneland et al., 2006, p. 11). Chinese development analysts such as Xu Weizhong are aware of Western nations' concern and nervousness. He argues, not without dry satisfaction, that while having to acknowledge that China is more popular than the West, they are jealous of the results obtained through Sino-African cooperation: 'They hope to strengthen co-operation with China on African issues and hope that by way of cooperating, China will join the Western track and have China play by Western rules, and share its costs in African affairs' (Xu, 2007).

Other analysts like Zhang Changlong echo the Chinese government's position on the World Bank, that is, not to interfere in the affairs of other countries. He argues that China must 'constrain the politicization of the World Bank Group' (2007, p. 32). In effect this means opposition to the notion of conditionality baked into aid programmes. This position, however, does not amount to Chinese fears of democratisation, as is argued by Paul Collier and others concerned about how the voting behaviour of the PRC in the UN Security Council obstructs development (2007, p. 186). It is first and foremost on the issue of territorial integrity that Chinese leaders are anxious not to set any precedents that may have implications for the People's Republic's ultimate goal of unification with Taiwan. There is, however, evident risks that friction rather than harmonisation between Western and Chinese views on development in Africa will grow. Chinese policy-makers are perturbed by the demands and complaints directed against them from Western governments, while at the same time – as reflected by the quotation above – they feel that they currently have the upper hand. In articles and at conferences, researchers and experts have for some time also been occupied with 'refuting the false theory of China engaging in neo-colonialism in Africa', something they are at pains to describe as being stirred up by Western countries (Zhan, 2006).

'Effective governance' and democracy

As the OECD has argued in a report, the rise of both India and China presents both risks and opportunities for African countries. The hunger for oil and minerals presents short-term opportunities, while there are serious long-term risks related to weak governance standards which may lead to failure to invest in other non-traditional sectors, as there is a growing trade dependency on China and India in Africa (OECD, 2006).[10] The risk of a deterioration of good governance and less respect for human rights, including workers' rights, due to the government's wish to have Chinese investors flocking in was brought up by several of my interviewees from NGOs in Zambia.[11] Therefore Deborah Brautigam is probably incorrect in saying scholars should move away from viewing ODA as an extension of foreign policy (1998, p. 3). In China's case, at least, increasing dependence on overseas natural resources makes the boundaries between trade, aid policy and diplomacy hard to disentangle. According to the Chinese development scholar Xu Weizhong, the strategic interest of China in Africa rests on these three pillars: (1) political interest, as a rising China needs the support from African nations; (2) economic interest, as China's need for energy resources and foreign markets increase and (3) the need for reunification of the motherland, as Africa can contribute to containing Taiwanese independence (Xu, 2007, p. 318). In a similar vein, Japan attempted to increase its influence over Africa in the 1980s instrumentally, driven by the hunt for natural resources. Tokyo was also motivated by economic interests, but especially in the case of Africa, this resource and energy rationale was supported by the use of foreign aid for a key diplomatic motive, laying the foundation for a permanent seat on the UN Security Council. It is quite likely that Asian overseas investment and aid will transform development patterns and loyalties in sub-Saharan Africa, and in turn the West will be impacted. A notable example is when Chinese scholars argue that there is a need to strike a balance between democratic politics and the politics of stability. If you have too much of either ingredient, they say, in the given cultural and socio-economic context, it may invite instability. Democratic disarray and political instability make a state of affairs that in the Chinese mind-set amounts to the same as negative GDP growth. He Wenping for example argues that:

It looks as if 'democracy' not at all is the miracle drug for every conceivable disease, and if applied it takes effect. Having 'democracy' does not automatically mean there is political development. One can definitely not easily equal 'democracy' with political development. Only a democracy that accounts for both order, i.e. social stability and rule by law, and effectiveness, i.e. economic development, can forcefully push for political development. (He, 2005)

While by no means writing off the merits of democracy or democratisation, she wants us to assess critically the merits of promoting democracy in all places and at any time. She brings up South Africa, Namibia, Botswana, Mauritius, Mali, Mozambique, Senegal and Ghana as countries that have acquired the right balance between democracy and stability, and thus shown how democratisation should sometimes be expanded in order to get the appropriate level of efficiency to promote development. Especially important are the establishment of the rule of law, expansion of popular participation in politics, a growing rights consciousness and the supervision of ruling parties by public opinion. But nonetheless, He Wenping also sees the need to temper democratic ambitions in unfavourable contexts. She observes that democracy has in some countries sped up and revived age-old African tribalism or local nationalism and thus proclaims that when 'democracy' cannot coordinate the relationship between effectiveness (economic development) and order (social stability and the rule of law) well, reversal and setbacks in the democratisation process can't be avoided. With a technocrat's glasses she views the contemporary African situation: 'Even if the logic of development means that nation-building and economic construction must be carried out in advance, yet third world countries too, at the same time, confront the strong wish and demands of people to participate in politics and economic distribution' (He, 2005, p. 279).

Interestingly, she's a realist in so far as brakes can rarely be applied to the development of democratic popular process in today's world. The technocratic logic of China's top leaders, however, does not play out well in smaller nations with a different colonial experience and political culture to China. And she holds that even if it is difficult, Africa must go forward while negotiating between a plethora of different demands from both domestic and international scenes. To He this means that African nations can neither use tradition as an excuse for hindering political development, nor can they reject tradition wholesale in replacing it with Western culture without considering the alternatives. This is where China presents a viable model to consider, perhaps to absorb some valuable experiences and digest them. She advocates that African countries should learn from 'advanced modern Eastern and Western political culture', in order to create a brand new African political culture.

China as an alternative development model

Should China perhaps be viewed as a golden opportunity for Africa to become a more developed part of the global economy, or even as a new model for development? Representatives of NGOs in Zambia and Tanzania take a more sober, sometimes cynical, approach to this issue: 'I think that only having one superpower is bad. The United States is a devil, but we can do with another devil! This would do well to balance off the United States.'[12] Thus, Hebron Mwakagenda executive director of the Leadership Forum in Tanzania responded to my question if China should be regarded as developmental model for Tanzanians to emulate.

Apparently, and to some extent contradicting arguments in the Western mass media that African state officials and officialdom believe China is a 'gigantic good' offsetting the 'evil' conditionalities imposed by Western financial institutions and ODA, this attitude is also shared by at least some government officials: 'We do not see China as a model as such – to copy. We can learn some things from their development, but we cannot copy. First, they have a different line of command; from the top down. They have only one party.'[13] This view is echoed by other of my interviewees people like Yusuf Dodia, who has adopted a pragmatic yet sceptical approach to Chinese aid and trade. When interviewed Dodia described Zambia as having gone through its own transition from a socialist economy to a market economy, but he was sure that China was no economic, cultural or political model to follow for Zambia.

The American law scholar Randy Peerenboom also discusses this issue and the view of China as a possible paradigm for developing states. He argues, although rather incorrectly I believe, that: 'China has attempted to persuade other countries to follow its lead' (2007, p. 9).[14] Peerenboom does not give any clue as to which Chinese leader tried to convince a particular foreign leader that China's route to development is the correct one. China's leaders are careful not to promote their views on development too hard, but Chinese scholars' views on these matters reflect deliberations among the foreign policy elite. The Africanist Li Zhibiao, for example, has argued for caution on the part of African development specialists and leaders: 'If African nations really want to study and learn from the Chinese experience, firstly, they must thoroughly understand the differences between their national situation and China's. Secondly, they must in earnest research the complete contents of China's and even other countries developmental experience.'

This is a far cry from telling people that your model of success is a 'one size fits all' solution to be emulated everywhere. Another Chinese Africanist, Liu Hongwu, is of a similar opinion when he observes how some view China as the new saviour that will reduce Africa's poverty, which he believes to be as ridiculous as when people in the past regarded the West as Africa's saviour (Liu, 2007, p. 12). The same argument is also heard from China's government agencies. The Chinese government's State Council Leading Group Office of Poverty Alleviation and Development, for example, has, like China's Africa watchers also stressed the importance of formulating policies that are context specific, as opposed to a fixed model. As the factors causing poverty vary, different approaches are needed in different regions in China. Gradual reform is also seen as key, to introduce pilot projects on a small scale to test different development ideas on a local level (Davies, 2007, p. 34). This, together with a multidimensional approach to poverty reduction, with a focus on capacity-building of farmers and a long-term focus where growth is coupled with poverty reduction, were said to be key lessons. Likewise, Li Zhibiao admonishes African nations that they must consider their own situation and not copy mechanically from others. While Li does not want to paint an overly rosy picture of the results brought by the post-Mao economic reforms, he still believes there are few pillars of wisdom in the Chinese reform experience that Africa can study. First, he argues that it is important to undertake gradual economic reform in order to avoid the outbreak of severe unrest. Second, he believes an opening up to the outside world is necessary as the Chinese reforms were carried out against the background of rapidly developing globalisation. Without opening up China could not have made use of foreign direct investment. Therefore Peerenboom is right, on the other hand, when he argues that China's developmental path does not provide a detailed blueprint to be followed slavishly by other developing nations (2007, p. 21). Rather than buying wholesale into advice from the World Bank and IMF, China has adapted basic economic principles according to its own circumstances and perceived needs. The question now is if China will continue to reduce poverty on a global scale by actively engaging in other Third World countries, through investing, becoming an important donor of foreign aid and giving loans at favourable terms. Numerous developing countries, both authoritarian and democratic, look to China and invite experts from there to lecture on law, economics and politics (ibid., p. 9).

The problem for African countries may be that they look to China as a wholesale model to follow, which may be bad for several reasons. There are many Chinese who caution against this. Is there one 'Chinese model' they ask. As argued by Li Zhibiao:

> Apart from the setting up of special economic zones, ever since the start of the reforms, there has been a surge in many local develop- ment models: rather successful ones have been 'the Suzhou model,' 'the Wenzhou model,' and the Dongguan model,' and different models have different characteristics. The Suzhou model is an eco- nomic development model led by the government. The Wenzhou model is an economic development model guided by the market; the Dongguan model on the other hand, is a model making use of for- eign investment to develop the manufacturing industry. (Li, 2007)

This is also what Randall Peerenboom judges to be the most impor- tant lesson for other countries looking to China as a model. He argues that one of the keys to China's success story has been the willingness to experiment and then to evaluate the results free of economic, nor- mative, or political dogma' (Peerenboom, 2007, p. 290). Following the same line of thought we find He Wenping, who argues that there are many successful cases of rapid development of economies and society in the world besides China. To her, all these are valuable for African countries to study (2005). Thus, at a time when many are contrasting how much Western aid is following the Washington consensus and principles of good governance to an emerging Beijing consensus, usu- ally referring to market reforms without democracy and an emphasis on self-determination and sovereignty, it is useful to refer to sociologist Huang Ping. Huang, an editor of China's most famous intellectual jour- nal *Dushu*, has argued that there is no such thing as a 'Beijing consen- sus', or a 'Beijing model', as there is actually not much of consensus of anything in Beijing (2006, p. 55).

Chinese and African views on corruption and conditionality

During the much-highlighted FOCAC meeting between 48 African heads of state and China's leaders in Beijing in November 2006, the PRC promised to increase its ODA to Africa. China was to sign debt relief agreements with 33 African countries by the end of 2007. Beijing also stated it was to double aid and interest-free loans, and that preferential loans worth US$3 billion would also be provided to develop infrastructure. According to a Chinese official within the Ministry of Commerce, all of the new aid packages destined for African countries were offered selflessly and there 'were no political strings attached nor interference in internal affairs'.[15]

Some pundits are dead certain that China is not prepared to support civil liberties and rights in Africa beyond those it provides to its own citizens. They argue that 'China is exporting some of its most dysfunctional domestic practices, including corruption, bad lending, disregard for labor rights and poor environmental standards' (Klein-Ahlbrandt and Small, 2007). Other scholars are less sure, although they correctly observe that accountability and transparency are definitely not 'core values' in Sino-African cooperation (Melber, 2007, p. 9). Some researchers even point out the exact opposite – that Chinese experts are invited to developing countries to lecture on China's experience, and that PRC government officials even lecture fellow Third World nations on how to combat corruption and strive for good governance (Peerenboom, 2007). Contrary to most Western observers, Chinese analysts do not necessarily view the prevalence of endemic corrupt practices as an inherent problem of autocratic politics. The scholar He Wenping at the Chinese Academy of Social Sciences (CASS) argues that there are many power holders who 'utilize the loophole of having democracy but not rule by law' making it possible for them to engage in large-scale graft and practise corruption (He, 2005).

One thing is evident, though; the Chinese aid specialists are definitely concerned with how Chinese money is spent. They certainly don't see squandering of their resources as unproblematic. At least in this regard, although definitely not in other aspects, their focus on 'effective governance' is bound soon to amount to pretty much the same as the anti-corruption principle of good governance. The methods and contents of the aid packages are still different of course and do not come without different socio-political implications, not least when it comes to the issue of human rights. According to Chinese officials within the Ministry of Commerce, the fact that China does not give aid in cash but in kind means that there is less risk of corruption (Davies, 2007, p. 64). Although this method of avoiding corruption may be feasible for some time and in some places, when Chinese labour is also included in the package, it may create equally strong sentiments and reactions in African labour markets and civil society (Polgreen and French, 2007). Moreover, the Chinese insistence on building shiny new infrastructure with its own materials and manpower, in return for the output from the drilling of oil and digging of precious minerals, may indeed prove a bad recipe. In order to develop domestic African industries, not just tending toward income and support by Indian and Chinese companies and government agencies, a more proactive strategy is needed by African governments.

The problem for China in Africa may be that the Chinese underestimate many of the latent potential conflicts and security threats as well as the defects of the various political systems on the continent and thus may find themselves involved on a scale and depth they did not at first anticipate. They have no strategy to tackle corruption problems resulting from a lack of transparency, and this may become a bigger problem as the volume of ODA grows (Gill et al., 2006, p. 11). As a matter of fact, many representatives of civil society organisations in, for example, Zambia and Tanzania are very concerned about deals being made by their governments and China behind closed doors. As argued by the Zambian development consultant Stephen Muyakwa: 'The main problem really is transparency as the deals are not open to scrutiny. They are signed with the government, and we have serious problems with corruption. You know, how can we know if Chinese aid is not pickpocketed by officials?'[16]

Muyakwa's argument and irritation about deals made in the dark are shared by an overwhelming majority of the persons I interviewed during fieldwork in Zambia and Tanzania in July 2008. This goes to show that China's 'effective governance' may turn into 'bad governance' because of neglect of corruption and embezzlement, and this is perhaps the greatest lacuna in current Chinese aid policy and developmental strategy for Africa. Nevertheless, this is still an open-ended story. If the Chinese really learn how to deal with African realities better than the European colonial powers did, and the US and the Soviets later did during the Cold War, there may be some potential for China to contribute to global equity through becoming a solid partner in taking the industrial revolution to African nations, too.

'Aid with Chinese characteristics', or rather, the Chinese perspective on development assistance cannot be viewed in isolation, as aid is integrated with other components. China's engagement with Africa should instead be viewed as part of a matrix in which aid, social stability and government-to-government cooperation guides the course that bilateral relations with developing nations should take. Therefore, it comes as no surprise that China in its aid programmes in Africa works closely with traditional state actors and agencies. This, however, is likely to become a problem of increasing magnitude for the Chinese government. Reactions in the Chinese media and among ordinary citizens to kidnappings in Nigeria in 2007 and 2008 and the killing of Chinese oil workers with the state-owned company China Petroleum and Chemical Corporation in Ethiopia in April 2007 were characterised by outrage. The Chinese engagement in Sudan is another case that seriously impacts on Chinese policy-makers concerned with 'distortion' of China's image in 'the court of global public opinion'. Actress Mia Farrow's warning that the Beijing Olympics would perhaps be remembered by future generations as 'the genocide Olympics' (Farrow, 2007), was definitely contrary to image the government wanted to project to the world in the run-up to the games. These and other cases illustrate how China, with its ever-increasing integration in global economic value and resource chains, is now drawn into largely unanticipated debates and conflicts. Because of the rise of public opinion on China's Internet and alternative channels of information, Chinese citizens have already been discussing the pace of domestic political reform and the nature of China's overseas engagement and bilateral relations (Lagerkvist, 2005). Questions that 'netizens' have been asking one another include what is needed to prevent the loss of Chinese lives in conflict-ridden and war-prone areas of the world, and what measures China should take in order to prevent casualties when drilling for oil in, say, Congo, Sudan or Nigeria. It is plausible to anticipate that with an increasing global presence and the concomitant demands of using its great power responsibly, domestic debates will begin to deal with issues such as China needing to project its power abroad, perhaps even including breaking away from its long-standing emphasis and arch-conservative conception of sovereignty and territorial integrity (Zhang, 2006).

Concluding remarks

As referred to at the beginning of this chapter, prime minister Wen Jiabao's solemn words about the rights of countries to 'independently choose their own development path' show that Beijing now, in the light of its own reform experience, acknowledges *and* advocates that indigenous contexts should determine what developmental model to choose. This is actually a change if compared to the period preceding the 1978 economic reforms, when Chinese aid workers self-assuredly propagated their (already failing) model of planned economy. Today, rather ironically in the light of poverty reduction unprecedented in the history of mankind, they are unwilling to force-feed their experiences of 'a market economy with Chinese characteristics' to other nations. Chinese ODA to Africa has moved from being ideologically motivated to being driven by economic concerns.

It is quite likely that Asian overseas investment and aid will transform development patterns and loyalties in sub-Saharan Africa, and in turn the West will be impacted. Apart from that of not accepting diplomatic ties or cooperation with Taiwan, China's policy of attaching no significant strings or conditions to its ODA, and not interfering with domestic policies, does challenge the Western ideals and policies aimed at promoting democratisation and good governance. However, the Western mass media and research based on secondary sources have hitherto simplistically described Chinese ODA, natural resource extraction and investment in Africa as being an assault on national economies, stifling civil society and supporting only dictators. The Africans are viewed as passive and/or ignorant about the menace originating in the East.

The only way to really find out what is going on is to listen to the African and Chinese voices and writings on this subject matter. As shown in this chapter, African views of Chinese trade and aid are very sober. Although they are quite optimistic about China's increasing role, they do not picture China as a golden model of effective governance and they hold no illusions that China will become the saviour of a continent lagging behind all the others economically. This is also true for the more positive views of Chinese investments held by government officials. Likewise, Chinese analysts are sober and careful not to paint China's investment and ODA as panaceas quickly speeding up human development in Africa. This is not to say that there are no differences between Chinese and Western aid. There are. This is clear when Chinese scholars argue that there is a need to strike a balance between democratic politics and the politics of stability. If you have too much of either ingredient, they say, in the given cultural and socio-economic context, it may invite instability. Nonetheless, as shown in this chapter, China's Africa watchers are on the whole a cautious cohort, and do not want to project any false hopes into bilateral relationships with African countries. This is a sharp turn from the earlier phase of Chinese development assistance in the 1960s and 1970s when 'emissaries of socialism' went to Africa convinced that China's solutions would also fit African problems.

Today we also hear quite often how Chinese officials in general are more interested in learning from other donors with a longer experience of providing aid. The view is that China is a newcomer and has a lot to learn (Davies, 2007). This open-minded attitude among Chinese officials is derived from newfound confidence in China's role in globalisation processes (Lagerkvist, 2006). This willingness to learn from the outside world extends to other sectors of Chinese society and the business world today, including the policy elite that coordinates and designs foreign aid programmes. This may bode well for the harmonisation of various views on aid and developmental models. Needless to say, it is not going to be easy to align the national interests of developed democracies as the US and the EU countries on the one hand, and on the other a developing democracy like India and authoritarian ruled China. Nevertheless, the outset could be much worse, and there is as yet hardly any sign of a clash between democracies and autocracies on African soil. We are now witnessing more competition, but that is not necessarily bad. Although it does not come without economic and political risks for both China and African states, there is reason to be positive about China's increased role and higher profile in Africa. For one thing, Africa is no longer in the shadow of the global media focus. The spotlight is on Africa – which is good. An Africa forgotten and forsaken, outside the attention and global trade flows, is what Africans and the rest of the world should worry about.

Notes

1. Full text of Chinese Premier Wen Jiabao's speech at the UN High-Level Meeting on the Millennium Development Goals, http://english.peopledaily.com.cn/90001/90776/90883/6507164.html, last accessed 29 October 2008.
2. For this chapter I have examined articles in the Chinese scientific journal *Xiya Feizhou* (Journal of West Asian and African Studies) from between 2004 and 2007, and the limited academic literature that exists in Chinese on African studies.
3. A recent exception is the report by Penny Davies (2007).
4. Interview in Lusaka, 23 July 2008.
5. Interview in Lusaka, 23 July 2008.
6. Interview in Lusaka, 24 July 2008.
7. See remarks made by South Africa's former president, Thabo Mbeki: China Faces Charges of Colonialism in Africa. *International Herald Tribune*, 28 January 2007, http://iht.com/articles/2007/01/28/news/sudan.php, last accessed 21 October 2007. Mbeki's real apprehension was also relayed to the author in an interview with South Africa's Ambassador to Sweden, June 2007 in Stockholm.
8. Interview in Dar-es Salaam, 28 July 2008.
9. See Ministry of Foreign Affairs (2006).
10. OECD (2006).
11. Interviews with representatives M. Mwila, L. Habasonda, M. Sitali and M. Dominique, in Lusaka, 22–25 July 2008.
12. Interview in Dar-es Salaam, 25 July 2008.
13. Interview in Dar-es Salaam, 28 July 2008.

14. See my arguments that Chinese leaders have neither the will, nor the capacity, to market a distinctly Chinese model to the world in Lagerkvist, J. (2008). What China does, however, is to defend its own developmental strategy against perceived attacks from the Western world; see *China Daily* (2008).
15. See China to Fulfill Its Sino-African Forum Pledges, 29 February 2007.
16. Interview in Lusaka, 23 July 2008.

References

Alden, Chris (2007). *China in Africa*. London: Zed Books.
Brautigam, D. (1998). *Chinese Aid and African Development: Exporting Green Revolution*. Ipswich: Macmillan.
China Daily (2008). Games Proves Validity of the China Model. Available at: http://www.chinadaily.com.cn/opinion/2008–09/23/content_7049796.htm (accessed 31 October 2008).
China to Fulfill Its Sino-African Forum Pledges. Available at: www.chinaview.cn (accessed 29 February 2007).
Collier, P. (2007). *The Bottom Billion*. Oxford: Oxford University Press.
Davies, P. (2007). *China and the End of Poverty in Africa: Towards Mutual Benefit?* Sundbyberg: Diakonia.
Farrow, M. (2007). China Can Do More on Darfur. *The Wall Street Journal*, 5 October.
Gill, B., C. Huang, and J. S. Morrison (2006). China's Expanding Role in Africa: Implications for the United States. A Report of the CSIS Delegation to China on China-Africa-U.S. Relations November 28–December 1. *CSIS Report*.
He, W. (2005). Jielun: zai minzhu biange zhong tuijin feizhou de zhengzhi fazhan (Conclusion: Promoting Political Development through Democratic Change in Africa) in *Feizhou guojia. Minzhuhua jincheng yanjiu* (Research on the Democratic Progress of African Countries), Beijing: Shishi chubanshe (Current Affairs Publishing), pp. 375–84.
Huang Ping (2006). '"Beijing gongshi" haishi "Zhongguo jingyan",' ('"Beijing Consensus", or "Chinese Experiences", or what?') in *Quanqiuhua: shehui fazhan yu shehui gongzheng (Globalization: Social Development and Social Justice)*, Beijing: Social Sciences Academic Press.
International Herald Tribune (28 January 2007). China Faces Charges of Colonialism in Africa. Available at: http://iht.com/articles/2007/01/28/news/sudan.php (accessed 21 October 2007).
Kleine-Ahlbrandt, S. and A. Small (2007). China Jumps In. *International Herald Tribune*, 1 February. Available at: http://www.iht.com/bin/print.php?id=4431580.
Kurlantzick, J. (2007). *Charm Offensive*. Binghampton: Caravan Books.
Lagerkvist, J. (2005). The Rise of Online Public Opinion in the PRC. *China: An International Journal*. vol. 3, no. 1, March 2005, pp. 119–30.
Lagerkvist, J. (ed.) (2006). Introduction, in special issue on 'Chinese Perceptions of globalization'. *Contemporary Chinese Thought*, 37, no. 4.
Lagerkvist, J. (2008). The Limits of the China Model, *Glasshouse Forum*, p. 9. Available at: www.glasshouseforum.org (accessed 31 October 2008).
Li, Z. (2007). Feizhou guojia ruhe jiejian zhongguo de fazhan jingyan, (How should African Nations Draw Lessons from China's Development Experience). *Xiya feizhou*, (West Asia and Africa), no. 4, pp. 49–55.

Liu, H. (2007). Zhongfei jiaowang: wenmingshi zhi yiyi, (Sino-African Exchanges: The Importance of the History of Civilizations). *Xiya feizhou, (West Asia and Africa)*, no. 1, pp. 11–15.

McLeary, P. (2007). A Different Kind of Great Game. *Foreign Policy*, March. Available at: http://www.foreignpolicy.com/story/cms.php?story_id=3744&print=1.

Melber, H. (2007). The (not so) New Kid on the Block: China and the Scramble for Africa's Resources, in *China in Africa*, Henning Melber, Margaret C. Lee and Sanusha Naidu (eds), Current African Issues, no. 35.

Ministry of Foreign Affairs (January 2006). China's African Policy. Available at: http://www.fmprc.gov.cn/eng/zxxx/t230615.htm (accessed 14 November 2007).

Minzhuhua jincheng yanjiu (Research on the Democratic Progress of African countries) (2005). Bejing: Shishi chubanshe (Current Affairs Publishing), pp. 375–84.

Naim, M. (2007). Help Not Wanted. *The New York Times*, 15 February.

OECD (2006). *The Rise of China and India: What's in It for Africa?* OECD, Development Centre Studies.

Peerenboom, R. (2007). *China Modernizes: Threat to the West or Model for the Rest?* Oxford: Oxford University Press.

Polgreen, L. and H. French (2007). In Africa, China Is Both Benefactor and Competitor. *The New York Times*, 20 August.

Ramos, J. C. (2004). *The Beijing Consensus*. London: Foreign Policy Centre.

Taylor, I. (2006). China's Oil Diplomacy in Africa. *International Affairs*, 82, no. 5, pp. 937–59.

Tjönneland, E. N., B. Brandtzaeg, Å. Kolås, G. le Pere (2006). China in Africa: Implications for Norwegian and Development Policies. *CMI Report*, 2006, p. 15.

UN (2006). *Millennium Project Report*. Available at: http://www.unmillenniumproject.org/reports/fullreport.htm (accessed 12 Feb 2010).

Xu, W. (2007). Cong zhong-fei hezuo luntan Beijing fenghui kan zhongfei guanxi de fazhan (Viewing the Development of Sino-African Relations in the Light of the Sino-African Co-operation Summit Meeting), in *Shijie fazhan zhuangkuan, 2007, guowuyuan fazhan yanjiu zhongxin shijie fazhan yanjiusuo bian* (The State of World Development, 2007, Edited by the State Council's World Development Institute), pp. 313–21. Beijing: Shishi chubanshe.

Zhan, S. (2006). 'dangqian zhongfeiguanxi mingan wenti' yantaohui zhaokai, (Convening a Conference on 'Sensitive Issues in Contemporary Sino-African Relations'), *Xiya feizhou*, no. 9, pp. 67–8.

Zhang, C. (2007). Lun shijie yinhang jituan zhili jiegou de gaige (Discussing Reforms of the Administrative Structure of the World Bank Group), *Guoji guanxi (International Review)* 6, pp. 27–33.

Zhang, W. (2006). China's National Interests in the Course of Globalization, in the special issue on 'Chinese Perceptions of Globalization'. *Contemporary Chinese Thought* 37, no. 4, summer.

8

Chinese Foreign Aid: The Tale of a Silent Enterprise

Yahia Mohamed Mahmoud

Introduction

Much of what had been written on China's foreign assistance in Western academia and mass media before the 1990s focused on the politico-ideological dimensions of this assistance and on China's aspirations to the leadership of the Third World (e.g., Hutchison, 1976; Larkin, 1971; Lin, 1989). In contrast, since the late 1990s, the focus has shifted towards China's geo-strategic move into Africa in order to guarantee access to natural resources, especially oil, for its expanding economy, and how this might be a threat to Western interests in the continent (e.g., Jiang, 2004). No matter how accurate and relevant these views are, they represent an obstacle to a nuanced understanding of the width and the depth of this engagement. Besides simplifying the nature of this enterprise, these views belittle and ignore other interesting dimensions of this assistance, such as its variation and impacts at different levels. Of special significance is the diversity of the Chinese assistance package, which involves political solidarity, development assistance, trade relations, foreign direct investment (FDI) and, to some degree, technological transfer.

Nevertheless, some efforts have been made to map and evaluate local effects of China's assistance to Africa (see Bartke 1975, 1989; Brautigam, 1998; Copper, 1976; Mahmoud, 2007). These authors underline issues that might help us to develop and adapt new schemes for future foreign assistance. It is important to note though that China's foreign assistance is far from being a full success story. China's aid has at times 'succeeded in fostering economic development to the extent that it can be seen as a model. Yet Peking has also met some disastrous and embarrassing failures' (Copper, 1976, p. 115). Just like its Western counterparts,

China's international assistance is plagued with many failures, but both its successes and failures are slightly different from those that characterise Western aid and it is exactly this that makes it a relevant subject to study.

This chapter is an attempt to map and shed light on some of the effects of China's assistance to Africa. It draws largely on Mahmoud (2007) and it uses three categories of qualitative interviews carried out between 2002 and 2006. The first of these were made with Chinese, African and European scholars, the second with Chinese and African civil servants and technicians involved in Sino-African cooperation and the third with African households affected by Chinese development assistance. Besides the interviews, sources that range from agreements to technical reports have been used.

Based on the analysis of these materials we discerned and explored what we tentatively called the three pillars of China's foreign assistance: continuity, diversity and unity.

The issue of continuity is reflected not only at the politico-diplomatic levels in which China has a persistent strategy, but also at local levels where different kinds of projects have been developed. Many critics of Western foreign aid have pointed out that short-term assistance is one of the causes of its failure. In the Chinese case one can observe almost the opposite. Some agricultural projects in West Africa have been developed and assisted by Chinese personnel for more than 30 years.[1]

In matters of diversity, China's technical assistance has reached a wide range of fields that are relevant for economic development. Through the material gathered we find medical assistance, agricultural projects, infrastructure development, educational and cultural cooperation, military assistance and training, scientific cooperation and high technology projects.

Finally, the subject of unity refers to how all this assistance is interrelated and has a common engine for coordination, namely the Chinese state apparatus. In the specific case of the assistance to Africa five ministries have been involved: the Ministry of Foreign Affairs, the Ministry of Foreign Trade and Economic Cooperation (MOFTEC), the Ministry of Health Care, the Ministry of Agriculture and that of Finance.[2] It seems that both centralisation and political continuity have made it possible for China to persist and diversify its assistance in several African countries. In the remainder of this chapter, the second section is a reflection on the evolution of China's foreign aid. The third takes up the two forms that this foreign aid assumes, namely bilateral and multilateral aid. The fourth briefly presents how China's assistance to Africa is perceived with suspicion by some observers. The fifth section focuses on the assistance being made in the field of agricultural development. Finally the sixth and seventh present two case studies, Mauritania and Mali, and the final section ties up the main arguments of this chapter.

An enduring aid strategy: From politics to economics

As mentioned earlier, China's foreign assistance programme started in the 1950s and went through different stages of geographic expansion and diversification. In the early years, a handful of Asian countries and liberation movements in Africa and elsewhere, with more or less clear ideological and political affiliations with China, represented the main bulk of recipients. Several issues, widely discussed by Western scholars, have been central in this initial stage. First, China was deploying efforts to gain diplomatic support in the issue of Taiwan. Second, China was engaged in the endeavour not only to compete and counter the influence of the West, especially the US, but also that of the Soviet Union after 1958 (see Mahmoud, 2007). Third, after the Sino-Soviet split in the late 1950s, Chinese leaders were very fond of the idea of a world divided into three geopolitical spheres. In matters of foreign policy, China did everything possible to ally itself to the Third World, playing a leading role in the Non Aligned Movement and at the level of the UN. All these were undeniably components of the international relations that characterised the Cold War period and can serve as explanatory variables to help to understand the movements of foreign aid. Nevertheless, they were far from being exclusive to China's foreign aid programme. What seem to have characterised China's assistance were pragmatism and persistence:

> There were certain periods when China was thoroughly absorbed by her own problems that she had no time for international involvement. However, it should be noted that the implementation of economic aid on the whole has at no time suffered from the domestic situation, and even during the Cultural Revolution the projects already begun were continued. (Bartke, 1975, p. 18)

Initially China's assistance involved a significant amount of financial donations and loans at low interest rates, but in the 1960s China started offering technical expertise in different fields. Two fields in which China had a millenary tradition and expertise dominated this endeavour, namely agriculture and textiles. From the 1960s on, Chinese engineers and technicians have been involved in the construction of textile mills and a variety of agricultural projects in South and South-east Asia, the Middle East, Africa and the Balkans. By 1972 China had sent over 22,000 technicians abroad (Copper, 1976).

Another important initiative in China's assistance took place in the field of health care. Since 1963 China has been sending medical groups to different developing countries. Bartke (1975) asserts that by the end of 1973, Chinese medical teams had accomplished 70 working years in 13 countries, attended 3 million patients and carried out 20,000 surgical operations. According to the Chinese Ministry of Health, by the end of 2005, China had dispatched more than 15,000 medical doctors to 47 African countries and these had attended about 170 million patients. In 2004, around 950 medical doctors were working in 36 African countries. Moreover, since 2000, China and several African countries have been cooperating in research on, and treatment of, infectious diseases, as well as the training of health care professionals.[3] By the mid-1970s China's aid to Africa was, as Table 8.1 indicates, covering a wide range of fields.

Many of these projects have survived the test of time and are still running today. By 1980, China had given around US$9 billion of aid to more than 70 countries in five continents, which was by far the largest amount given by any non-OPEC developing country (OECD, 1987). Until 1972 the major recipients of Chinese aid were in Asia. However, after the American recognition of the People's Republic of China, this situation changed. The African continent became the main recipient, absorbing almost 50 per cent of all Chinese foreign aid. Between just June 1971 and December 1973 the number of African countries receiving Chinese assistance grew from 13 to 29 (see Bartke, 1975). By June 2000 China had implemented 640 projects in more than 47 African countries in a variety of fields (see Mahmoud, 2007).

During the past 50 years, many economic, political and social-development changes have taken place in China. In matters of foreign policy, the Maoist period was characterised by concentrating the decision-making process in the hands of few leaders. Despite all the openings during Deng Xiaoping's reforms, and the inclusion of a broader elite in the shaping of foreign affairs, the ultimate decision-making stayed highly centralised. Today, the making of foreign policy has become more decentralised and institutionalised (see Medeiros and Fravel, 2003). Still, China's foreign strategy towards Africa has been tainted by some sense of consistency. There are, of course, those who argue that China's involvement in Africa cooled down during the 1980s only to revive in the 1990s after the Tiananmen Square events, as China

Table 8.1   Chinese aid projects in Africa according to branches in the early 1970s

	Completed	Ongoing	Planned
Heavy industry	1		
Mining	2		1
Oil industry	1	1	
Light industry	63	9	28
Textile mills	13	9	15
Broadcasting stations	9		
Buildings	31	4	6
Power stations	7		5
Hydroelectric			
Thermoelectric	2		2
Electrification	3		4
Transport	12	8	4
Roads			
Railway lines	1	91	2
Bridges	11		
Miscellaneous	2		
Medical aid	4	10	
Medical groups			
Hospitals	7	3	
Pharmaceutical plants	3		
Agriculture	16	9	13
Irrigation and water supply	10	4	6
Other projects	6		11
Total	200	61	90

Source: Bartke (1975), p. 204.

needed support from African countries to face the Western critique (see Lin, 1989; Taylor, 1998).

During the 1980s China's foreign assistance did not escape the reforms that were affecting the economic and political strategies of the country. The motto of *mutual-benefit* became suddenly central in the jargon of Sino-African cooperation. The exploration initiated by Chinese state-owned companies and the creation of joint ventures seeking economic profit started reshaping Sino-African cooperation. By the mid-1990s the Chinese cooperation strategy for Africa was acquiring its new structure. From 1995 on, several issues received higher priority:

1. Preferential loans to African enterprises.
2. Promotion of cooperation between Chinese and African companies.

3. Increased participation and project administration by Chinese banks.
4. Combination of governmental efforts with those of enterprises from both sides.

After the first Sino-African forum,[4] the expansion of this new kind of cooperation intensified. For instance, in early 2000 China initiated 46 cooperative projects in 21 African countries through the creation of joint ventures, and by the end of the same year Chinese companies had invested US$660 million in 485 projects (see Ting'en, 2003). Between January and March 2005, Chinese enterprises in Africa won contracts worth US$1.53 billion and achieved a turnover of US$890 million. By the end of March 2005, the accumulated value of labour service contracts by Chinese enterprises in Africa had reached US$34.13 billion with a total turnover of US$23.59 billion and 74,000 Chinese workers were involved in these contracts (see Jianwei, 2005).

The above developments are a consistent part of China's global interactions. Chinese FDI outflows to all continents have grown since 1980 (Table 8.2).

Between 1979 and 2002 Africa occupied the third place in attracting Chinese capital. Much indicates, though, that these patterns have been fluctuating. For instance, between January and November 2004 Latin America received the lion's share attracting 49.3 per cent of China's FDI (see Gottschalk, 2006).

In addition, the more China becomes a part of the global economic system the more its FDI will grow. Chinese firms are acquiring assets abroad

Table 8.2   China's FDI Outflows 1979–2002

Rank	Region	1979–2002	
		Number of projects	Cumulative investment value (US$ millions)
	Total	6960	9340.0
1	Asia	3672	5482.3
2	North America	847	1270.5
3	Africa	585	818.1
4	Latin America	362	658.2
5	Europe	1194	561.1
6	Oceania	300	549.8

Source: Ministry of Commerce of China (2003) *The Almanac of China's Foreign Trade and Economic Cooperation.*

Table 8.3 Chinese enterprises' overseas investments

Why invest overseas? (%)	What is the most attractive factor in host country? (%)	Where is your priority region? (%)
Expanding overseas markets (47.1)	Host country's privileged policies (32.0)	Africa (32.0)
Better profits (16.9)	Requiring relatively small amount of investment (28.7)	South-east Asia (20.0) Latin America (18.0)
Sluggish demand in China (14.5)	Cheap labour (22.5)	Middle East (9.3)
Export to Third Country (12.1)	Cheap land and proximity to raw materials (8.5)	Eastern Europe (8.7) Central Asia (8.0) Others (4.0)

Source: Research Team of MOFTEC's Offshore Plant Project, 'Inward Flow Should be Accompanied by Outward Flow: Policy Analysis of China's Offshore Plant Operations,' *International Trade*, 5 (2000), pp. 9–13 (in Chinese), cited in Mark Yaolin Wang (2002), The Motivations behind China's Government-Initiated Industrial Investment Overseas, *Pacific Affairs* 75, no. 2, pp. 187–206.

to help them to improve their competitiveness. Some of the firms that began their international economic activities in Africa have ended up expanding their business or moving them to other regions.[5] According to the Chinese Ministry of Commerce (2003) among the top 30 recipients of FDI between 1979 and 2002 were 11 developing Asian countries, six African and three Latin American ones. However, the popularity of Africa among Chinese investors seems to be growing (see Table 8.3).

China's economic expansion poses both opportunities for, and pressures on, the international economic system. This does not apply exclusively to developing countries but also to developed ones. However, developing countries will be facing the biggest challenges. First, the pace and growth of the Chinese economy is imposing adjustment strategies on many Third World regions in order for them to keep up with global changes. Second, China's growing involvement in the shaping of global trade rules may give it a central position that many developing countries must take into consideration. Third, China and other Asian actors may represent, from now on, viable alternatives to the hegemony of the US-led Bretton-Woods institutions (see Humphrey and Messner, 2006).

Today, China's cooperation with Africa is both qualitatively and quantitatively different from that of the 1960s, but much of the present collaboration has been possible thanks to the long-term political relationships that China has maintained and developed through the years. Despite its vigorous participation in international organisations, China has relied strongly on its bilateral relations to build and implement its foreign policy. Due to the speed and the extent of international interactions today, China is learning how to deal with many issues through multilateral mechanisms.[6] Consequently a development in China's assistance to Africa is an attempt to find multilateral strategies that complement the bilateral ones.

From bilateralism to multilateralism

Foreign relations in China have a very long tradition, but until recently they have relied on bilateral links. The country's recent economic and political developments, which have widened China's international network of interactions, are forcing vigorous engagement in international organisations. International Relations, for instance, emerged as an autonomous academic discipline as late as the 1980s, but the field has been expanding ever since (see Chan, 1998, 1999; Xinning, 2001). Still, 'Beijing lacks substantial experience in multilateralism – although this is changing in recent years – and also harbors suspicion toward multilateral fora and thus often opts for reliance on bilateralism. China has likely already drawn many positive lessons from its experience in multilateralism' (Glaser, 2001, p. 4).

In the case of Africa, bilateralism was China's leading strategy until the second half of the 1990s. In the early days, China supported several liberation movements and newborn nation states in Africa. The milestone in Sino-African relations was achieved by Zhou Enlai in his visit to ten African countries between 1963 and 1964. Just as important was Jiang Zemin's African tour in 1996, during which he proposed a Five Point programme to develop long-term relationships and cooperation with all African countries. After Jiang's visit, intensive efforts were deployed to create a multilateral platform for Sino-African coordination in economic cooperation, and it was not long before concrete steps were made. The Forum on China-Africa Cooperation (FOCAC) was established in 2000 on the basis of 'equal negotiation, enhancing understanding, increasing consensus, strengthening friendship and promoting cooperation' (FOCAC, 2000). One of the main purposes of the forum was to adapt to and meet the requirements of economic globalisation and seek co-development through negotiation and cooperation. On 10 October of the same year, the forum held its first Ministerial Conference in Beijing. President Jiang Zemin, four African presidents, the Secretary-General of the Organization of African Unity and around 80 foreign ministers and ministers in charge of international economic cooperation affairs from 45 African countries attended, along with representatives of 17 international and regional organisations, heads of NGOs and entrepreneurs (see FOCAC, 2000).

The forum formulated an integral programme for cooperation in economic and social development. The conference defined 19 areas of cooperation ranging from trade, investment and agriculture to health care and debt cancellation. China and several African countries established ministerial commissions to plan and coordinate the implementation of follow-up measures. In the following three years, exchanges intensified at all levels, with more than 30 African leaders visiting China and high Chinese delegations visiting Africa. Dialogue mechanisms were also diversified, leading to regular bilateral interactions between foreign ministries and joint commissions on issues of economy, trade, science and technology.[7] Concerning international and regional affairs, China and several African countries are actively maintaining consultations on how to defend the legal rights and interests of developing countries through negotiation, cooperation and mutual support.[8]

On 15 December 2003, the second Ministerial Conference of FOCAC took place in Addis Ababa. Chinese premier Wen Jiabao, Ethiopian prime minister Meles Zenawi, six African presidents, three vice-presidents, two other prime ministers, the president of a senate, the president of the African Union Commission, and the representative of the UN Secretary-General attended the opening ceremony. More than 70 ministers from China and 44 African countries and representatives of various international and African organisations attended this event. Parallel to this, the first China-Africa Business Conference was held, where over 500 Chinese and African entrepreneurs negotiated and signed 21 cooperation agreements with a total value of US$1 billion. On 4 November 2006, the third conference took place with 48 leaders of African countries present. At the opening ceremony president Hu Jintao pledged that China would double its assistance to Africa by 2009 and announced a package of aid and assistance measures, including US$ 3 billion of preferential loans and US$2 billion of buyer's credit to Africa in the next three years. Priority was given to cooperation in agriculture, infrastructure, industry, fishing, information technology, public health and personnel training. The Chinese government also promised the cancellation of more debt owed by poor African countries. Parallel to this event, the 2nd Conference of Chinese and African Entrepreneurs concluded with 14 agreements signed between 11 Chinese enterprises and African governments and firms worth US$1.9 billion in total.[9]

Besides the creation of new multilateral spaces, such as FOCAC, China is also deploying efforts to expand her engagement with other regions through other international organisations. For instance, on 16 May 2006, during UN Food and Agriculture Organization's regional conference for Asia, the FAO and China forged a strategic alliance to improve food security in developing countries. Around 3000 Chinese experts and technicians would be provided during a six-year period to help improve the productivity of small-scale farmers and fishers. The main objective of this collaboration is to fulfil the goals of FAO's Special Programme for Food Security (SPFS), designed to improve the quality of life in some of the world's poorest nations. Today, more than 100 countries are involved in this programme, which is engaging more than 600 experts and technicians working with rural communities in over 30 countries. In this context, China is a major provider and at the time of writing has already signed agreements with Bangladesh, Ethiopia, Ghana, Mali, Mauritania and Nigeria, as well as with 14 Small Island Developing States under regional programmes.

The above is only the tip of the iceberg of China's expanding role in international affairs. As correctly noted by Kaplinsky (2006), the consequences for developing countries of the rise of new dynamic economies, especially those of China and India, have been widely ignored. Geopolitics claims that many of the historical developments of the last two centuries are tightly related to the rise of demands for commodities, markets and natural resources. The spectacular Chinese economic growth cannot escape these logics, and its need for raw materials, energy and markets is no secret. The official documents of the Sino-Africa cooperation address the issue of exploration, exploitation and development of the oil sector and other minerals.[10] It is highly legitimate, though, to ask if China's involvement in Africa will be any different from that of European colonialism or American neocolonialism. It is also relevant to ask if this development will create new collisions of interests between some Western countries and China on the African continent.

Chinese assistance to Africa: A Janus-faced engagement?

There is a widespread concern, particularly in the West, about China's growing economic and political role in the international arena. This concern is emphasised in the case of Africa. Many Western governments, researchers, non-governmental organisations (NGOs), mass media and actors in the private sector are sending a variety of warnings. These range from reminders of how the West is losing hegemony on the African continent to claims of a new 'yellow peril'. In the past few years, Western papers and scientific journals have been publishing articles on China's presence in Africa with suggestive titles such as: *New scramble for Africa, China's Africa's Safari, Friends or foragers?, Hunger for oil, Fueling the Dragon* and *La Chine à la conquête du continent noir,* to mention but a few.

Several arguments have been central to this concern, but the most frequent ones will be discussed below. The first relates to human rights, as China has been accused of disregarding human rights and legitimacy issues when supporting regimes in Africa, perhaps the most used examples being Zimbabwe and Sudan. Several Chinese companies have also been pointed out for their unkind treatment of employees. The second argument is related to environmental issues, a field in which China is considered still to have low standards (see Economy, 2004). It is argued that China's extensive exploitation of natural resources on the continent could lead to disastrous results. The third argument takes up the asymmetry in Sino-African interchanges. In this context, it is argued that Africa is once again playing its classical role of energy and raw material supplier, something detrimental to Africa. Furthermore, cheap Chinese products, especially textiles, might out-compete the nascent African industries, both in Africa and elsewhere (see Jenkins and Edwards, 2006a; Kaplinsky, 2005; Morris, 2006).[11]

From a distance these arguments might seem a genuine concern on behalf of Africa. Yet, a closer look reveals that what might have passed as concern on the parts of countries such as the UK, France and the US was more possibly a loss of their unchallenged political and economic hegemony. For centuries, these countries have interpreted and shaped African realities. For every historical period of this long domination there was a hegemonic discourse and a 'rationale'. As noted by an African diplomat in China 'the current discourse in the West is, in my view, a normal reaction to a new international situation. China is emerging as a strong economic actor in the international arena and this is a challenge, both economically and politically, for many Western countries'.[12]

Furthermore, the West has never been so engaged with, interested in and open to China as it is in present times. 'While we [Africans] are warned for our interchanges with China, western countries themselves are tightening their economic relations with China and the human rights record doesn't seem to be a hinder to those relations.'[13] Far from it, 'most Western countries, including the US, are developing cordial relations with China and these are marked by intensive economic interchange and mutual respect'.[14] While Chinese direct investment in Africa is still less than a billion dollars, American investment in that Asian country is 15 times higher (see Wilson, 2005). What is more, Sino-Western relations are expanding and diversifying and seem to be entering a phase of maturity. 'Chinese studies in the West, for instance, are booming and the interest in China, Chinese language and culture had never been so trendy among western researchers, students, and even average citizens.'[15]

For years, the West has limited its interchanges with Africa almost exclusively to raw materials. Several of the big oil producers on the continent depended highly on industrialised countries in Western Europe and North America for their exports. As already mentioned, the rise of new economies in the developing world, especially in Asia, is changing this picture. International energy consumption and trade are two fields in which China's growing participation seem to worry some industrialised countries highly.

In 2004 China became the second largest world consumer of petroleum products absorbing some 6.5 million barrels of oil a day. The largest consumer in the world, the US, consumed around 20 million barrels a day in the same year. However, China's oil demand was expected to average 7.4 million barrels per day in 2006. This issue of energy consumption is, in addition to that of international trade, one of the most sensitive topics in Sino-American relations (see Zweig and Jianhai, 2005).

China's growing demand for energy has led the country to diversify its oil supplies and participate actively in exploration for new sources. In the past few years, new partners in Latin America and Africa have become more important to China in this respect. In Africa, countries like Algeria, Angola, Chad, Gabon, Egypt, Equatorial Guinea, Libya, Nigeria and Sudan are among the most important suppliers.

China is playing an active role on the west coast of Africa, where the largest oil producers on the continent are concentrated. Chinese capital has a strong presence in the Nigerian and Angolan oil industries. However, China's engagement is not exclusively limited to traditional oil-producing countries. In several West African countries there are projects of oil exploration led by Chinese companies. For instance, in countries like Mauritania, the China National Petroleum Corporation (CNPC) is drilling the first onshore oil well. Mauritania is bound by four oil agreements with the CNPC. In Mali, the Chinese oil and gas firm Sinopec Corporation has been one of the international companies given exploration rights.[16]

Besides oil, the Chinese economy also demands a variety of minerals. For instance, China has now become the world's largest consumer of copper. In several African countries the Chinese are exploring, exploiting and developing industrial infrastructure in the mining sectors. Zambia, the Democratic Republic of the Congo and Sierra Leone are just a few examples (Menzie et al., 2005).

Simplistic ways of understanding and explaining international relations see the economic rise of China, and other developing countries, as a threat to Western interests in Africa, especially those of the US. However, this threat does not seem to be imminent:

> American interests are not yet seriously threatened. American oil companies still dominate in the offshore technology that is at the heart of West Africa's growing energy production. And the United States still imports substantially from African oil and gas producers, with the market controlled more by international price and demand than by individual country manipulations. But the United States does have to recognize that the United States, and the western nations altogether, cannot consider Africa any more their chasse garde as the French once considered francophone Africa. There is a new strategic framework operating on the continent and it demands new ways of operating. (Lyman, 2005, p. 4)

Accepting and adapting to this new international situation, where novel economic and political actors are emerging as important players, is an actual challenge for a Western world which had expected hegemony after the collapse of the bipolar structure. It is important to acknowledge that the rise of China's economy, equally to that of India and other Asian countries, is changing the strategic and economic possibilities on the African continent. This is not at all dissimilar to the impacts and effects that these economies are having in Latin America for instance (see Lyman, 2005; Wilson, 2005). Nevertheless, 'we need to listen to what the Africans themselves are saying about China's influence in their continent; we are not always as good at listening as we should be' (Wilson, 2005, p. 17).

What a strong Chinese presence in Africa might lead to is not only a concern in the West. Some of the African intellectuals I interviewed are also concerned about a replication of the uneven exchanges that characterise the continent's relation to other regions. A clear pattern of opinions could be discerned in the collected data. For most policy-makers and civil servants, Sino-African relations are perceived positively. A similar view is also found among different workers, technicians and peasants who have participated in Chinese projects. In opposition, there are the views of some scholars, journalists and NGOs' representatives who perceive China as exclusively seeking its own interests. This group points out several issues that are worth mentioning here. First, China's activities in Africa are leaving very little traces of human development as they always employ unqualified labour. Second, in some places, the influx of Chinese migrants might create future problems as they compete with the locals for the few existing economic possibilities.[17] Third, the relationship between China and several African countries is diminishing the possibilities for African countries to integrate into strong regional blocks, in order to strengthen their own position in the global economy and follow international trends.

No matter what the future will bring out of these developments, China is deploying resources in Africa and is doing it in a relatively novel way. This is an opportunity for China to show that engaging Africa in the global economy in a constructive way is not an impossible task. It is also very likely that effective assistance to Africa must be integral and coherent. There are some signs that China is moving in this direction. In the next section we will see some of the issues that characterise this aid strategy.

'Packaging' foreign aid: A shifting approach

Foreign aid has been switching from one strategy to another for a variety of reasons, but perhaps the most important of these are the changing views and political constellations in donor countries. These alterations have made it difficult for donors to have long-term programmes in Africa. In contrast, China's aid strategy has maintained continuity. What is more, this aid has gradually included means that could trigger dynamics in the African economy. Among these we can mention untied aid, debt cancellation, more trade, FDI and human resource development.

In terms of debt cancellation, China has paradoxically been well in advance of other countries, cancelling around RMB10 billion owed by African countries. In December 2003, China offered further debt relief to 31 African countries, as well as opening up the prospect of zero-tariff trade. In 2006 the Chinese government pledged to cancel all the interest-free government loans that matured at the end of 2005 owed by the highly indebted poor countries and the least developed countries in Africa.[18]

In matters of trade the rise is striking. In 1991, trade between China and Africa was only US$1.44 billion but rose dramatically to US$12.389 billion in 2002. For the same year, Chinese imports accounted for US$5.427 billion while its exports were US$6.962 billion. In 2005 the figures reached US$39.7 billion and in the first nine months of 2006 they were US$40.6 billion. During FOCAC 2006, Wen Jiabao proposed the target of US$100 billion by 2010. China is deploying substantial amounts of resources to reach that target. It has, for instance, set up new trade promotion centres in 11 African countries and established special funds to encourage and support Chinese investment in Africa. Following this strategy the Beijing Conference 2006 decided to set up a Sino-African development fund, which will amount to US$5 billion to encourage Chinese companies to invest in Africa and provide them with support. What is more, China is not exclusively engaging state-owned companies in this process. According to figures from the Exim Bank of China, among the 800 Chinese enterprises that invest in Africa, only about 100 are totally state-owned enterprises. Similarly, investment opportunities for African enterprises are being created. Investment in China from countries such as South Africa has increased continuously year by year.[19]

Sino-African cooperation has also made achievements in the development of human resources. Up until 2005 China had offered around 2000 scholarships to African students annually, but in 2006 pledged to double this number by the year 2009. In 2006 there were more than 3900 African professionals studying in China. Besides normal university scholarships, China organises a variety of seminars and training courses for various professionals. According to the Ministry of Commerce more than 11,000 professionals from Africa have received training in China since 2004.[20] In 2004 China hosted 2963 African trainees and in the following year 4887. Among the fields of specialisation were trade, agriculture, forestry, fisheries, health care, telecommunications, education and environmental protection.

China also sends experts, teachers and technicians to African countries in order to train locals in different fields. In 2005 the number of locals trained by the Chinese was approximately 7000. In 2006, China pledged to double that number and train 15,000 African professionals over the next three years. During the same period it is planning to build 30 hospitals and 30 malaria prevention and treatment centres. China also contributes to different kinds of African initiatives and cooperates with several organisations in developing human resources. On 26 July 2006, for instance, China handed over a US$500,000 grant to the Secretariat of the New Partnership for Africa's Development (NEPAD) to support its African Nurses and Midwives Post-Graduate Training Program, which was envisaged to be launched in Tanzania and Kenya.[21]

The issue of agriculture should play a central role in any responsible developmental attempt in Africa. Unfortunately, both the US and Europe had neglected this for a very long time. This is another field in which China is taking initiatives that might challenge the Western aid strategy.

Chinese agricultural assistance in Africa

Since its beginnings, China's aid strategy has put an emphasis on agriculture, and through the years it has signed agreements and developed extensive cooperation in this field. By the end of the 1980s nearly a quarter of China's aid programme was in the field of agriculture. Based on the role that this has played in China's own developmental experience a wide range of agricultural projects, experimental farms and agricultural stations were established in different parts of Africa.

Africa has been the continent that has profited most from China's agricultural assistance. More than 40 African countries have benefited from agro-technological pilot farms and experimental stations built with the help of China. By the early 1990s, of the more than 120 projects, 35 were in the field of rice and 24 were agricultural stations, used to test local conditions and develop the best methods of cultivation. At the time of writing, nearly 200 cooperation programmes have been carried out in this field and 23 projects in the fishing industry. Over the years, China has sent over 10,000 agro-technicians to Africa to train local farmers and provide technical assistance. In the mid-1980s, the Chinese government adopted an active role in mobilising funds and creating policies to encourage and engage more competitive enterprises, including private ones, to invest in Africa and diversify the cooperation. Several Chinese state-owned companies took a leading role in China's new strategy for Africa. Perhaps, the most successful is the China State Farm and Agribusiness Corporation (CSFAC).

Founded in 1980, the CSFAC is one of 120 state-owned large-scale experimental business groups. For over 20 years, the CSFAC has carried out a variety of projects in the fields of agriculture, light industry and trade, both in China and abroad. In the specific case of Africa, the CSFAC has established 11 agricultural projects in nine African countries occupying around 16,000 hectares. These projects produce and process a wide range of agricultural products, predominantly for national markets, but most importantly they provide thousands of jobs.

In West Africa, the CSFAC is operating in Guinea, Togo, Gabon, Ghana, Sierra Leone and Mali to mention but a few. In 1997 it founded the *Société Sino-Guinéenne de Coopération pour le Développement Agricole* (SIGUICODA) in cooperation with the Guinean government. The company developed the Koba Farm and ten minor projects attached to it.

For the past few years, the farm has been producing around 4000 tons of rice per year.[22] In 2003 the CSFAC introduced, in collaboration with the China Hybrid Rice Engineering Research Center, hybrid high-yield rice in Guinea with satisfactory results.[23]

In Togo the Agriculture Development Company Limited located at Mishanto is developing small-scale fish farming and promoting intermediate level poultry and pig farming. The Chinese government is also aiming at developing agricultural technical services and creating trade connections with neighbouring markets. In April 2006 a mission of Chinese experts arrived in Togo to help select new maize varieties and improve the varieties of rice. New resources have also been approved to finance a project for improving and upgrading water management in the Kara and Savannah regions in the northern part of the country (Tribune, 2006). Similarly, in Gabon the Gabon Orient Agriculture Developing Corporation has built a tapioca food factory and it intends to extend and develop Cassava farming and processing. The final goal of the company is to create an integrated business corporation dealing with planting, breeding, processing and trade.[24]

In other parts of the continent the CSFAC has been successful in identifying the most strategic products in which to invest. For instance, in the 1960s Africa's sisal output made up more than 60 per cent of the world total, but by mid 1990s this proportion had dropped to 20 per cent due to inefficient management, increasing competition in the international market and synthetic substitutes. For countries like Tanzania sisal had been an important crop, but by 2000 most local sisal farms had become wasteland (see for instance Sabea, 2001).[25]

In 2000, the CSFAC purchased two abandoned farms whose combined land amounted to 5900 hectares. By June 2002, the two farms were evaluated by the Tanzanian Ministry of Agriculture and Sisal Association as the best-managed sisal farms in Tanzania. The farms became also a stimulus to the local economy and provide around 400 jobs for local residents.[26]

The China-Zambian Friendship Farm near Lusaka is another example of CSFAC expansion in Africa. For years the farm's wheat yield stayed at around 400 kg per mu,[27] one of the highest in Zambia, and by the end of 2002 the farm had made a profit of more than US$1.5 million. Encouraged by this development, the corporation bought a second farm in Zambia for raising chickens, and another for growing vegetables and raising cattle, cows, chickens and fish to be sold in neighbouring cities.

It is perhaps timely to inquire what factors make Chinese commercial operations in Africa possible. Han Xiangshan attributes the CSFAC's success to four main factors. First, there is the support from African governments in the form of preferential policies for expanding the agricultural sector, tax exemption on agricultural machinery and production material imports, as well as tax rebates on fuel for agricultural use. Tanzania, for instance, reduced its annual land rent from 600 to 200 shillings per hectare. The second is Africa's fertile soil, abundant sunshine and rainfall, and the third is China's capability to meet the demands of Africa's agricultural market in terms of technology, management, machinery and equipment. Fourth, and according to Mr Han the most important, is the pre-project market research. Chinese companies are obliged to do thorough research into local markets before engaging in these projects.[28]

Besides its direct commercial interests, China has also been very keen on promoting similar technologies to those that, only 30 years ago, saved the Asian continent from the consequences of grain shortages. The country has been very active in diffusing and assisting hybrid rice production across the whole African continent. In West Africa for instance, Sierra Leone has been one of China's priorities in the region. The Chinese dispatched experts in September 2002 and December 2005 to study the possibility of establishing a technical hybrid rice research and production team in that country. Later on, another team was sent to Sierra Leone's Bo Agricultural Station to improve large-scale production and processing of hybrid rice. Similar efforts are also being deployed in other parts of the continent. In Mozambique, Chinese cooperation is working on increasing rice production from the current 100,000 tons to 500,000 tons. Experts from the China's Hybrid Rice Institute in Hunan have visited the southern part of Mozambique to consider a hybrid rice production project in Chókwe, Gaza province (GRAIN, 2006).

There are broad prospects for Sino-African agricultural cooperation, as Africa possesses abundant agricultural potentials and China the expertise and technology. Between 2006 and 2009 China planned to send 100 senior agricultural experts to Africa, set up ten special agricultural technology demonstration centres in different parts of the continent and build 100 rural schools. China's pragmatic approach resulted in a variety of ways to implement technical assistance.

What makes China's agricultural assistance in Africa interesting is the fact that many of the issues that China has been focusing on in this field are back on the international agenda today. Issues of food security, water management, technological transfer, small-scale farming and rural market development are central in the most recent proposals of institutions such as the World Bank (see World Bank, 2008).

As mentioned earlier, China's cooperation strategy in Africa has been characterised by a long-term relationship with African countries. In the next two sections we will look closely at how China's cooperation with Mauritania and Mali developed. This will be done in a manner that exemplifies the processes of continuity and diversification.

Chinese foreign aid in Mauritania

Mauritania belongs to the group of African countries that at an early stage took a clear stand on the issue of Taiwan and established diplomatic relations with the People's Republic of China on 19 July 1965. Since the establishment of those relations, every Mauritanian president, with one exception, has visited China. In 1967 the two countries signed their first agreement on economic and technical cooperation, which has led to more than 20 agreements and protocols in different fields and a fruitful cooperation.[29] Of the 367 aid projects that China had completed in Africa by 1987, 20 were in Mauritania and, as shown in Table 8.4, only four African countries had benefited more.

China's cooperation with Mauritania has touched almost every field, but until the mid-1980s its most relevant part had been concentrated on infrastructural projects. This is not at all surprising if we take into consideration that until the early 1960s the country's infrastructure was literally non-existent.[30]

In the field of health care three important projects can be mentioned, namely two hospitals and a national health centre with a variety of departments.[31] Several projects in the field of culture and sport have been built by the Chinese, a youth house in 1970, a cultural centre in

Table 8.4 Chinese projects in Africa by the late 1980s

The 5 Biggest African recipients of Chinese aid in terms of projects up until 1987

Country	Number of projects
Tanzania	53
Mali	23
Sierra Leone	22
Guinea	21
Mauritania	20

Source: Adapted from Bartke (1989).

1972 and a football stadium in 1983 with a capacity for 10,000 spectators.[32] Chinese cooperation was also behind several water supply projects and wells in different parts of the country, as well as an electric power station in Nouakchott that benefited thousands of the capital's inhabitants. In the mid-1970s several garment factories were built with the Chinese cooperation.[33] However, the two most crucial infrastructural projects are, in my view, the *Nouakchott Friendship Harbor* and the *M'pourie Experimental Farm*.[34]

Mauritania had, during the colonial period, relied on its sole port of Nouadhibou, located in the north-west part of the country and attached by railway to the iron mines of Zoureat, but with no useful links to the southern, central or eastern parts of the country. For years, several projects to build a port were contemplated but the nature of the coast and the amount of sand did not allow for simple solutions. In 1966 a small port was built close to Nouakchott, but soon was unable to cope with growing traffic.

The Mauritanian government turned to the People's Republic of China in order to build a deep-sea harbour and in October 1974 a cooperation agreement was signed. The preliminary work commenced in 1978 and on 17 September the 1986 the 'Port of Friendship' was inaugurated. The harbour is located 15 kilometres from the capital and can disembark three cargo ships of between 10,000 and 15,000 tons at the same time and handle 500,000 tons of cargo a year.[35]

This project was 'the most ambitious African aid project undertaken by China in Africa since its involvement in the building of the Tanzania-Zambia railway' (Bartke, 1989, p. 90). The project was a technical challenge for China and crucial for Mauritanian economy. 'More than 80 per cent of [the] economic interchanges with the rest of the world would have been for sure uncertain as [Mauritania] would have had to rely on the harbor of Nouadhibou (Porte Autonome) in the northern part of the country or that of Dakar in neighbouring Senegal.'[36]

Among the most important infrastructural projects presently ongoing is the International Airport of Nouakchott. According to the National Bank of Mauritania, on 6 June the 2005 a Chinese loan of US$136 million had been registered for this goal.[37]

Besides these infrastructural projects Mauritania has also benefited from the Chinese medical teams which have been visiting the country since 1968. The Chinese health care workers are appreciated in Mauritania. 'They are very devoted, hardworking and competent. Besides, they bring to us many experiences and practices that differ from ours. For all the years that I worked with the Chinese medical teams I have never had any difficulties in taking them to the most remote places and to the hardest conditions that exist in our desert land. Their motto has always been to serve the needed no matter where they live and the use to say if the needed can't come to us we go where they are.'[38] In 2004 there were 27 health care workers in Mauritania[39] and China was donating medical equipment and medicines on a regular basis.[40]

According to data from the National Bank of Mauritania, China had supported different projects with RMB135 million between March 1995 and January 2002. In addition, according to the same source, China donated US$1.5 million in foreign debt alleviation within that same time frame.[41]

Since 1982, the Chinese government has encouraged its companies to undertake contract projects in Mauritania and in 1984 the bilateral Agreement on Establishing Joint Committee of Economy and Trade was signed. The volume of trade between the two countries rose from US$34 million in 2001 to US$78 million in 2005.[42] Since 1991 Sino-Mauritanian cooperation in the fishing industry has gradually been growing and in 2004 there were 800 Chinese workers in the fishing sector in Mauritania.[43] As already mentioned, a new growth sector in Sino-Mauritanian collaboration is oil exploration and exploitation. In 2005, of 1000 Chinese persons working in Mauritania, 113 were in road construction and the oil sector.[44]

During Li Zhaoxing's visit to Mauritania in May 2006, the two countries signed an agreement that guaranteed a technical subsidy of RMB 20 million to Mauritania. On this occasion, the Mauritanian minister of foreign affairs, Ahmed ould Sid'Ahmed, affirmed that the Sino-Mauritanian relations had reached a mature stage and they proceeded to deepen the economic cooperation in fisheries, transportation, culture, sport and commercial exchanges. When the Chinese foreign minister drew up a summary of this cooperation, he emphasised that it could serve as a model for cooperation between China and other African countries. He also declared that China would continue to bring support and aid to Mauritania as well as to encourage important Chinese enterprises to invest there.[45]

Similarly, during a meeting with the Mauritanian head of state on 4 November 2006, president Hu Jintao revealed that China would deepen its cooperation with Mauritania in the fields of telecommunications, science, technology and human resources in order to find common efforts for development.[46]

Chinese foreign aid in Mali

Similarly to the case of Mauritania, the Republic of Mali has had a resolute relationship with the People's Republic of China. On 25 October 1960, the two countries established diplomatic relations and ever since, their ties have been solid. In 1961 the two countries signed their first agreement on economic and technical cooperation and in January 2006 the number of agreements and protocols reached more than 35. China has provided Mali with assistance in a variety of fields such as agriculture, textiles, manufacturing, infrastructure and health care. Until 1987 Mali was one of the countries that most profited from Chinese assistance, at least in terms of the number of projects, surpassed only by Tanzania.[47]

In the agricultural domain this cooperation has achieved important results in tea, sugar, rice and cotton production. Chinese assistance has been characterised by pragmatic and sequential development in this field, as the setting-up of every plantation has been followed by the construction of processing infrastructure. In 1962, studies for the development of a tea plantation in Mali started with Chinese assistance. The exploration took place in different points in the country and finally a spot near Sikasso, in the south-east was chosen.[48]

In the field of sugar, the Chinese began the development of a plantation in Segou, which in 1966 reached the extent of more than 1000 hectares. Simultaneously, Mali's first sugar refinery was built in the district with Chinese assistance. Ten years later another sugar plantation and a refinery were constructed in Siribala. In the mid-1980s joint ventures and private enterprises started to dominate,[49] and in this new context new infrastructure was developed with two plantations and two refineries. This time, the Chinese had more of a presence in the forms of production management, labour organisation and financial affairs.[50] After more than ten years of existence, the Sukala S.A., a Sino-Malian joint venture[51] that produces sugar and alcohol, is generating economic returns for its shareholders and for the Malian economy. For instance, the tax returns amounted to CFAF17 billion and the company provided nearly 10,000 jobs.[52]

In 1962, Chinese experts arrived in Mali for the first time in order to assist in the cultivation of paddy fields. In the mid-1970s, at least two rice mills were constructed with Chinese assistance at Sevare and N'debougou. The latter had a capacity of 18,750 tons of rice annually. Today, rice has an important place in the Malian agricultural industry occupying 3 per cent of the cultivated areas in Mali. These are mainly found in the interior of the Niger River delta. The production from rice paddies increased from 185,000 tons in 1960 to 276,000 tons in 1990 and, later on, from 492,000 tons in 2000 to 900,000 in 2005. The country has become to some extent an exporter of rice to neighbouring countries. In 2003, for instance, Mali produced around 697,000 tons of paddy-rice, thereby covering 80 per cent of its national needs. However, while the competitiveness of Malian rice is improving and its exports to other West African countries are growing, imports from Asia are still high.[53]

In the field of infrastructure, China has been constructing buildings, roads and bridges. The biggest Chinese actors dominating this field are the Chinese National Overseas Engineering Corporation (COVEC), the China State Construction Engineering Corporation (CSCEC) and the Compagnie de Géo-ingénierie de Chine (CGA). These companies are winning the great majority of contracts for infrastructural projects that the Malian government announces for international bidding and consequently their presence in the country is growing. For instance, three of the eight branches that COVEC has in north-west Africa are located in Mali. One of these (COMATEX Malienne des Textiles) operates in the field of textiles and is on its way to producing for the international market.[54]

In January 2006, Chinese Foreign Minister Li Zhaoxing and his Malian counterpart Moctar Ouane signed an agreement in Bamako on economic and technological cooperation. China and Mali agreed to enhance cooperative ties in several fields. First, both countries will intensify political dialogue and consultations on key issues in the UN and other international organisations. Second, to promote economic and trade cooperation, China will take further steps to encourage investment in Mali, while Mali will increase direct export of cotton and other products to China. Third, both countries will actively explore ways to promote cooperation in agriculture, telecommunications services, health care, culture, tourism and services, giving priority to projects fundamental to Mali's economic and social development.

In the field of health care Mali and China have a long history of cooperation. Since December 1967 the two countries have signed protocols concerning medical assistance every two years. From February 1968 to July 2002, China sent 34 medical teams to Mali with a total of 581 medical personnel, who treated more than 7 million patients and performed more than 135,000 surgical operations. In 2006 there were 31 medical workers in the hospitals of Kati, Sikasso and Markala.[55]

Concluding remarks

The effects of China's assistance to Africa have been widely ignored by Western academia. We have argued in this chapter that a closer look at the hundreds of Chinese projects in Africa might teach us significant lessons on how to assist and collaborate with African countries and communities on issues of economic and technological development. Despite all kinds of shifts and changes, both at domestic and international levels, China's aid strategy has kept some sense of consistency. One can discern the following characteristics in China's foreign aid: continuity, diversity and unity over space and time.

Despite a clear line of continuity, this cooperation has shifted from a politico-ideologically centred model to a more economically centred one. In the former case, supplying the partner with what it needed was the most important point, while in the latter economic rationality and *mutual benefit* became the main driving forces. However, during this process of transformation Sino-African interaction has been characterised by a dialogue between equal partners. Besides the qualitative changes, there are also changes in magnitude. When China began its foreign assistance programme in the 1950s and 1960s it was a poor country with very limited resources, but this has gradually changed since the mid-1980s. China's impressive economic growth, in the last two decades or so, has led the country's economy to a wider interconnection with the world and consequently to an expansion of China's economic interests all over the globe. In the specific case of Africa, since the late 1990s China has been moving towards the creation of mechanisms of coordination for its cooperation with Africa. As has been argued in the third section this has led to the successful organisation of FOCAC 2000 and 2006, at which virtually all African governments were represented.

Nonetheless, several voices are critical of the ways in which China is doing business all over the world. In the specific case of Africa there are both external and internal voices that represent this scepticism. The main arguments of these voices, which were related to human rights and environmental issues, have been presented and discussed. Some concern about the rapid growth of Chinese economic activities and how these might affect Western interests in Africa can also be seen. However, many Western politicians do not seem to find the contradictions between the Chinese and Western presence in the continent worrying at the moment. Furthermore, both the US and EU are negotiating ways of collaborating with China in Africa.[56]

The fifth section considered what this author views as the most important lesson from observing the Chinese assistance, namely that it has the character of a 'package'. In most African countries, China has touched upon the most acute and sensitive issues for development, such as health care, food security, debt cancellation, human resources and infrastructural development. There is no doubt that these fields have received assistance from many other donors, but often in very fragmented and uncoordinated ways. It seems that the difference lies in the fact that Chinese assistance is still coordinated by a state apparatus that enjoys a high degree of centralisation in this matter. Paradoxically, this centralisation created the conditions for the Chinese state to make priorities, coordinate its overall activities and integrate its assistance. However, there are no guarantees that this will continue this way.

As the shift to *mutual benefit* cooperation took place, much of the agricultural infrastructure projects created in the previous phase was turned into joint ventures or totally managed by Chinese state-owned companies, and some of them became commercial success stories. However, most of them play a vital role for the populations of villages and neighbouring communities. In the sixth section, a brief presentation of some of the economic activities that are taking place in the field of agriculture was made and a discussion of how some of these are expanding rapidly was undertaken.

It is perhaps in this field that China has some lessons that could enrich the present Western engagement with African agriculture. These lessons range from the transfer of simple agricultural technologies to the creation and development of rural infrastructure and markets.

Notes

1. For some examples, see Mahmoud (2007).
2. Personal conversation with Zhou Hong at the Chinese Academy of Social Sciences (CASS).
3. Interview with Zheng Xin, Chinese Ministry of Health Care.
4. For more details on the forum, see the next section.
5. Interview with Yang Shuzeng, Chinese Embassy in Côte d'Ivoire.
6. Interview with Ai Ping, China's Ambassador in Ethiopia.
7. Interview with Zhang Yi, MOFTEC.
8. Interview with Professor Yang Lihua, Institute of West Asian and African Studies. CASS.
9. See FOCAC (2006).
10. See FOCAC (2000, 2006).
11. It is worthwhile noting here that Chinese Premier Wen Jiabao assured South African President Thabo Mbeki on 22 June 2006 that China is willing to restrict its textile exports to South Africa (see FOCAC, 2006).

12. Interview with Mr Barikalla ould Abdallahi, Financial Affairs, Embassy of Mauritania in Beijing.
13. Interview with Mr Ahmed ould Mahmoud: Ministry of Foreign Affairs of Mauritania.
14. Interview with Professor M. Diallo: Center for Development Studies Nouakchott.
15. Ibid.
16. Interview with Ahmed ould Mahmoud, Mauritanian Ministry of Foreign Affairs.
17. Interview with Dr Keita (see Mahmoud, 2007).
18. See FOCAC (2006).
19. See FOCAC (2006).
20. Xinhua (2006), Beijing, 20 October.
21. See FOCAC (2006).
22. Interview with Yang Shuzeng (see Mahmoud, 2007).
23. Interview with Zhang Yi, MOFTEC. (see Mahmoud, 2007).
24. Interview with Yang Shuzeng.
25. See also Fruitful Agricultural Cooperation. Available at: http://www.china. org.cn/english/features/China-Africa/82040.htm (accessed 17 Mar 2007).
26. Ibid.
27. (1 mu = 1/15 hectare).
28. See Fruitful Agricultural Cooperation. Available at: http://www.china.org. cn/english/features/China-Africa/82040.htm (accessed 17 Mar 2007).
29. Interview with the first secretary of China's Embassy in Mauritania.
30. For further details on Mauritania's situation at independence (see Mahmoud, 2007).
31. For details of these see Bartke (1992).
32. Turned later on into a sports complex.
33. Interview with the first secretary of China's Embassy in Mauritania (see also Eadie and Grizzell, 1979).
34. For a detailed study of this farm see Mahmoud (2007).
35. Interview with the first secretary of China's Embassy in Mauritania.
36. Interview with Mr Ahmed ould Mahmoud: Ministry of Foreign Affairs, Mauritania.
37. Interview with Dr Mohamed ould Tayeb at the National Bank, Mauritania.
38. Interview with Dr Cheik Lekbir.
39. Interview with the personnel at Chinese Embassy in Nouakchott.
40. Interview with Dr Cheik Lekbir.
41. Interview with Dr Mohamed ould Tayeb at the National Bank, Mauritania.
42. For more details see Mahmoud (2007).
43. Interview with the personnel at Chinese Embassy in Nouakchott.
44. Interview with the personnel at Chinese Embassy in Mauritania.
45. AFP, 23 May 2006.
46. Xinhua News Agency delivered by Newstex.
47. See Table 8.4.
48. For a detailed study of this farm see Mahmoud (2007).
49 See the section An Enduring Aid Strategy, this chapter.
50. See Bartke (1989) for earlier technical details of all these projects.
51. In 2004, 60 per cent of SUKALA was Chinese-owned.

212 Challenging the Aid Paradigm

52. Interview with Yang Guang, CLETC.
53. Interview with Abdoulaye Keita.
54. See Mahmoud (2007).
55. Interview with the personnel at Chinese Embassy in Bamako.
56. See the *Africa-China-U.S. Trilateral Dialogue* and *Challenges for EU-China Cooperation in Africa*.

References

Bartke, W. (1975). *China's Economic Aid*. Delhi: Vikas.
Bartke, W. (1989). *The Economic Aid of the People's Republic of China to Developing and Socialist Countries*. Munich, London, New York, Paris: K.G. Saur.
Bartke, W. (1992). *The Agreements of the People's Republic of China with Foreign Countries, 1949–1990*. München, New York: Saur.
Brautigam, D. (1998). *Chinese Aid and African Development: Exporting the Green Revolution*. Basingstoke: Macmillan.
Chan, G. (1998). *International Studies in China: An Annotated Bibliography*. New York: Nova Science Publishers.
Chan, G. (1999). *Chinese Perspectives on International Relations: A Framework for Analysis*. Basingstoke: Macmillan.
Copper, J. (1976). *China's Foreign Aid: An instrument of Peking's Foreign Policy*. Lexington, MA and Toronto: D.C. Heath.
Council on Foreign Relations (2007). *Africa-China-U.S. Trilateral Dialogue: Summary Report*. Washington DC: The Brenthurst Foundation.
Eadi, G. A. and D. M. Grizzell (1979). China's Foreign Aid 1975–78. *The China Quarterly* 2, no. 77, pp. 217–34.
Economy, E. (2004). *The River Runs Black: The Environmental Challenge to China's Future*. Ithaca, NY: Cornell University Press.
FOCAC (2000). *Documents and Speeches. Forum on China-Africa Cooperation, Ministerial Conference Beijing 2000*. Beijing: FOCAC.
FOCAC (2006). *Ministerial Conference, Beijing 2006. Documents and Speeches*. Available at: http://english.focacsummit.org/ (accessed 15 Nov. 2006).
Glaser, B. (2001). Discussion of Four Contradictions Constraining China's Foreign Policy Behavior. *Journal of Contemporary China* 10, no. 27, pp. 303–8.
Gottschalk, R. (2006). The Asian Drivers: Financial Flows into and out of Asia – Implications for Developing Countries. *IDS Bulletin* 1, no. 37, pp. 98–106.
GRAIN (2006). China's Mission to Bring Hybrid Rice Production to Africa. *Hybrid Rice Blog*. Available at: http://www.grain.org/hybridrice/?lid=166 (accessed 7 Dec. 2006).
Humphrey, J. and D. Messner (2006). China and India as Emerging Global Governance Actors: Challenges for Developed and Developing Countries. *IDS Bulletin* 1, no. 37, pp. 107–14.
Hutchison, A. (1976). *China's African Revolution*. Boulder: Westview Press.
Jenkins, R. and C. Edwards (2006). The Economic Impacts of China and India on sub-Saharan Africa: Trends and Prospects. *Journal of Asian Economics* 17, no. 2, pp. 207–25.
Jiang, C. (2004). Oil: A New Dimension in Sino-African Relations. *African Geopolitics* 14, no. 2, pp. 65–77. Available at: http://www.african-geopolitics.org/home_english.htm (accessed 18 Jan. 2005).

Jianwei, Q. (2005). *Talking Points at the Consultation between the Secretariat of Chinese Follow-up Committee of the Forum on China-Africa Cooperation (FOCAC) and African Diplomatic Envoys in China.* Beijing: FOCAC.

Kaplinsky, R. (2005). *Globalization, Poverty and Inequality: Between a Hard Rock and a Hard Place.* London: Polity Press.

Kaplinsky, R. (2006). Introduction. *IDS Bulletin,* 37, no. 1, p. 1. Lin, Y. (1989). Peking's African Policy in the 1980s. *Issues and Studies* 25, no. 4.

Larkin, B. D. (1971). *China and Africa 1949–1970: The Foreign Policy of the People's Republic of China.* Berkeley: University of California Press.

Lyman, P. (2005). *China's Rising role in Africa.* Presentation to the US-China Commission July 21. Washington: US-China Commission.

Mahmoud, Y. (2007). *Chinese Development Assistance and West African Agriculture: A Shifting Approach to Foreign Aid?* Lund: Lund University.

Medeiros, E. and M. T. Fravel (2003). China's New Diplomacy. *Foreign Affairs,* 82, no. 6, pp. 22–35.

Menzie, D., P.-K. Tse, M. Fenton, J. Jorgenson and H. van Oss (2005). China's Growing Appetite for Minerals. *U.S. Geological Survey.* Available at : http://www.minecon.com/proceedings05/presentations/menzie.pdf (accessed 7 July 2006).

Morris, M. (2006). China's Dominance of Global Clothing and Textiles: Is Preferential Trade Access an Answer for Sub-Saharan Africa? *IDS Bulletin* 1, no. 37, pp. 89–97.

OECD. (1987). *The Aid Program of China.* Paris: OECD Publications.

Sabea, H. (2001). Reviving the Dead: Entangled Histories in the Privatisation of the Tanzanian Sisal Industry. *Journal of the International African Institute* 71, no. 2, pp. 286–313.

Solana, J. (2007). Challenges for EU-China Cooperation in Africa. *China Daily,* 7 February.

Taylor, I. (1998). China's Foreign Policy towards Africa in the 1990s. *The Journal of Modern African Studies* 36, no. 3, pp. 443–60.

Ting'en, L. (2003). Opininons on further Developing Sino-African Agricultural Investment and Cooperation. *West Asia and Africa* 138 no. 1, pp. 9–13.

La Tribune Economique du Togo (2006). La Chine en vedette. *La Tribune Economique du Togo* 3, p. 1.

Wilson III, E. (2005). China's Influence in Africa: Implications for U.S. Policy. *Testimony before the Sub-committee on Africa, Human Rights and International Operations U.S. House of Representatives July 28, 2005.* Washington DC: House of Respresentatives.

World Bank (2008). *World Development Report: Agriculture for Development.* Washington DC: World Bank. (ISBN-13:9780821368077) 365 pp.

Xinhua (2006). China Trains More than 11,000 African Professionals. Available at: http://www.china.org.cn/english/2006/Oct/185229/htm (accessed 10 Dec 2006).

Xinning, S. (2001). Building International Relations Theory with Chinese Characteristics. *Journal of Contemporary China* 10, no. 26, pp. 61–74.

Zweig, D. and Bi Jianhai (2005). China's Global Hunt for Energy. *Foreign Affairs* 84, no. 5, pp. 25–37.

9

China in Africa: Any Impact on Development and Aid?

Henning Melber

From an African perspective globalisation is not a new phenomenon. It started with the slave trade. After the days of the transatlantic human trafficking various subsequent more or less direct and brutal forms of exploitation characterised the relationships of Africans with the rest of the world. These were then modified by means of formal decolonisation processes. The 'winds of change' – as the then British prime minister Harold Macmillan dubbed the rapid transfer from direct colonial rule to political sovereignty under local African governments from the late 1950s – created sovereign states. Their societies, however, remain to a large extent characterised by the structural legacy of an externally oriented economic system, the beneficiaries of which continue to be based mostly outside the countries, with only limited participation of – all too often parasitic – local elites, who exploit political control over national wealth for their own gains.

Given this history of African relations to the outside world, some (if not most) of the recent critical accounts of the expansion of Chinese interests into African countries and societies and their collaboration with a few local beneficiaries have a hypocritical flavour or bear traces of amnesia. After all, the Chinese penetration is only another facet of capitalist patterns of exploitation and corresponding exchange relations. One is therefore tempted to wonder if the concern expressed is actually at times not more about the Western interests at stake than about the welfare of the African people. While this critical observation does not exonerate the at times appallingly blunt self-interest of Chinese expansion into Africa, it does question the credibility of those critics who find no similar words for the other forms of imperialism, which for far too long have shared responsibility for the state of misery many African people are in. This chapter, although critical on some aspects of the current forms of Chinese-African relations, therefore concurs with the following observation:

> Many commentators, especially segments of the western media, tend to take one example of China's less positive engagement with Africa and project this onto the entire 'China-Africa' relationship. I am not arguing that these are not critical concerns, but this crude extrapolation is part of a move to demonise China's presence on the continent in order to represent 'western' approaches as morally and ethically superior. (Mohan, 2008, pp. 155–6)

Given the centuries of exploitation of the continent it should come as no surprise that many among the most wretched of the Earth's population pin their hopes onto a new actor, who – claiming to represent the global South – seems to offer an alternative. This might at the present conjuncture be more wishful thinking than a justified assessment based on socio-economic and political reality. But it can be seen as an understandable projection by those who for far too long have been kept at the receiving end. Such kind of anti-thesis is, however, a rather uncritical if not a predictable embrace by those analysts who welcome the Chinese charm offensive solely as a window of opportunity.

The new hunger for raw materials to fuel further industrialisation processes in countries outside the continent had since the turn of the century offered several African economies new opportunities for more favourable terms of trade and trade balances. World market prices for many African resources boomed and strategic minerals as well as energy supplies became sought-after precious goods. Unfortunately, their existence does not add to the security of the local population, which at times seems to be more cursed than blessed by the natural wealth in its vicinity. While economic growth might be seen as a necessary condition for poverty reduction, it is in itself certainly not enough to secure it. Instead, national socio-economic policies deliberately pursuing such an aim (including fair and wide distribution of accumulated wealth and investment of revenue income into public infrastructure and services supporting – if not empowering – the poor and thereby investing in local potential to run the economy) remain a challenge.

What can be termed the new Scramble for Africa's natural resources (cf. Southall and Melber, 2009) has so far therefore accelerated economic growth, but not necessarily contributed to a redistribution of wealth. Despite the recent relative bonanza at least in some (although not all)

African countries, poverty remains a structurally embedded phenomenon and thus a continuous challenge.

With the collapse of the global financial system and its effects on the emerging industrial economies, too, the gospel of growth seems to have reached new limitations. The recession becoming effective towards the end of 2008 has affected manufacturing and other forms of production and services not just in the EU, the US and other OECD countries. The honeymoon seems over for all those who participated in the recent rush and thereby contributed to the rising world market prices for raw materials. With industrial production in decline, prices, as much as demand, will drop again. The African continent once again remains at the receiving end of this process. At the time of writing, the end of the downward spiral was not in sight, so this chapter will limit its focus to an analysis until mid-2008.

Africa since the end of the Cold War

The collapse of the Soviet empire and the end of a more than 40-year period of bloc confrontation was by no means 'the end of history'. It was the beginning of a new global order for hegemonic rule with far-reaching consequences for African governments, too. Gone were the days when in the midst of a Cold War some manoeuvring space for limited opportunistic bargaining existed, which allowed for a bit of strategic positioning. Not that this was necessarily to the betterment of the African people: all too often, this constellation encouraged and protected self-enrichment schemes for dictators and small local cliques lacking any legitimacy among the ordinary people. They were part of the externally dominated and determined structure of exploitation through forms of rent-seeking or sinecure capitalism, as examples from A (like Angola) to Z (like Zaire) document. The bipolar world order was in no way a suitable breeding ground for development 'from below'. It offered parasitic agents the opportunity to position themselves as satellites in return for their own gains within the East-West polarisation.

The consolidation of US dominance during the 1990s and its impact on the global order also resulted in several changes for the African continent. A regionally interlinked 'appeasement strategy (with the Russian retreat from Afghanistan and the Cuban withdrawal from Angola) secured in southern Africa the final decolonisation, of Namibia (1990), and paved the way for an end to apartheid and democratic elections in South Africa (1994). During this period the economic paradigms represented by the international financial institutions (the World Bank and the IMF) assumed the dominant power of definition. The notion of 'good governance' emerged as the gospel (Abrahamsen, 2000), a powerful instrument that allowed development policies to be placed firmly under the ownership of the donor countries and international institutions. The World Trade Organization (WTO) emerged as the broker for regulating comprehensively the global exchange relations of goods. It also expanded and defined property rights, once again in the interest of the powerful in the industrialised states and thereby further marginalised and excluded indigenous interests in the global South.

Large parts of conventional developmental paradigms and discourses continue to cultivate within the OECD countries the notion that regional collaboration is a positive factor and a suitable tool also towards economic growth and socio-political stability. At the same time, while they have not abandoned such gospel, donor countries and in particular the US and the EU are through their trade-related initiatives actively involved in preventing any supportive environment for enhancing regional cooperation. In the case of the EU this is even – despite all the emphasis on coherence – in contradiction to the priorities on the agendas of some of its member states, as formulated in their national ODA strategies (cf. Hettne, Söderbaum and Stälgren, 2008, p. 59).

Under the paradigm of the WTO, a newly structured economic reality gains momentum. It organises trade relations in a way that replaces or at least undermines regional dimensions by either bilateral or, increasingly, continental and/or global arrangements, under which ownership clearly lies outside any regional configuration's primary sphere of influence. Emerging features that since the turn of the century have pointed in such a direction include a further enhancement of bi- and multilateral trade agreements between external agencies and individual African states. This has a potentially divisive impact on regional integration issues, as with the US-American African Growth and Opportunity Act (AGOA) and the EU's Economic Partnership Agreements (EPAs), but also increasingly so with bilateral initiatives from new actors such as the so-called BRIC countries (Brazil, Russia, India and China) and not least South Africa as a main actor within the continent.

At the beginning of this century significant intra-African dynamics complemented the shifting global rearrangements, reinforcing the dominance of the industrialised world within the regulation of the global market system. The new democratically elected and legitimised governments in South Africa and Nigeria, as the two economic powerhouses on the continent south of the Sahara, left behind their pariah status. Based on internal and international acceptance, they resumed leadership roles in international policy arenas. At the turn of the millennium presidents Thabo Mbeki and Olusegun Obasanjo emerged (with active support from Senegal, Algeria and Egypt) as new figureheads representing the collective interests of the South and Africa in particular vis-à-vis the industrialised Western countries. Originally tasked to negotiate debt cancellation arrangements, they moved on to seek new forms of interaction based on the acknowledged socioeconomic premises defined by the WTO. As kind of junior partners in the global market they became the architects of the New Partnership for Africa's Development (NEPAD), which has since its establishment received several critical appraisals (see, e.g., Bond, 2002; Melber, 2002, 2004; Taylor, 2005).

After an incubation period and presumably intensive political negotiations behind closed doors this blueprint was upgraded to the status of an official economic programme and institution of the African Union (AU). The AU itself was a parallel transformation of the Organization of African Unity (OAU). In the course of its change it underwent some significant corrections to the established pillars on which the continental policy had been built. Most importantly it moved away from the erstwhile almost holy principle of non-intervention in the internal affairs of member states and replaced the notion of non-interference with one of non-indifference.

With a lot of confidence, trust and substantive political support offered by the G8 after its 2001 summit in Genoa, the NEPAD architects could bring back home the reassuring message that the industrial West was on board and willing to support the initiative. This contributed to its acceptance both in Africa and by the UN system, which in a General Assembly resolution officially recognised NEPAD as the economic programme for Africa. While this looks like a success story, the critical policy issues were to some extent at the same time aborted or at best watered down. The good governance discourse in line with the new unipolar world system and to some extent imposed by the Western capitalist hegemony – was after all not only cosmetic rhetoric, but in some parts a meaningful deviation from past practices of unquestioned autocratic rule by African despots and oligarchies.

The AU constitution was adopted at the same summit in Durban in 2002 as NEPAD was incorporated. It introduced a collective responsibility that had so far been absent, justifying joint intervention for specified reasons. This has since provided several results, as cases like Darfur, the Democratic Republic of Congo (DRC), the Ivory Coast, Liberia and Togo among others have shown in different ways (and with varying degrees of success), all seeking to contribute to conflict reduction or enhanced legitimacy of political systems. It also paved the way for a direct involvement of African armies in peace-keeping operations within the continent (cf. Aning, Bergholm and Mehler, 2008). In contrast to this new active role and responsibility, which have been realised, the African Peer Review Mechanism (APRM) conceptualised by NEPAD has so far not met expectations as a cornerstone for enhancing the notion of good governance (Fombad and Kebonang, 2006).

The disappointment over the discrepancy between the newly claimed responsibility and the non-delivery in reality was maybe biggest when it came to the complete absence of any determined policy action by the NEPAD initiators in the case of Zimbabwe. Despite such setbacks, the demand for democracy, human rights and respect for constitutional principles articulated by the NEPAD blueprint as a prerequisite for sustainable socio-economic development might have been a contributing factor to the emerging new phenomenon of an increasing number of African heads of state more or less voluntarily (and peacefully) vacating their offices as a result of elections or the end of their terms in office (cf. Southall and Melber, 2006) – even though enough rotten apples remain in the basket.

Towards a new scramble in Africa?

Systematic new efforts to access African markets and tap into its local resources became visible with the adoption of AGOA by the outgoing Clinton administration. AGOA is US legislation and as law – in contrast to any form of a negotiated agreement – a unilaterally decreed act. Sole ownership and power of definition therefore rests with the US administration, which is free to interpret and apply AGOA according to its understanding alone. Originally adopted as Title I of the Trade and Development Act of 2000 as part of the 'trade not aid' paradigm, AGOA has since then been extended twice by President Bush. The benefits of AGOA differ among African countries according to their resources. Through this initiative the US openly underlined the relevance of the African dimension for its external trade relations (Africa ranks higher than Eastern Europe in the US trade balance). The breakdown of the AGOA trade volume, however, also discloses that with the exception of a few smaller niches (e.g., the temporary opportunities created for a locally based – though not owned – African textile industry with preferential access to the US market) the trade volume is mainly composed of exported US-manufactured high tech goods and machinery and imported oil, strategic minerals and other natural resources to meet the demands of US-based industries.

Initial empirical findings presented by Thompson (2004, p. 468) showed only narrow positive impacts of AGOA in a total of six out of 37 eligible countries, mainly from increased exports in the textile and apparel sectors: Kenya, Lesotho, Madagascar, Mauritius, Swaziland and South Africa. Only in Kenya and South Africa were exports from other sectors (primarily agricultural products) able to rise substantially under AGOA. Ironically, the best opportunities created under AGOA so far from an 'African' perspective were those that provided short-term profits for Asian – not least Chinese – investments in short-lived textile and apparel production for the US market (Kaplinsky, 2008). With the Multi-Fibre Agreement (MFA) coming into effect at the beginning of 2005, the textile and apparel industries in China, India and other Asian countries were, in accordance with the liberalisation under WTO rules, able to start competing with the AGOA-favoured African products. The predictable result was a massive decline and in some cases the ultimate collapse of the Africa-based industry seeking temporary gains:

> The simple facts are that the full incorporation of China and Eastern Europe into the world trading system over the next decade will more than double the number of workers in the global economy in just ten years time. The AGOA legislation passed in 2004 provides some preferential access for certain categories of African textiles until 2008, but there is no evidence that any African state will be able to build up viable domestic textile industries capable of competing with Chinese producers before that deadline. (Martin, 2004, p. 589)

Once the AGOA bonanza is over, the winners will again have been those with the internationally operating capital and the handful of local compradors.

Soon after AGOA was enacted, the trade department at the European Commission headquarters in Brussels initiated negotiations for a rearrangement of its relations with the ACP countries of Africa, the Caribbean and the Pacific through newly designed EPAs. The declared aim was to enter a post-Cotonou Agreement phase, meeting demands for WTO compatibility. The EPA negotiations have since then failed to come to satisfactory new arrangements with many of the ACP countries. During their intended period of completion in 2006/2007 negotiations instead entered critical stages as they met resistance of many of the designated partner states. These were afraid of losing out on trade preferences and felt that Brussels was seeking to impose a one-sided trade regime in its own interests, which by redrawing the map of regional configurations in Africa to comply with EU expectations would deny the declared partners the right to autonomous negotiations. Both AGOA and the EPAs claim to be trade as aid. In contrast to such noble declarations, they seem to be guided more by the desire to secure continued access to relevant markets and exchange patterns, not least in their own interests (cf. Melber, 2005). Farrell (2008) points to the discrepancies between the emphasis on ideals and values in the official discourse by EU policy makers and the practical impacts of the shift in emphasis from aid to trade as a means of increased 'hegemonic control'.

EPAs not only seek to replace the previous Cotonou Agreement by means of sub-regional separate negotiations but also aim towards compatibility between EU-ACP trade relations and the WTO. Bond (2004, p. 226) warns that the emerging regime of harsher 'reciprocal liberalization', suggested and pursued under the EPA negotiations in stricter compliance with the WTO than its statutes would actually require, will replace the close trade links existing through 'preferential agreements that tied so many African countries to their former colonial masters via cash-crop exports' and that 'what meagre organic African industry and services remained after two decades of structural adjustment will probably be lost to European scale economies and technological sophistication'. The EU is accused of using the EPA negotiations to push through agreements on a number of sensitive matters (such as investment, procurement and competition policy) that were rejected by developing countries at the WTO negotiations during 2003. EPAs are about much more than only the suggested reciprocity within a narrowly defined WTO compliance: 'Non-tariff barriers, such as environmental standards or sanitary and phytosanitary provisions (EU consumer protection policy) are crucial issues in the negotiations' (Grimm, 2005, p. 25). It is of growing concern that these agreements would reduce the policy space for African governments (Ochieng and Sharman, 2004, p. 3) and that they could be used for exerting pressure in cases of political non-compliance.

The EU negotiated separate accords with different regions, and each country had to decide which bloc to join. This first weakened the ACP countries, which are now denied a collective bargaining power, and even divided hitherto established regional economic configurations, and this has been quantified by Lee (2009) as being tantamount to a repartitioning and recolonisation of Africa. It is not far-fetched to see that there is an inbuilt conflict between regionalism as it exists and the negotiations for new multilateral processes. Countries might differ over the relative advantages of benefits from the continued protection of regional arrangements and those of the creation of individual preferential access within other trade agreements.

The predictable outcome of the negotiated agreements is a 'shrinking of development space' (Wade, 2003). To avoid such pseudo-partnerships, he argues, a shift in balance 'from the drive to homogenize trading commitments to other states towards granting states reasonable scope to choose appropriate levels of national protection' is required. A development strategy would therefore have to operate in a zone where internal and external (regional) integration would reinforce rather than undermine each other. Instead, issues of integration have largely dropped out of the development agenda as the free trade paradigm dominates the discourse.

The negotiations on future EPAs introduced serious implementation problems and a negative impact on regionalism within the ACP group and its African member states (Kohnert, 2008, p. 14). Hurt (2004, p. 165) had already pointed out the capacity problems that confronted regional organisations within Africa when entering the negotiations. A further complication is the fact that all of these regional configurations consist of a mix of least developed countries (LDCs) and non-LDCs. Likely results include the further fragmentation of the process of regional integration and a division of ACP states into regional groups, which might 'enable the EU to target its trade restrictions more effectively on products that it chooses not to liberalize' (ibid., p. 166). Critics maintain that, 'it would be an act of foolish optimism to expect integrity or honesty in the EU's trade policy' (Goodison and Stoneman, 2004, p. 734). Instead, the EPA initiative:

> has created new regional groupings that are inconsistent with, and undermine, existing African economic and political blocs. Reducing regional integration to trade liberalisation undermines the broader socio-economic and political objectives of existing bodies. (Ochieng and Sharman, 2004, p. 3)

As a study exploring the possible gains for LDCs under the emerging world trade regime has warned: 'it is important that EU's future policy for free trade agreements regarding developing countries within the ACP group, does not work counter to or hinder regional economic cooperation and integration, which can provide better preconditions for regional trade including the LDCs of each region' (de Vylder

Nyander and Laanatza, 2001, p. 161). This requires more than merely an opening up to the global economy. The EU needs to revisit matters of regional economic collaboration and seek involvement of the majority of the African population in these countries (Kivimäki and Laakso, 2002, p. 176). The current initiatives by the EU fail to live up to such needs.

The challenge is to contribute towards sustainable development by offering the African partners a global environment conducive to securing them a fairer share in the world economy and the international policymaking processes. Taking such a responsibility seriously, the G8, the EU and other OECD countries would have to stop the pursuance of their protectionist trade policies. Agrarian subsidies and other distorting interventions in their economic spheres should come to an end as an initial contribution towards a more competitive general environment. Only on such a basis, might scenarios for fairer partnerships be discussed, negotiated and entered. It has been suggested by Hurt (2004, p. 171) that the currently dominant neoliberalism in trade is to a large extent compatible with the interests of a political elite, as well as those of an outward-oriented faction of capitalism both within the EU and (though to a lesser extent) in African states, and that the international environment made it more difficult to redefine African-European relations positively. Kohnert (2008) suggests that the economic relations negotiated by the EU with Africa contribute to a continued dominance traded for aid. It is not easy to counteract such conclusion convincingly. As a matter of fact, 'much remains to be done before this benevolent European actor can present itself credibly to the world' (Hettne, Söderbaum and Stälgren, 2008, p. 54).

While some believe that ACP countries have in essence 'nothing to gain and everything to lose from the EPA negotiations' (Brown, 2005, p. 9), the EU also has more to lose than to gain – at least in terms of reputation and acceptance concerning its policy on Africa. In the absence of sufficient capacity among the ACP countries to negotiate meaningfully the EU proposals viv-à-vis the 'well oiled trade negotiation machinery of the EU' (Grimm, 2005, p. 24), many among those at the receiving end felt forced into a process they actually resisted. The EU-ACP process, which unfolded within the EPA negotiations, was not convincing as evidence for claims that the EU would not ignore the interests of the ACP countries, nor did it meet the criteria for coherence with other fundamental principles of development paradigms and policies of the EU and its member countries, such as support to regional integration. At a time of intensified rivalry between the 'have lots' among the countries of the world in order to consolidate their particular interests within the regions of the 'have-nots', EU policy risks a credibility loss.

The speech by the then Tanzanian President Benjamin Mkapa delivered on 31 August 2005 at the headquarters of the AU, in which he explicitly took EU policies to task and warned of the devastating consequences of further globalisation, is an indication of the growing sentiments since then. As he added: 'I urge African leaders to think afresh about the place of our continent in a rapidly globalising world.' The new offensive pursued by China is only the most visible sign of growing interests of external actors in the continent. In a short time, India, Brazil and Russia (as well as a number of other actors such as Malaysia and Mexico) are likely to add further pressure to the scramble for limited markets and resources. Of particular interest in this accelerated global competition for resources is access to, and control over, potential energy supplies. On offer, in particular, are oil, natural gas and uranium from the African continent, which has emerged as 'a vital arena of strategic and geopolitical competition' and 'the final frontier' (Klare and Volman, 2006, p. 297).

This new stage of competing forces on the continent has resulted in a plethora of recent analyses dealing mainly, if not exclusively, with the Chinese impact and practices (cf. Mohan, 2008; Taylor, 2007). With the exception of the current controversies around the EPAs and the emerging concerns over increased US-led military control over the continent, European and US policies and interests seem to feature much less prominently. Such a selected narrative tends to downplay if not ignore the damaging external effects that the existing socio-economic imbalances and power structures created and consolidated long since. It appears at times that the criticism raised against China and other potential emerging competitors is more an indication of an increasing fear of losing out on their own interests than of being motivated by a genuine concern for the African people.

A recent example for the new situation and the interests guiding decision-making was the discussion around the European-African summit in December 2007 in Lisbon. Most EU member states were prepared to accept the presence of Zimbabwe's president Robert Mugabe in violation of their own previously agreed sanctions. This was partly motivated by a concern that his exclusion could result in a boycott by most African countries, weakening Europe's status among African governments and thereby strengthening Chinese influence. One does not need to balance the arguments and seek a convincing answer to the dilemma. Suffice it to note that China's presence in Africa has far-reaching effects that are also visible in this regard. No longer being a subject exclusively to the sphere of influence of the Western states, African countries can gain new operational space. While this might strengthen their negotiating power and be favourable to economic interests seeking to achieve maximum gains, it has also provoked the fear 'that the political consequences for democracy, human rights, and conflict prevention will be overwhelmingly negative' (Tull, 2006a, p. 36; see also Tull, 2006b).

China's expansion into Africa

After the Bandung Conference in the mid-1950s, Chinese foreign policy included ambitions for a hegemonic role in the South as part of the Sino-Soviet rivalry and competition. It also pursued a proactive, interventionist dimension with regard to African countries in its support to liberation movements and governments in newly independent states (cf. Alden and Alves, 2008). This expansionist policy under the flag of anti-imperialism was at times guided by disastrous misjudgements and resulted in costly, and not just financially, adventures under chairman Mao (cf. Chang and Halliday, 2006). More recently, Chinese foreign policy has shifted slightly from cultivating an isolationist tendency towards a more active (although preferably still low-profile) policy of going abroad more openly and aggressively. This has been, not least, the result of a domestic industrialisation process and its inherent expansionist tendencies: as a mode of production it is based on the growth paradigm, which results in an ever-growing demand for supplies of resources to fuel the industrial mass production of goods.

Such demand by emerging economies of this calibre contributed to dramatic increases in world market prices, which positively affected the terms of trade for at least some resource-rich African countries. The beneficiaries were not only Africans, but also new enterprises established under foreign ownership to participate in and profit from the boom. Chinese multinational companies have mushroomed on the African continent (cf. Corkin, 2007). They have left major footprints in the energy sector, notably through operations by Sinopec in Angola, the China National Offshore Oil Corporation (CNOOC) in Nigeria and Kenya and the China National Petroleum Corporation (CNPC) in Sudan. In the telecommunications sector the state-owned Zhong Xing Telecommunication Equipment Company Limited (ZTE) and the private multinational Huawei are challenging the dominance of British, French and South African companies. Chinese companies have secured major government tenders in the construction sector in several African countries. They have moved on from the early days, when they earned a reputation for building sports stadiums as a sign of friendship (and most prominently the railway line connecting Zambia with Tanzania), and now build not only more sports complexes and railway lines, but also state houses and government offices, major roads, dams, harbours, airports and other infrastructural projects. 'Following the "going global" strategy and dove-tailing with the Chinese government's foreign aid programs to African countries, these projects are often financed by Chinese government loans' (ibid., p. 21). Empirical evidence on the multiple forms of Chinese political and economic expansion into sub-Saharan Africa is growing (cf. numerous examples in Mehler, Melber and van Walraven, 2008 and the six case studies in Centre for Chinese Studies, 2007).

By 2007 China already ranked as the third biggest trading partner with Africa, behind the US and France, but ahead of the UK. While having a volume of US$5 billion with Africa in 1997, Sino-African trade was hitting US$55.5 billion in 2006 and is estimated by a senior economist at the Chinese Ministry of Commerce to top the US$110 billion mark by 2011 (cf. Taylor, 2007, p. 379). The new trend suggests that China has become in the meantime 'a trade-driven industrial power integrated into the world system', which 'increasingly replicates in key ways long-standing developed-state policies' (Sautman and Hairong, 2007, pp. 77 and 78). This was illustrated during the US-Africa Business Summit in Cape Town in November 2007. Prof. Yang Guang from the Institute of West-Asian and African Studies of the Chinese Academy of Social Sciences informed the audience that the total number of Chinese companies operating on the continent by then exceeded 800. Some 100 of these companies were state owned, and most others received state support while operating privately. He further put the cumulative value of Chinese investments by the end of 2006 at a total of US$11.7 billion (Kilbey, 2007). According to Alden (2007, p. 14) Chinese companies operated in 49 out of the 53 countries on the continent, while joint ventures with local African firms amounted to some 480 enterprises.

Trade between China and Africa has accelerated since the turn of the century accordingly (the following figures are from Wang, 2007, p. 5). Africa's exports to China increased between 2001 and 2006 at over 40 per cent per annum to reach US$28.8 billion. During the same period imports from China quadrupled to US$26.7 billion, leaving a small trade surplus for Africa. The bulk of Sino-African trade (some 85 per cent) took place with sub-Saharan Africa. It reproduced a classically skewed pattern: raw materials on the one side (Africa), and (value added) manufactured products on the other (China). In 2006 oil and gas accounted for 62 per cent of Africa's exports to China. Oil supplied from Africa is currently estimated to cover one third of China's annual consumption. Non-petroleum minerals and metals rank second (13 per cent) on the export list. This means that 75 per cent of all exports to China are oil, gas, minerals and metals. In contrast, Africa imports mainly manufactured products from China (45 per cent), as well as machinery and transport equipment (31 per cent). This includes a considerable amount of weaponry: China ranks among the top suppliers of arms to African customers.

While African governments often welcome the new partners in business, there are also growing feelings among local people for a number of reasons: Chinese companies and their Chinese workers (who are often imported, too, and kept apart in separate compounds) are perceived as unwanted competition and a threat. The construction sector, in particular, in some African countries is affected and ailing due to government tenders handed to Chinese bidders, who manage to make more attractive offers. But the growing Chinese presence also negatively affects the local survival strategies of people without salaried employment battling to make a living. This includes a hitherto unknown competition for the hawkers and street vendors, who suffer from the effects of cheap Chinese goods sold locally in Chinese shops or even on the pavements at prices below those they can offer.

Against the background of such a mixed track record, a Chinese public relations exercise initiated at the World Social Forum in Nairobi at the end of January 2007 (in the Chinese-built sports arena on the outskirts of the capital) backfired, when the Chinese quasi-NGO representatives (known to be semi-official policy representatives of the government) were confronted with an outburst of anger by social activists from a variety of countries. They denounced the Chinese policy of bailing out despotic and authoritarian regimes under pressure (like Zimbabwe) through their economic deals and accused China of being worse than the old colonial and imperialist powers. While these had had forms of exploitation based on local labour, they accused the Chinese of generating extra profits even at the cost of the small traders and unskilled workers, who were victimised by the new competition and lost their last source of monetary income as a result of the Chinese operations (cf. Bello, 2007). It was a disastrous failure for the planned Chinese charm offensive and an obvious indicator of the growing frustration in some of the countries with a massive Chinese presence. A volume by African scholars and activists on the subject launched at the same occasion in Nairobi testifies further to the, at best, mixed reactions to the newly emerging constellation (cf. Manji and Marks, 2007). The social activists criticising Beijing's policy and the Chinese expansion into African societies are by no means less critical of Western imperialism (see also Guerrero and Manji, 2008). For many among them and numerous other people on the ground, it is the choice between the plague and the cholera, as a critical Gabonese observer of the Chinese impact on Gabon stated provocatively (Legault, 2008, p. 42).

Risks of the new multipolarity

Obviously, the current increase in external players seeking to secure and maintain access to and control over Africa's natural resources strengthens not only the economic but also the political bargaining role of African governments. With new rivals such as China, India, Brazil, Russia and a series of further countries at the threshold of meaningful domestic industrial production with orientation to exports and growing demands for imports, the competition for entering into favourable relations with African countries has increased. This in itself is not against the interests of African people. However it requires the relatively tiny elites who benefit from the current unequal structures to put their own interest in transnationally linked self-enrichment schemes behind the public interest and to be willing to create investment and exchange patterns that primarily provide benefits for the majority of the people. Admittedly, the chances for such a redefinition of the agenda might not be the best.

The dependency syndrome, which characterised North-South relations, might, however, have been replaced by a feeling of having alternative choices at hand. While this expands the action radius of African governments, it has not necessarily had a positive impact on improved governance. Quite the opposite: it might create new exit options to once again allow them to be able literally to get away with murder. Over and above this redrawing of the political map, highly reminiscent of the Cold War era, the economic realities have not really changed that much. A report based on six case studies presented by the Centre for Chinese Studies (2007, p. viii) observed:

> that the government, particularly the executive, in many cases in Africa is comprised of a political elite whose reality is very much removed from the rest of the population. This results in policy-makers and influential opinion-leaders crafting policy approaches that are not beneficial to the more impoverished sectors of the population.

The emerging new global trade and exchange patterns have despite new actors not displayed any meaningful qualitative structural changes. Chinese trade and investment in African countries is not significantly different from other neocolonial patterns and will not transform the structure of production or make for a new international division of labour. 'Indeed, such trade can only perpetuate the dependence of developing countries on exports of primary commodities' (Nayyar, 2008, p. 17). The Chinese track record emerging is not an indicator of a new trajectory, which would benefit the majority of African people. Even more, the Chinese foreign policy gospel of non-interference is an attractive tune for the autocratic leaders and oligarchies still in power, be it in Angola, the DRC, Sudan, Zimbabwe or similar societies still run to a large extent like the private property of elites. Guided by its gospel of non-intervention, China unscrupulously provides grants and loans to countries with dubious human rights records and is not choosy when it comes to its economic partnerships or to the funding modalities with regard to any checks and balances (Henderson, 2008, p. 12–13).

Transparency and accountability are certainly not among the core values cultivated in African-Chinese links, and Beijing's notion of human rights is at best dubious – although one should not forget that neither has the West been a role model in rigorously pursuing concerns over human rights violations (Breslin and Taylor, 2008; Taylor, 2008). The current 'risk investments' pursued by Chinese front companies might secure a foot in the door as an immediate aim, but the medium- to long-term interest will also lie in creating and operating within a calculable and investor-friendly environment with a relative stability. Put differently. 'China cannot afford to put all its eggs in government baskets' (Amosu, 2007), at least not so long as these governments are not held accountable by the rule of law in a society regulated by checks and balances. After all, 'China seeks, as do all investors, a stable and secure investment environment' (Mohan and Power, 2008, p. 37).

Notwithstanding such longer-term self-interest, the declared Chinese policy of non-interference does not presently abide well with transparency and accountability, the protection of human rights and the promotion of democracy. Nor does the European response to Chinese competition, if it means that the emphasis on such values and norms guiding cooperation is reduced. It is noteworthy, however, that Chinese foreign policy in terms of its international responsibilities seems to change and adapt rapidly. Leaving behind the earlier fundamentals of Chinese non-interference, 'China has moved from outright obstructionism and a defensive insistence on solidarity with the developing world to an attempt to balance its material needs with its acknowledged responsibilities as a major power' (Kleine-Ahlbrandt and Small, 2008, p. 56). Since the beginning of the century, Beijing has turned through its role in the UN peace-keeping operations into an active contributor to conflict resolution efforts (cf. He, 2007).

While this might contribute to more coherent collective efforts towards enhanced 'good governance' in political terms, the resource curse is still looming for those economies that currently benefit more from the unexpected conjuncture than one could have expected only a few years ago. The record windfall profits, positive terms of trade and trade balances and the unusual high economic growth rates do not necessarily indicate sustainable positive changes towards poverty reduction and secure livelihoods for the majority of the people. Inequalities and social disparities might well increase further in midst of a growing segment of beneficiaries who are able to siphon off the revenue for their own enrichment.

Institutional quality and sound economic policies remain substantial ingredients for a development paradigm benefiting the majority of people in the affected societies. Governing the access to resources through appropriate rent and revenue management policies as well as by improving policy design and implementation are as important as a diversification of the economy and the creation of human and social capital (Wohlmuth, 2007, p. 11f.). Relatively weak African states (which because of their structural weakness are at the same time strong in the sense of a lack of institutionalised control and checks and balances with regard to those who execute political power, allowing them to use the state as a private instrument in self-enrichment schemes) and their governments on the one hand and major international corporations on the other are very unequal partners. In many cases neither the governments nor the people in the resource-rich areas are aware of the cash flow generated by the exploitation of the raw materials, and they derive hardly any benefit (with the exception of odd accomplices in the business deals):

> In settings where initial political and economic institutions are relatively weak, dependence on primary commodities, especially natural resources such as oil, appears to have encouraged predatory government behaviour and rent-seeking, deterring the development of stable, democratic institutions that are conducive to growth. (Jerome and Wohlmuth, 2007, p. 201)

In the light of the new scramble, the question is not so much a choice between Europe, the US and China (or any other actors interested in

African resources). The challenge lies in setting a new course to make optimal use of the new scenario for the majority of the people on the continent. As Amosu (2007) concludes in a variation on the African proverb, which says when elephants are fighting, the grass is suffering: 'Don't focus so much on the elephants. The future of Africa lies with the grass.' This draws attention again to those who had always been at the receiving end of the unequal relationships, namely the majority of people in the African societies. Their agency is crucial, and their interests should matter more than those of any others. This also points in a direction, which should seek to transcend the focus beyond a reduced Sino-African dichotomy termed a reductionist 'dragon in the bush' perspective (Large, 2008). As summarised by Habib (2008, p. 274), there remain great dangers in the current competitive constellation:

> It demonstrates that all of the countries in the scramble are driven largely by national interests, and that their behaviour is conditioned far more by competition with each other than by the noble sentiments enshrined in their policy documents and press releases. The consequence is that this scramble is likely to repeat the results of its predecessor: neo-colonial relations, proxy wars, and, ultimately, political instability and economic devastation.

This echoes similar concerns expressed in an earlier report for the Development Committee of the European Parliament, which concludes with a sobering diagnosis:

> The current quandary is the result of a multi-layered security dilemma. All major actors involved in the new scramble for Africa are wary that their urgent domestic needs will be compromised if they distance themselves of their own opportunistic and self-centred policies. Short-term gains still prevail over long-term stability. (Holslag et al., 2007, p. 50)

To neutralise this 'destructive development', the authors identify a need for 'a comprehensive and open dialogue between Africa and all its partners' (ibid.; see also Holslag, 2007). In that logic, there is indeed another task, namely for crafting an African response to China, as identified by Le Pere (2008, pp. 34–6) in his more favourable assessment of China's engagement. The priorities he lists are: (1) a need to overcome the 'yellow peril' stereotype, (2) African involvement in harmonisation of bi- and multilateral donor activities in the continent, (3) urging

China to participate in the Extractive Industries Transparency Initiative (EITI), (4) the need for African governments to improve their regulatory frameworks and policies and (5) to establish a high-level continental coordinating body to guide and implement the Chinese-African cooperation agenda. Such steps would at least contribute to an African policy towards China, the absence of which so far has been a critical deficit. When articulating such a demand, however, one should also accept that there has so far not been any truly coherent African policy on other matters, given the variety of political regimes and interests on the continent.

Effects on development and aid

Chinese expansion into Africa has not only resulted in intensified economic and political links to a series of African countries, as illustrated among other things by the establishment of a China-Africa Joint Chamber of Commerce in 2005 with the support of UN Development Programme and the impressive Beijing Summit of the Forum on China-Africa Cooperation (FOCAC) in early November 2006, which assembled a hitherto unprecedented number of African heads of state outside the continent. Significantly, in May 2007, the African Development Bank held its annual board meeting in Shanghai. Complementing these events, which underpin the Chinese charm offensive and illustrate its diplomatic skills, China has emerged in an increasingly active role as a provider of mainly bilateral support (cf. Davies et al., 2008). While China is careful not to call it aid, it clearly corresponds to this, despite having different packaging, priorities and nuances to Western development assistance. A series of agreements, often based on loans for the implementation of a wide range of mainly infrastructural projects, testify to the new Chinese engagement as a donor country, which at the same time provides know-how, equipment and labour for the work it finances. There are concerns that China's lending strategy might lead to another debt trap and new forms of dependency. These have in one assessment been considered as unjustified (Reisen and Ndoye, 2008), while in another one have been seen as a reason for demanding established internationally recognised legal standards for responsible lending (Huse and Muyakwa, 2008). Be that as it may, with the Chinese presence in Africa a new global player also in the role of a donor has not really arrived but has become visible to the extent that others react.

The aid architecture that emerged with the independent states as a programmatically defined commitment during the 1960s has been through a variety of changes since then. Despite continuous South-South collaboration dating back to the Bandung Conference in the mid-1950s, and notwithstanding socialist internationalism, aid had always been perceived as a Western approach to assisting the African countries in a process termed development. Rarely, though, have these initiatives provided reasons for satisfaction and resulted in success. Half a century into decolonisation, the challenges have remained the same to a large extent. With new powerful actors joining and challenging the earlier established network of external relations between African countries and the rest of the world, one needs to revisit the aid and development paradigms to see if and how they change or how the changing economic relationships impact on defined priorities and potential collaboration among old and new donor countries (for the first such assessments see Asche and Schüller, 2008; Davies, 2007; Goldstein et al., 2006; Tjønneland et al., 2006).

Several fundamentals of the current aid paradigm and policies are under scrutiny when taking into consideration the Chinese 'constructive engagement' in Africa (Corkin and Burke, 2008). These include among others the following essentials:

- the role played by multilateralism versus bilateral relations among states;
- the balance between collective responsibility and national sovereignty; and
- the prominence and preference given to either hard (infrastructural) or soft (good governance and institutional capacity building) priorities.

These areas touch upon earlier debates dating back to the days of the developmental state policy of the 1970s. The official notion propagated then (largely by governments accountable mainly to themselves) had demanded development first, human rights and democracy later. It contrasted with the later, post-Cold War era understanding that there is no sustainable development without institutionalised democratic norms and the entrenchment of human rights and their corresponding values. It remains to be seen if the proponents of the two views find a way to shift towards convergence of these priorities in one coherent framework, which gives sufficient recognition and space for implementing both complementary factors to induce and promote sustainable development for the benefit of a majority of the people in the countries, or if a confrontation over the priorities gains the upper hand. Put differently, the question is if the external stakeholders move back into geopolitics reminiscent of the earlier Cold War period or if the ground is laid more for a realpolitik seeking benefits for all stakeholders, not least the hitherto marginalised at the receiving end.

In a stock taking exercise, Thorborg (2008, p. 14) compiles a list of 15 interrelated and overlapping characteristics she considers as typical features for an alternative Chinese development model based on the Beijing consensus. These encompass *inter alia*: continued preference for entering bilateral relations; adherence to a one China policy as the only conditionality without any further strings attached; involvement of Chinese labour in construction work and other Chinese projects in the countries; no compliance with local labour regulations for either the Chinese or the African workers; the use of Chinese equipment; a mixture of trade, aid and loans and bilateralism on a government-to-government level guided by dignified and respectful dialogue with the African leaders. She concludes:

> if China is prepared to encourage more multi-laterality and if African states through the AU can work out common strategies a more equal and win-win relationship could ensue. If China as well would be prepared to both cooperate more with NGOs in African countries and with other donors efficiency could be increased contributing to China's 'peaceful rise'. (ibid., p. 15)

This corresponds with similar mildly optimistic expectations as articulated in other preliminary assessments (cf. Davies, 2007; Tjønneland et al., 2006). Ampiah and Naidu (2008, p. 338) emphasise a related forward-looking approach in their summary conclusions, stressing the need for recognition of an 'enlightened selfishness' as the guiding principle for an evolving partnership to bring about maximum good for Africa's people. This could in their view be the bedrock, 'and not what seems to be the current state of play of minimum benefits for the few "enlightened political and economic elites".' There seems to be evidence that the new players on the continent might indeed provide additional windows of opportunity (McCormick, 2008). The question remains, to what extent this might be in response to earlier negative perceptions a kind of positive wishful thinking in the absence of little comforting concrete evidence so far. What most authors agree upon at this stage is the urgent need for more thorough and empirically sound studies, which investigate the realities within countries before drawing general conclusions based on vague assumptions. Many also share the hope that the major global players find sufficient common ground to act within a defined framework of shared interests:

> in their common interest of maintaining an open global economic system, the EU and China stand the best chance of fruitful co-operation if they work through multilateral channels, or together help to draw up new international rules. Such an approach would increase the chances of a multi-polar world emerging in a multilateral form, rather than in the shape of two or more hostile camps. (Grant and Barysch, 2008, p. 104)

The question remains to be answered, if this also reflects the legitimate interests of all those who remain outside or at the receiving end of such an alliance. China was already a signatory to the Paris Declaration on Aid Effectiveness adopted on 2 March 2005. This committed her to the principles of ownership of recipients, alignment of aid to national priorities and harmonisation and coherence among donor countries. It is not clear, however, if China signed up in its capacity as a recipient rather than as a donor country (Davies, 2007, p. 13). The Accra Agenda for Action, endorsed on 4 September 2008 by ministers of developing and donor countries and heads of multi- and bilateral development institutions attending the Third High Level Forum on Aid Effectiveness stressed that 'all development actors will work in more inclusive partnerships'. It further stated the intention to 'reduce the fragmentation of aid by improving the complementarity of donors' efforts and the division of labour among donors'. It also welcomes all development actors and states in article 19. d):

> South-South co-operation on development aims to observe the principle of non-interference in internal affairs, equality among developing partners and respect for their independence, national sovereignty, cultural diversity and identity and local content. It plays an important role in international development co-operation and is a valuable complement to North-South co-operation.

This sounds as if there is a lot of goodwill, and intentions to find a common denominator. – The question remains, again, in whose interest? China, at times considered as the most successful developing country in the current era of globalisation, has called its own programme of socio-economic transformation and reform *Gai Ge Kai Feng*, meaning, 'change the system, open the door'. This includes the privatisation of large parts of the economy, the liberalisation of trade and investment and the development of high quality infrastructure guided by market principles (cf. Dollar, 2008). This, after all, sounds not too different from the Western development discourse. It is at least questionable if this is good news for Africa. For Guttal (2008, p. 34) 'China's current aid and foreign investment practices have begun to dangerously resemble colonialism'. There are similar concerned and critical voices more reluctant than others to argue in favour of a welcoming embrace for a new global player who might not change the rules of the game but ultimately play along and join the existing club. Their motive is not to protect the Western or Northern interests that are possibly at stake. On the contrary, their fear is that China in the end merely offers more of the same, instead of being a true alternative. China's role in future deals and its collaboration with African partners should therefore finally simply be measured against the words of one of her former leaders. In his speech at a special session of the UN General Assembly, Deng Xiaoping stated in 1974:

> If capitalism is restored in a big socialist country, it will inevitably become a superpower. (...) If one day China should change her colour and turn into a superpower, if she too should play the tyrant in the world, and everywhere subject others to her bullying, aggression and exploitation, the people of the world should identify her as social-imperialism, expose it, oppose it and work together with the Chinese people to overthrow it. (Quoted in Manji and Marks, 2007, p. ix)

References

Abrahamsen, R. (2000). *Disciplining Democracy. Development Discourse and Good Governance in Africa*. London and New York: Zed Books.

Alden, C. (2007). *China in Africa*. London: Zed Books.

Alden, C., and A. C. Alves (2008). History & Identity in the Construction of China's Africa Policy. *African Affairs*, 107, no. 426, pp. 43–58.

Amosu, A. (2007). China in Africa: It's (Still) the Governance, Stupid. *Foreign Policy in Focus*, 9 March. Available at: http://www.fpif.org/fpiftxt/40658 (accessed 12 March 2007).

Ampiah and S. Naidu (2008). The Sino-African Relationship. Towards an Evolving Partnership? in *Crouching Tiger, Hidden Dragon? Africa and China* (eds) K. Ampiah and S. Naidu. Scottsville: University of KwaZulu-Natal Press.

Aning, K., L. Bergholm and A. Mehler (2008). *The United Nations, Security and Peacekeeping in Africa. Lessons and Perspectives*. Uppsala: The Dag Hammarskjöld Foundation.

Asche, H. and M. Schüller (2008). *China's Engagement in Africa – Opportunities and Risks for Development.* Eschborn: Deutsche Gesellschaft für Technische Zusammenarbeit.

Bello, W. (2007). China Provokes Debate in Africa. *Foreign Policy in Focus,* 9 March. Available at: http://www.fpif.org/fpiftxt/4065 (accessed 12 March 2007).

Bond, P. (ed.) (2002). *Fanon's Warning. A Civil Society Reader on The New Partnership for Africa's Development.* Trenton, NJ: Africa World Press.

Bond, P. (2004). *South Africa and Global Apartheid. Continental and International Policies and Politics.* Uppsala: The Nordic Africa Institute.

Breslin, S. and I. Taylor (2008). Explaining the Rise of 'Human Rights' in Analyses of Sino-African Relations. *Review of African Political Economy,* no. 115, pp. 59–71.

Brown, O. (2005). *EU Trade Policy and Conflict.* Winnipeg: International Institute for Sustainable Development.

Centre for Chinese Studies (2007). *China's Engagement of Africa: Preliminary Scoping of African Case Studies. Angola, Ethiopia, Gabon, Uganda, South Africa, Zambia.* Stellenbosch: Centre for Chinese Studies.

Chang, J. and J. Halliday (2006). *Mao. The Unknown Story.* London: Vintage.

Corkin, L. (2007). China's Emerging Multinationals in Africa. *The Africa Journal,* Spring, pp. 20–22.

Corkin, L. and C. Burke (2008). Constructive Engagement: An overview of China's role in Africa's Construction Industries, in *New Impulses from the South: China's Engagement of Africa* (eds) H. Edinger with H. Herman and J. Jansson. Stellenbosch: Centre for Chinese Studies.

Davies, M. with H. Edinger, N. Tay and S. Naidu (2008). *How China Delivers Development Assistance to Africa.* Stellenbosch: Centre for Chinese Studies.

Davies, P. (2007). *China and the End Of Poverty in Africa – Towards Mutual Benefit?* Stockholm: Diakonia.

de Vylder, S., G. A. Nyander and M. Laanatza (2001). *The Least Developed Countries and World Trade.* Stockholm: Swedish International Development Cooperation Agency.

Dollar, D. (2008). *Lessons from China for Africa.* Washington: The World Bank.

Farrell, M. (2008). EU-Africa: From Lomé to EPA, in *EU and the Global South* (eds) F. Söderbaum and P. Stålgren. Boulder and London: Lynne Rienner.

Fombad, C. M. and Z. Kebonang (2006). *AU, NEPAD and the APRM. Democratisation Efforts Explored.* Uppsala: The Nordic Africa Institute.

Goldstein, A., N. Pinaud, H. Reisen and X. Chen (2006). *The Rise of China and India. What's in it for Africa?* Paris: OECD Development Centre.

Goodison, P. and C. Stoneman (2004). Europe: Partner or Exploiter of Africa? The G-90 & the ACP. *Review of African Political Economy* 31, no. 102, pp. 725–34.

Grant, C. with K. Barysch (2008). *Can Europe and China Shape A New World Order?* London: Centre for European Reform.

Grimm, S. (2005). African-European Relations, in *Africa Yearbook 2004. Politics, Economy and Society South of the Sahara* (eds) A. Mehler, H. Melber and K. van Walraven. Brill: Leiden.

Guerrero, D.-G. and F. Manji (eds) (2008). *China's New Role in Africa and the South. A Search for a New Perspective.* Cape Town, Nairobi and Oxford: Fahamu and Bangkok: Focus on the Global South.

Guttal, S. (2008). Client and Competitor: China and International Financial Institutions, in *China's New Role in Africa and the South. A Search for a New Perspective* (eds) D.-G. Guerrero and F. Manji. Cape Town, Nairobi and Oxford: Fahamu and Bangkok: Focus on the Global South.

Habib, A. (2008). Western Hegemony, Asian Ascendancy and the New Scramble for Africa, in *Crouching Tiger, Hidden Dragon? Africa and China* (eds) K. Ampiah and S. Naidu. Scottsville: University of KwaZulu-Natal Press.

He, Y. (2007). *China's Changing Policy on UN Peacekeeping Operations.* Stockholm: Institute for Security & Development Policy.

Henderson, J. (2008). *China and the Future of the Developing World: The Coming Global Asian Era and Its Consequences.* Helsinki: UNU-Wider.

Hettne, B., F. Söderbaum and P. Stålgren (2008). *The EU as a Global Actor in the South.* Stockholm: Swedish Institute for European Policy Studies.

Holslag, J. (2007). *Friendly Giant? China's Evolving Africa Policy.* Brussels: Brussels Institute of Contemporary China Studies.

Holslag, J., G. Geeraerts, J. Gorus and S. Smis (2007). *China's Resource And Energy Policy in Sub-Saharan Africa. Report for the Development Committee of the European Parliament.* Brussels: Vrije Universiteit.

Hurt, S. R. (2004). The European Union's External Relations with Africa after the Cold War: Aspects of Continuity and Change, in *Africa in International Politics. External Involvement on the Continent* (eds) I. Taylor and P. Williams. London and New York: Routledge.

Huse, M. D. and S. L. Muyakwa (2008). *China in Africa: Lending, Policy Space and Governance.* Norwegian Campaign for Debt Cancellation and Norwegian Council for Africa.

Jerome, A. and K. Wohlmuth (2007). Nigeria's Commodity Dependence and Options for Diversification. An Introduction' in *Africa – Commodity Dependence, Resource Curse and Export Diversification* (eds) K. Wohlmuth et al. Berlin: LIT.

Kaplinsky, R. (2008). What Does the Rise of China Do for Industrialisation in Sub-Saharan Africa? *Review of African Political Economy,* no. 115, pp. 7–22.

Kilbey, H. (2007). Why China Beats Its Competitors. Allafrica.com News, 16 November. Available at: ⟨http://allafrica.com/stories/200711160638.html⟩ (accessed 17 November 2007).

Kivimäki, T. and L. Laakso (2002). Conclusions and Recommendations, in *Regional Integration for Conflict Prevention and Peace Building in Africa. Europe, SADC and ECOWAS* (ed.) L. Laakso. Helsinki: University of Helsinki/ Department of Political Sciences.

Klare, M. and D. Volman (2006). America, China & the Scramble for Africa's Oil. *Review of African Political Economy,* no. 108, pp. 297–309.

Kleine-Ahlbrandt, S. and A. Small (2008). China's New Dictatorship Diplomacy. Is Beijing Parting With Pariahs? *Foreign Affairs* 87, no. 1, pp. 38–56.

Kohnert, D. (2008). *EU-African Economic Relations: Continuing Dominance, Traded for Aid?* Hamburg: German Institute of Global and Area Studies.

Large, D. (2008). Beyond 'Dragon in the Bush': The study of China-Africa relations. *African Affairs* 107, no. 426, pp. 45–61.

Le Pere, G. (2008). The Geo-Strategic Dimensions of the Sino-African Relationship, in *Crouching Tiger, Hidden Dragon? Africa and China* (eds) K. Ampiah and S. Naidu. Scottsville: University of KwaZulu-Natal Press.

Lee, M. C. (2009). Trade Relations between the EU and Sub-Saharan Africa Under the Cotonou Agreement: Repartitioning and Economically Recolonizing the Continent? in *A New Scramble for Africa? Imperialism and Development in Africa* (eds) R. Southall and H. Melber. Durban: University KwaZulu-Natal Press and London: Merlin Press.

Legault, G. L. (2008). Africa's Newest Friends. *China Rights Forum*, no. 1, pp. 40–2.

Manji, F. and S. Marks (eds) (2007). *African Perspectives on China in Africa*. Nairobi and Oxford: Fahamu.

Martin, W. G. (2004). Beyond Bush: The Future of Popular Movements & US Africa Policy. *Review of African Political Economy*, no. 102, pp. 585–97.

McCormick, D. (2008). China & India as Africa's New Donors: The Impact of Aid on Development. *Review of African Political Economy*, no. 115, pp. 73–92.

Mehler, A., H. Melber and K. van Walraven (eds) (2008). *Africa Yearbook. Volume 4: Politics, Economy and Society South of the Sahara in 2007*. Leiden: Brill.

Melber, H. (2002). The New Partnership for Africa's Development (NEPAD) – Old Wine in New Bottles? *Forum for Development Studies*, 29, no. 1, pp. 186–209.

Melber, H. (2004). *The G8 and NePAD – More Than An Elite Pact?* Leipzig: University of Leipzig.

Melber, H. (ed.) (2005). *Trade, Development, Cooperation. What Future for Africa?* Uppsala: The Nordic Africa Institute.

Mohan, G. (2008). China in Africa: A Review Essay. *Review of African Political Economy*, no. 115, pp. 155–66.

Mohan, G. and M. Power (2008). New African Choices? The Politics of Chinese Engagement. *Review of African Political Economy*, no. 115, pp. 23–42.

Nayyar, D. (2008). *China, India, Brazil and South Africa in the World Economy. Engines of Growth?* Helsinki: UNU-WIDER.

Ochieng, H. and T. Sharman (2004). *Trade Traps. Why EU-ACP Economic Partnership Agreements Pose a Threat to Africa's Development*. London: Actionaid International.

Reisen, H. and S. Ndoye (2008). *Prudent versus Imprudent Lending to Africa: From Debt Relief to Emerging Lenders*. Paris: OECD Development Centre.

Sautman, B. and Y. Hairong (2007). Friends and Interests: China's Distinctive Links with Africa. *African Studies Review*, 50, no. 3, pp. 75–114.

Southall, R. and H. Melber (eds) (2006). *The Legacies of Power. Leadership Transition and the Role of Former Presidents in African Politics*. Cape Town: HSRC Press and Uppsala: Nordic Africa Institute.

Southall, R. and H. Melber (eds) (2009). *A New Scramble for Africa? Imperialism and Development in Africa*. Scottsville: University of KwaZulu-Natal Press and London: Merlin Press.

Taylor, I. (2005). *NEPAD. Towards Africa's Development or Another False Start?* Boulder and London: Lynne Rienner.

Taylor, I. (2007). China and Africa: Towards the Development of a Literature. *Afrika Spectrum* 42, no. 2, pp. 379–88.

Taylor, I. (2008). Sino-African Relations and the Problem of Human Rights. *African Affairs* 107, no. 426, pp. 63–87.

Teklu, D. (2005). Mkapa Accuses the West for Paralysing African Economy. *The Daily Monitor* (Ethiopia), 1 September.

Thompson, C. B. (2004). US Trade with Africa: African Growth & Opportunity?, *Review of African Political Economy*, no. 101, pp. 457–74.

Thorborg, M. (2008). *Business as Usual or Yellow Man's Burden – Chinese Labour and Development Policies in Africa*. Paper presented to the 12th EADI Conference, Geneva, 24–28 June.

Tjønneland, E. N. with B. Brandtzæg, Å. Kolås and G. Le Pere (2006). *China in Africa – Implications for Norwegian Foreign and Development Policies*. Bergen: Chr. Michelsen Institute.

Tull, D. M. (2006a). China and Africa in *China's Rise: The Return of Geopolitics?* Berlin: Stiftung Wissenschaft und Politik.

Tull, D. M. (2006b). China's engagement in Africa: scope, significances and consequences. *Journal of Modern African Studies*, 44, no. 3, pp. 459–79.

Wade, R. H. (2003). *What Strategies Are Viable for Developing Countries Today? The World Trade Organization and The Shrinking of 'Development Space'*. London: Crisis State Programme/Development Research Centre, London School of Economics.

Wang, J. -Y. (2007). *What Drives China's Growing Role in Africa?* Washington: International Monetary Fund.

Wohlmuth, K. (2007). Abundance of Natural Resources and Vulnerability to Crises, Conflicts and Disasters – An Introduction, in *Africa – Commodity Dependence, Resource Curse and Export Diversification* (eds) K. Wohlmuth et al. Berlin: LIT.

10
Conclusion: The *'Bios'* and *'Geo'* of Contemporary Development-Security Policy

Jens Stilhoff Sörensen

The chapters in this volume problematised and examined various dimensions of the current juncture of international aid. The first part approached the Western and mainstream paradigm by interrogating and challenging the very foundations of development as a project, by investigating it in terms of a historical and contemporary practice within liberal governance and by questioning core foundations as well as recent trends such as the turn to neoliberalism, the emergence of sustainable development and the accompanying focus on civil society and NGOs. Further, it explored the connection between development and security issues and their reframing into a development-security nexus. In this context a crucial theoretical insight and 'lens' was the *biopolitics of development* – a politics over life *through* development – and the shift from a focus on building nation states in former colonies and promoting modernisation and global material convergence towards a focus on populations and life. Rich language and terminology reflect this shift where development takes *life* rather than *states* as its referent: we thus have the language of *'state fragility'*, *'human security'*, *'human development'*, *'humanitarian intervention'* and *'civil society'*. This language, and thus policy shift, has been crucial in re-extending the Western sovereign frontier in the periphery, that is, in penetrating aid-receiving societies.

So what is aid? Moreover, what is 'development' in a context of what is now labelled the 'development-security nexus'? As the latter concept signals, and Chapter 2, in particular, analysed, we need to understand it in terms of a security technology. International aid and development form a security technology operating as a dimension of a wider compact of global liberal governance. It cannot be understood in isolation from this wider context of international political economy or from the governmental rationality of liberalism. What does it secure? From the viewpoint of liberalism and especially *actually existing liberalism* as practice (as opposed to actually existing socialism) it secures the present moment and unfolding of global capitalism and thereby a foundation of liberalism more generally. Capitalism and liberalism are interconnected, but not interchangeable, concepts. Capitalism is an economic *and social* system, a mode of organising ownership, production and distribution in society, with certain consequences with regard to utilisation of resources and stratification in society. It has an inherent logic and dynamic of creation-destruction and recurring waves of accumulation by dispossession. Liberalism, by contrast, is an ethos of government as well as a political ideology (or theory) that embraces capitalism as the best system to guarantee individual freedom. Liberalism, in a way, is more complex and comes in many varieties but generally embraces a certain conception of the economy and of man as *homo oeconomicus*.

A capitalist state does not have to be liberal, as is evident in the example of authoritarian-capitalist China. Biopolitics, in turn, is a governing technology that is inherent in – but not exclusive to – liberalism.

Historical capitalism has had different stages, of which colonialism was one. While the late nineteenth-century colonial expansion was a specific method of imperialism which used political control to secure economic control, thus ensuring further capitalist expansion, it was also through the experience of empire that liberalism encountered and developed strategies for how to relate to 'the other' *non-liberal* form of life. When the colonies became free a new way of managing and relating to the 'periphery' and non-liberal life was required, and this new way was 'development'. In the binary geopolitics of the Cold War the emphasis was on building nation states and reining them into the right 'camp'. Although this strategic framework fostered a clustering of client-state dependency on one of the superpowers and its respective development models, the emphasis on state-led modernisation did create some space for autonomy for those states. Since the Soviet Union's retreat from Africa in 1989 and its collapse in 1991 this geopolitical game is no longer a concern. The liberal model is all there is. The present moment of global capitalism (and *actually existing liberalism*) is neoliberalism. Contemporary aid and development-security strategies aim to secure global neoliberalism, or what we may call neoliberal imperialism. First, it needs to ensure that states open up their markets to free trade and especially to foreign investment so that surplus capital can find profitable outlets. However, the reign of the free market brings social dislocation, tensions and imbalances in terms of social inequality, exploitation and poverty. Such dislocation and tensions need to be controlled, mitigated and contained. There is thereby a second concern for security, which becomes its main referent, namely *life*. There are various ways of breaking up the biological continuum of 'life' in order to divide and categorise it. Race is one way of doing so; the distinction between *liberal* and *non-liberal* life, between *developed, civilised* and *non-developed, under-developed or non-civilised* is another. Thus, development is a liberal biopolitical technology that *divides, separates* and reproduces this division and then *secures* non-liberal life (and thereby liberal life as well). Chapter 2 explored this in some detail and made a distinction between modernisation and development. The project of state-led modernisation, and state- and nation-building, during the 1950s, 1960s and 1970s, was attacked ideologically from different standpoints. Most successful, and instrumental, in breaking it down were *sustainable development philosophy* and *neoliberalism*. Although coming from different viewpoints they could combine well. Here, as explored in Chapter 2 and especially in Chapter 3, the NGO movement played a crucial role. The increasing focus on NGOs since the 1980s and the emerging language of *civil society* since the 1990s, critically discussed in Chapter 4, should be understood in this context. The language of sustainable development and civil society belongs not just to the liberal tradition more generally, but is adjoined to its neoliberal version. Sustainable development supports the idea of local self-reliance, rather than modernisation, convergence and global equality, and helps secure non-liberal life *in situ*. It is instrumental in re-territorialising and containing non-liberal life, thus securing liberal life itself from the potential danger and global disorder posed by non-liberal life. From another viewpoint it also preserves a latent, potential and future reserve army for global capitalism.

The shifting contours and proclamations of recent decades of development and aid policy could thereby be analysed as stages within the same neoliberal paradigm. Structural Adjustment and first-generation reform gave way to a focus on institutions, their reshaping in a neoliberal fashion and their empowerment to address security issues including border control, poverty management and comprehensive development.

As discussed in Chapter 2, the continuous reinvention of development has been marked by grand proclamations appearing every one or two decades. The most recent grand proclamation for this decade was the 'Millennium Development Goals' (MDG), followed by the 'Paris Declaration' of 2005 and the recent (2008) 'Accra agenda for action'. The MDG have received considerable attention, but their content is an extension of the 'human security'/'human development' paradigm established a decade earlier, which was scrutinised in the first part of this volume. The MDG articulated several of the key points of 'human security-development', such as how to promote 'sustainable development' and strengthening institutions and domestic efforts for poverty reduction. They also targeted some particular areas such as gender equality, maternal health and the reduction of child mortality and combating diseases such as HIV and malaria, and outlined a set of targets and indicators. Thus, rather than a shift or new departure, it was a paradigm *consolidation*, extension and proclamation, and it was successful in bringing a great number of governments – thus international consensus – towards the mainstream objective.

There *are* variations within a paradigm. While not much discussed in this volume, the Western mainstream paradigm contains differences and strictures that are contested, mediated and negotiated. For example, the US has generally had a much stronger emphasis on rapidly imposing privatisation, opening up for foreign investment and take-overs, as well as on the ritual of elections and on conditionality on certain issues, whereas the EU in some cases has favoured local cooperatives as alternative to immediate privatisation (for example in Kosovo). Again, this varies between countries and the region involved. Under the George W. Bush administration the US moved onto a stronger bilateral track and implemented a policy of replacing loans with grants to states that fulfilled certain criteria of liberal and neoliberal reform. The initiative was formulated in 2002 as the 'Millennium Challenge Account', and a new government agency 'The Millennium Challenge Corporation' (MCC) was created in 2004 to implement the agenda. Again, rather than being a new departure the MCC embodies a consolidation and deepening of US bilateral neoliberal reform pressure accompanied by poverty management security strategies. Replacing credits and loans with grants allows a stronger control over the reform process in the recipient country. States have to compete for these grants and are measured on a number of performance criteria which they have to fulfil in order to qualify. Among these criteria are various measures of 'good governance', open and free trade policy, fiscal policy, etc. The initiative is coated in the language of aid efficiency, ownership, accountability, and so on, but it is also a strong statement that aid should be provided on the basis of *desert*, rather than on strict humanitarian or solidarity grounds.

The extension of the Western or liberal sovereign frontier has been greatly facilitated by the doctrine of humanitarian intervention, by the language of state fragility and by current engagements in peace-building and state-building in international protectorates or areas of direct military intervention, such as Iraq, Afghanistan, Bosnia-Hercegovina (BiH) and Kosovo.

While each single mission varies in mandate and rationale there is a common denominator in how the above-mentioned aid, or development-security, paradigm informs all reform packages, initiatives and operations. Thus, as discussed in the introduction, the promotion of neoliberal reform and the free-market economy is prevalent in all cases, and now enshrined in the new constitutions of Iraq, BiH and Kosovo alike, accompanied by an emphasis on institutional capacity-building, good governance, poverty management and civil society. The introduction discussed these features in what has been called 'governance states', but given the overall human development-security paradigm analysed in Part I of this volume, the type of state being promoted may be termed a 'human security state' (as opposed to a 'developmental state'). Such international state-building for peace-building has been ongoing in over a dozen countries since the 1990s: for example BiH since 1995, Kosovo since 1999, Afghanistan since 2001 and Iraq since 2003.

While interventions have often, but not always, been able to claim some success in stopping open armed conflict, the track record in terms of promoting reconciliation, democratisation, development and stable institutions is much weaker. The result of the current paradigm has been gloomy at best. The accumulating evidence is beginning to reveal a policy that acts in the name of development and security but that is incapable of providing either. Instead we may have to conclude that the current paradigm has gone beyond development and security and is one of constant crisis management; it is continuously reinventing and extending itself, operating on the effects of its own making.

The second part of this volume moved to another challenge, posed by an emerging, *actually existing* alternative model of aid and development. It began, in Chapter 5, by analysing Asian models of aid where, in spite of variations, a number of common features were noted, such as a higher general reliance on the state as a crucial agent for economic development. It then moved to an extensive treatment of Chinese aid and its deepening involvement in Africa.

Much academic, political and media attention with regard to China's involvement in Africa has centred on geopolitical struggle and a coming – or already ongoing – resource war. There is undeniably a worrying reality to this 'new Scramble for Africa'. The unipolar moment and the paradigmatic shift to a biopolitical development-security have certainly not rendered geopolitics irrelevant. The US has continuously been engaged in grabbing and securing natural resources such as oil and would not be so active in the Middle East without its presence there; the Bush administration's full-spectrum dominance doctrine, pre-emptive war and thrust into Central Asia, as well as the Russian response to the Georgian crisis (and Kosovo's independence) all remind us that geopolitics and geo-strategy remain important features of international relations. China's interest in natural resources in Africa is no anachronism. Nor is the fact that it is buying agricultural land there for its own food production. This may have a troublesome colonial ring to it, but it is hardly an unfamiliar pattern to Western historical and contemporary interests and policies. Whereas China buys land and brings workers to cultivate it for the Chinese food market, the EU subsidises a domestic overproduction of agricultural products which are dumped on African markets and thereby contribute to their destruction. The imposition of free trade through the WTO is in this context equally exploitative.

The new strategic framework that has emerged in Africa does provide new opportunities for African states in terms of bargaining positions, and has enabled countries like Angola to take a tougher stance towards the World Bank by relying on Chinese loans. The Chinese model of investment and loans is reminiscent of the Western modernisation paradigm of the 1950s, 1960s and 1970s, and suggests that an alternative model may again be possible – that there may be an alternative 'globalisation model'. The rise of a new group of actors with the BRIC countries (Brazil, Russia, India and China) may increase bargaining space and the spectrum of opportunity. But, as Chapter 9 warned us, this may be so more for the governments and elite groups, rather than for the people of the continent. A troubling scenario is that a new 'authoritarian-capitalist' competition may provide bargaining spaces for elite groups and governments in the periphery, whereas the general capitalist dynamic as such continues to marginalise groups upon which security technologies of the Western sustainable development kind are employed, causing an ever-continuing need for crisis management. The question would then arise whether there is, or will be, an authoritarian-capitalist biopolitics as well as a liberal one and whether there will be a convergence or a clash between them.

Index